Women
in Design

Published in 2019
by Laurence King Publishing Ltd
361–373 City Road
London EC1V 1LR
United Kingdom

Tel: +44 20 7841 6900
Fax: +44 20 7841 6910
E-mail: enquiries@laurenceking.com
www.laurenceking.com

A catalogue record for this book is
available from the British Library

ISBN: 978-1-78627-531-8

Designed by BLOK
www.blokdesign.co.uk

Printed in China

Women in Design

From Aino Aalto to Eva Zeisel

**CHARLOTTE FIELL &
CLEMENTINE FIELL**

This book is, first and foremost, a celebration of some truly remarkable women whose careers in design have been exceptional. They can rightly be called exceptional because, despite the odds stacked against them, the women featured here created significant bodies of work within what was – and to a certain extent still is – the male-dominated field of design. By highlighting their extraordinary achievements, our intention is to contextualize the role of women in design over the last one hundred years or so in order to trace how the status of female designers has evolved, while at the same time assessing where it stands today. In the past, all too often the work of female designers was overlooked in the literature on design, while also being woefully under-represented in exhibitions and museum collections. This book seeks to redress these outstanding omissions.

The primary reasons for this paucity of representation are that – as in other male-dominated professions – women were often either largely excluded from certain areas of endeavour or had no option but to take on subordinate roles. Women designers and their work have, also, all too often been assessed through the lens of the patriarchy, meaning they have either been entirely defined by their gender or their contributions have been subsumed under that of their 'more famous' husbands, brothers, fathers or lovers. This book attempts to tell a very different story, one that appraises their activities within the wider landscape of the feminist movement – both past and present. It is only now that women designers working in developed free-market economies are beginning to enjoy anything like equality with their male counterparts when it comes to professional access and recognition, let alone parity of remuneration. As for women living elsewhere in the world, having any kind of professional career, let alone one in design, is still often largely an impossible dream.

RALLYING AGAINST THE ODDS

The publication of this book was inspired by two things: first, the centenary of the Votes for Women legislation that was enacted in Britain and the USA in 1918 and 1920 respectively, which seemed like a good marker in time to look back and assess just how far women's rights have come over the intervening period, especially with regards to design practice. And, secondly, it was motivated by some pretty shocking statistics that have emerged over the last few years, revealing a gender imbalance of professional opportunity within the design industry.

In 2018 the Design Council in the UK published 'The Design Economy 2018'[1] report, which found that only 22 per cent of the UK's design workforce are women, despite the fact the 63 per cent of all students on creative arts and design courses in the UK are female. These two figures suggest there is a clear discrepancy between men and women when it comes to design career prospects, leading to an almost 1-in-3 attrition rate of design-trained women as they transition from student life to professional practice and then presumably into long-term partnerships or marriage and motherhood. This discovery was backed up by later research undertaken by Kerning the Gap, a mentoring network that promotes gender equality in the design industry, which found that in the UK, although 70 per cent of graphic design students are women, only 11 per cent of creative directors are female – starkly revealing a gendered disproportion of opportunity at the highest levels of professional practice. And this is by no means only a British problem but an international one, for it has been estimated by the American author and activist, Kat Gordon, that, worldwide, only 3 per cent of creative directors are women,[2] suggesting the chances of high-level success in that sector of the design world are horribly skewed against women. This is due to a whole host of reasons including lack of support during motherhood, misogynistic assumptions about women's technical abilities and an entrenched gender bias of often male-dominated award juries, which have a tendency to function as cliquey boys' clubs.

Yet, as the recent #MeToo and Time's Up movements suggest, times are changing in the world of workplace gender politics and increasing numbers of people are finally waking up to the glaring injustices faced by women in all spheres of life and calling time on them. And part of this is a growing questioning of why so many women still struggle to find proper recognition in the world of design.

But recognition is by no means the only issue here, for, perhaps even more troubling, is the fact that women working as product and fashion designers in Britain are, on average, paid 18.3 per cent less than their male counterparts,[3] despite making up 64 per cent of that subsector's workforce, and only 17 per cent of design managers in the UK are female.[4] In America, the statistics are just as worrying, with women accounting for nearly half of all architecture graduates in 2017 but only 22 per cent of licensed architects and only 17 per cent of partners/principals.[5] Quite simply, the design world has a problem and the first step to solving any problem is to identify it, which is where this book comes in.

By focussing on women's design achievements, both historical and contemporary, we do not suggest that there is any qualitative difference in creative capacity between the genders. Nor does this book seek to emphasize, as one well-known French female designer mistakenly thought, the 'gender difference in creative artists'.[6] Rather, it strives to highlight discrimination and gender-equality obstacles that still exist for women in the design industry. It also seeks to demonstrate how, time and again, women have been able to bring a more empathetic feminine sensibility to design thinking that has led to better, more human-centric, solutions. But more than this, we hope that, by telling the inspirational stories of women designers who have succeeded within their different fields of endeavour – often against seemingly insurmountable odds – this book will motivate those who seek to follow in their illustrious footsteps.

Today, as in the past, many women involved in design are not actually designers, but work as entrepreneurs, product researchers, manufacturing engineers, material scientists, curators, educators, writers and publicists, however, we knew that there was not sufficient scope in this publication to survey their contributions. That said, we did give preference to designers who have also operated in these areas, such as Estrid Ericson who founded Svenskt Tenn, Carlotta de Bevilacqua, the current vice-president of Artemide, and Neri Oxman who heads the Mediated Matter research group at the MIT Media Lab. Making our selection as international and multidisciplinary as possible, we were also determined not to fall prey to multicultural tokenism. The role of women in design reflects strongly the status of women's rights and, so, it is fundamentally a 'First World' story. To gloss over this glaring fact would be a betrayal of the vast number of women around the world who are still denied the basic self-determining freedoms of education and employment that women in developed societies largely take for granted. One can only hope that, in the future, gender equality will be realized universally and, as a result, we will see more women designers emerge from countries not known for their advocacy of human rights, let alone women's rights.

THE CRITERA FOR SELECTION

One of the biggest challenges we faced when researching this book was deciding who to include, because there were more than enough notable women designers to fill this publication and a similarly sized sister volume, too. We have, therefore, attempted to make our selection as objective and broad as possible in order to produce what we believe to be the most representative and insightful sampling of women in design. We have focused on women designers from the past who were acknowledged trailblazers in their day and who left an important mark on design history, and also on today's women designers who, through their different pioneering approaches, are having an undeniable impact on contemporary design and its professional practice. We also took great care to focus on designers whose stories shed light on what it was like to be a woman working in design in the past, or what it is like now. Certainly, the one-hundred-plus designers that made the final cut can all be said to have helped break down the prejudice that women have faced in design practice thanks to the intelligence and innovation of their work.

The role of women in design mirrors the wider history of women's rights – as women have gained greater emancipation, doors have opened to them professionally within the design world. The women's rights movement originated in the Enlightenment in eighteenth-century Europe and America, which produced a groundswell of libertarian ideas, including universal suffrage and equality between the sexes. This led to better education for women, at least in the upper echelons of society, whose academic rigour helped counter the pervasive notion that all females were innately inferior, childlike and feeble of mind, body and spirit. The Blue Stockings Society, founded in England around 1750, reflected this new, small but influential, group of highly educated women who preferred reading, writing and intellectual debate to card games and gossiping.

From this intellectual awakening emerged some of the first professional women designers, who produced designs for Josiah Wedgwood's Etruria ceramics factory in Stoke-on-Trent in the 1780s. Drawn from the ranks of the aristocracy and high society,[1] these early female design practitioners created designs that were intended to appeal specifically to a burgeoning female consumer market. Essentially highly skilled amateur artists, Lady Diana Beauclerk (the Duke of Marlborough's daughter), Emma Crewe (daughter of one of Wedgwood's best clients) and Lady Elizabeth Templetown, devised decorative motifs that were translated into the enduringly popular Neoclassical bas-relief motifs that adorned Wedgwood's Jasperware pieces.

A decade or so later, the English writer and philosopher Mary Wollstonecraft wrote *A Vindication of the Rights of Woman*. This radical text, published in 1792, laid the foundations of feminism by promoting the cause of female education and arguing for the increased participation of women in society.[2]

FEMALE EDUCATION AND THE ARTS AND CRAFTS MOVEMENT

In the following century, these nascent feminist ideas continued to take hold, leading to the establishment of design institutions specifically for women – in 1842, for example, an offshoot of the Government School of Design[3] in London, known as the Royal Female School of Art, was established, to teach design as part of its arts-and-crafts curriculum. The following year, in the United States, the Philadelphia School of Design for Women was founded with the aim of providing vocational training to ensure its students would have the necessary skills to gain meaningful employment, leading to greater financial independence and social empowerment.

In America, the emergence of women in architectural practice can be traced to Harriet Irwin, the first women to patent a plan for a dwelling in 1869 despite having received no formal training. In 1878 Mary Page graduated from the University of Illinois, becoming America's first female architecture graduate.[4] In Britain, Ethel and Bessie Charles were the first female students to train at the renowned Bartlett School of Architecture in 1892, with the former, six years later, becoming the first woman to be elected a member of the Royal Institute of British Architecture.

It was, however, the Arts and Crafts Movement that did the most to propel forward the cause of women designers. Ideologically inspired by William Morris's socially progressive writings, the Arts and Crafts Movement had an egalitarian ethos and many of its associates were also involved with the suffrage movement. Morris's utopian novel, *News from Nowhere*, published in 1890, evoked a pastoral, non-industrialized communistic paradise set in the future, in which women and men were equals and contractual marriage no longer existed. Yet, in this vision of a more humane society, domestic work was still regarded as the woman's domain, although the female pursuit of knowledge was very much encouraged. Inspired by these sentiments, many women associated with the Arts and Crafts Movement actively acquired design and craft skills, and went on to work as designers of mainly textiles, jewellery and books.

In Arts and Crafts circles, many women took on the role of supportive comrade-wives to their more famous husbands, either practising design themselves or becoming philanthropically involved in design-related educational causes. Elizabeth Waterhouse, for instance, whose husband, Alfred, was a leading architect, organized the weekly Yattendon class in Berkshire that ran from 1890 to 1914 and taught young men metalworking skills. Many of the repoussé copper and brass pieces made there were actually designed by Waterhouse herself. As a means of counteracting the capitalist exploitation of factory workers, the Arts and Crafts Movement also promoted the revival of handicrafts practised within the home, the consequence being that a significant number of women became skilled hobbyist designer-makers.

The Arts and Crafts community steadfastly encouraged the involvement of female amateurs and students through the founding of organizations including the Home Arts and Industries Association, established by Eglantyne Louisa Jebb in 1884. These organizations allowed women to take a more active role as creators. Those that came from the ranks of the upper and middle classes were, however, dismissively referred to as 'Dear Emilys' by the guildsmen associated with Charles Robert Ashbee's Guild of Handicraft, mainly because, by not charging proper piece-time rates for their homemade wares, the women undercut the work of trained men who were reliant on their craft skills for their livelihoods. The result of this was that both the Guild of Handicraft and the Art Workers' Guild made a point of excluding women from their membership, with the latter rather condescendingly holding regular 'ladies' nights'. Female members were not allowed into its ranks until the 1960s – some 70 years after its founding.

Despite this, however, there were a number of key women designers associated with the British Arts and Crafts Movement who worked professionally, producing innovative designs for which they became renowned. It was these high-profile designers – including, among others, May Morris, Georgie Gaskin and Margaret Macdonald Mackintosh – who helped establish the wider acceptance of women, albeit only in certain 'women's disciplines', namely textiles, jewellery and book design. In 1907 May Morris and Mary Elizabeth Taylor founded the Women's Guild of Arts, which functioned as a vital platform for the exchange of ideas among women designers.

Another important early champion of women in design was the Arts and Crafts Exhibition Society, founded by Walter Crane in 1887. It mounted regular decorative art exhibitions that invariably included the work of women designers. As Imogen Hart at the Yale Center for British Art notes, the organization 'also contributed to an international re-evaluation of the status of decorative arts',[5] thereby propagating a more holistic understanding of design across the genders. The designs included in the society's exhibitions were often featured in *The Studio* magazine, one of the most influential design journals of the day. It was crucial in disseminating recognition of the creative ingenuity and technical proficiency among women designers across Britain, Europe and America.

A number of women designers also carved out meaningful careers under the auspices of the American Arts and Crafts Movement, including Florence Koehler and Marie Zimmermann, alongside a vast number of middle- and upper-class women who occupied, as cultural historian Catherine Zipf has put it, a 'middle ground'[6] that bridged professional and domestic practice. In line with the international rise of National Romanticism, movements reviving indigenous craft and design also appeared across continental Europe, especially in Scandinavia, and even Russia. The noted Russian painter and illustrator, Yelena Polenova, designed a number of interesting Slavophile pieces of furniture, executed in the Abramtsevo Colony workshops near Moscow in the 1880s and early 1890s, which demonstrated an acceptance of women designers in international artistic circles. From the last quarter of the nineteenth century up to the outbreak of World War I, however, the vast majority of women working in the design field, and especially those from the lower echelons of society, were employed either as artisans to execute designs created by men or as assistants in design studios where their creative input went largely unattributed, whether at the Tiffany Studios in New York or at the Wiener Werkstätte in Vienna. Their smaller hands enabled them to execute finer and more delicate work, upon which much of the decorative arts at that time relied.

STRIDES FORWARD AND THE SUFFRAGIST MOVEMENT

A number of high-profile female design pioneers did, nevertheless, emerge. In fashion, Louise Chéruit, Jeanne Lanvin and Lucile (Lady Duff-Gordon) were amongst the foremost couturiers of their day. In textile design, both May Morris and Märta Måås-Fjetterström made similarly significant contributions, while Elsie de Wolfe completely redefined the concept of interior design. Alongside these female-centric design triumphs, there were also three notable female design innovators who made their mark with their inventions within the more macho worlds of packaging, aeronautical and product design. They include the self-taught engineer Margaret E. Knight, who patented a machine in 1871 for the mass production of flat-bottom brown paper bags, which, to this day, remain a feature of American grocery stores; the early aviator, E. Lilian Todd, who designed and built her own aeroplane in 1906, becoming the world's first female aircraft designer; and the Dresden housewife, Melitta Bentz, who devised and patented an ingenious coffee filter in 1908, which remains in production. This inventive trio must, however, be considered outliers and, today, their achievements are barely remembered.

Although there had been growing agitation for women's rights throughout the nineteenth century, it was not until the first decade and a half of the twentieth century that this was transformed into real strategic action. This period saw the rise of the women's suffrage movement in both Europe and America, beginning with peaceful protests. In Britain, when these failed to bring about any real change, more militant tactics were employed by the movement's activists. They began by heckling politicians in the street and, when this was met with imprisonment, they countered with hunger strikes. This led the authorities to adopt force-feeding, a practice tantamount to torture. The suffering of the imprisoned

women in Britain stoked the flames of both sympathy and militancy, compelling swathes of the nations' mothers, daughters and wives to join the Suffragettes' cause, and even futher radicalized some of the movement's key members. It provoked a spat of arson attacks and bomb planting across the country, with private, unoccupied property owned by men the primary target. By 1913, the Suffragette insurgency had grown into an unstoppable force, in the face of political intransigence. The outbreak of World War I, in 1914, transformed the political landscape in Britain almost overnight, with 1 million women entering the nation's workforce during the course of the conflict, proving their professional mettle to any doubters. This was repeated across Europe and in America. Although many women had previously worked in factories and in clerical jobs, their numbers now increased vastly, while the roles they took on were beefed up, both physically and intellectually. Increasing numbers of women also worked on the land, in hospitals or in transport, and, even more significantly for our purposes, in what had been male-dominated industries, such as munitions production and shipbuilding, in which they often performed vital engineering roles.

WOMEN DESIGNERS IN THE MODERN, INDUSTRIAL AGE

The Great War led to women over the age of 30, who also met a property threshold, gaining the vote in Britain in 1918. This was a validation of the essential contribution women had made during the war years and breached centuries of female political oppression. That same year, women in Germany, Poland and Russia also won the right to vote, while a year later similar legislation was passed in Sweden, the Netherlands and Belgium. In 1920 American women also attained this right, after years of strong opposition, especially from brewers and distillers, who feared it would lead to prohibition. Their opposers were mainly drawn from the German–American community and, in the aftermath of the war, strong anti-German sentiment significantly bolstered the suffragist cause in the United States leading to this historic right-to-vote legislation. That same year, alcohol prohibition was indeed introduced largely due to efforts of the Woman's Christian Temperance Union – revealing the increasing political clout of women.

Despite the fact of women's suffrage, the war did not have a lasting effect on female employment opportunities, with women invariably forced to return to their pre-war occupations or domestic lives, as men, returning from the front, resumed their previous employment. Nevertheless, the conflict had changed the female mindset, having given many women a belief in their own abilities. Another outcome of the war was an imbalance in numbers of women versus men, because so many young men had lost their lives during the conflict. The number of unmarried women needing to support themselves consequently rose dramatically, with many seeking careers within the design industries in one capacity or another.

Thanks to greater emancipation during the interwar period, more women began to make names for themselves in the design world, which around this time witnessed the international rise of Modernism. In Germany, the Bauhaus, founded in 1919, had a number of female students who became acknowledged Modernist pioneers within their design disciplines. Even at this seemingly enlightened institution – the manifesto of which stated that it welcomed 'any person of good repute, without regard to age or sex'[7] – there was a strong culture of gender bias. Its founder and first director, Walter Gropius, believed that women were only suited to two-dimensional design, because he thought they were, unlike men, incapable of thinking three-dimensionally. Marianne Brandt's innovative designs created in the school's metal workshop well and truly trashed that notion. Nevertheless, female students – who accounted for around half the student body at the Bauhaus – after completing the preliminary course, were customarily sent straight to the weaving workshop, which became a sort of de facto women's facility. Most of the departments at the Bauhaus remained virtually closed to women, with architecture never admitting a single female student.

The 1920s, however, did see a number of women designers come to the fore despite continuing misogynistic attitudes. It was a period of unbridled optimism, as people wanting to distance themselves from the emotional rawness of the recent past embraced the thrilling new world of technological progress and sought to remake society. Certainly, the home was becoming increasingly seen as the women's design realm, as German architect Bruno Taut's *The New Home: the Woman as Creator*, published in 1924, made emphatically clear. Aimed at German housewives, it argued that Modernism could be a vehicle for important social change that would free women from the slavery of domestic labour through functional efficiency. It called for 'planned order'[8] and the purging of mementos and any other kind of 'historic junk'[9] within domestic environments. In this spirit of rationalism, two years later Margarete Schütte-Lihotzky designed the Frankfurt Kitchen, a milestone in purposeful domestic planning based on time-and-motion studies that became the blueprint for today's built-in kitchens. By putting state-of-the-art design theory into three-dimensional practice, Schütte-Lihotzky's Frankfurt Kitchen ensured her legacy as a one of the great pioneers of Modernism.

The 1920s also witnessed a radical shift in fashion design, with boyish silhouettes replacing the womanly pre-war Edwardian look, a highly practical move given that more young women were entering the workforce. Fashions became looser and the resulting freedom of movement mirrored the freer lifestyles that these young women were experiencing. It culminated in the so-called Flapper Vote law – or, as it was officially known, the Representation of the People (Equal Franchise) Act – being passed in Britain in 1928, allowing all women over the age of 21 to vote.

Gabrielle 'Coco' Chanel's workwear-inspired clothing made from easy-to-wear jersey, and her iconic little black dresses, reflected the era's new pared-down yet practical aesthetic, as did the tubular metal furniture of Charlotte Perriand, designed in collaboration with architects Le Corbusier and Pierre Jeanneret, which was showcased as Living Equipment at the 1929 Autumn Salon in Paris. Likewise, Anni Albers's woven textiles, and the furniture and interiors designed by Lilly Reich during the interwar period, epitomized the strict formal restraint of Modernism, which sought to eliminate the decoratively superfluous in order to attain a design purity that would, it was hoped, possess a timeless universality. A more stylistic interpretation of Modernism was seen in the Art Deco designs of the painter Sonia Delaunay and interior-designer Eileen Gray during the 1920s, which had an undeniable modish chic and brought them international recognition during their lifetimes.

WOMEN DESIGNERS AND THE 1930S DEPRESSION

The Wall Street Crash of 1929, and ensuing Great Depression of the 1930s, enhanced the professional status of female designers, especially in the United States. For, although during this so-called Design Decade all leading professional industrial-design consultants in America were men – Raymond Loewy, Henry Dreyfuss, Walter Dorwin Teague, et al. – a few women also began to be successful in the field of product design. Among them were Anne Swainson, head of Montgomery Ward's Bureau of Design for many years, and Belle Kogan, who ran her own studio and worked for various companies designing mass-produced Art Moderne homewares in plastics, metal and ceramics. The Depression also saw a surge in the production of 'hostess wares', as people trying to save money were more inclined to entertain at home. Women were ideally suited to designing such products.

In Germany, during the 1930s, Marianne Brandt, Lilly Reich and Eva Zeisel also made inroads into design for industrial production. Brandt, for instance, designed a host of innovative and highly rational lighting products, as well as homewares. Reich, along with her partner, architect Ludwig Mies van de Rohe, developed tubular-metal furniture pieces for large-scale manufacture. It was, however, Zeisel who had the most interesting career trajectory. She worked first in Germany and Russia, then the United States and designed innovative homewares for the whole of her long career, once noting, 'Men have no concept of how to design things for the home. Women should design the things they use.'[10] Her comment speaks volumes about how the home was seen as the woman's natural domain and also how patriarchal she found the design industry.

The 1930s also saw women in interior design, with Dorothy Draper helping to professionalize the decorating business in the United States, while adding an influential and distinctively feminine flair to American interiors. The surrealistic fashions of Elsa Schiaparelli likewise created an international stir, and she became the first women designer to grace the cover of *Time* magazine, in August 1934 – something her rival Coco Chanel never achieved. The early lives of these two extraordinary women of fashion make an interesting contrast: Schiaparelli, a descendant of the all-powerful Medici family, was born in the Palazzo Corsini in Rome, whereas Chanel was born in a workhouse, the daughter of a peasant and a street vendor. Successful women designers have tended to come from either end of the socio-economic spectrum: they have either been nurtured by affluent families that valued female education for its own sake, or they have grown up in impoverished circumstances, in which disadvantage prompted a desire to strike out and make their way in the world. Another predictor of success is birth order, women who were either only children (as was Draper) or the eldest child, especially if their father died young, seemingly far more likely to go on to successful design careers, presumably because they assumed the familial mantle of 'eldest son'. Certainly, the international celebrity of Draper, Chanel and Schiaparelli during the

1930s bolstered the profile of women designers significantly in the public imagination, opening more doors for those who followed.

In stark contrast to the flamboyant designs of Draper and Schiaparelli and the rigidly Modernist designs of Perriand, Reich and Brandt, in Scandinavia the 1930s witnessed a new, softer and more humane interpretation of Modernism, pioneered by Aino Aalto, alongside her husband, Alvar. They would prove to be enormously influential, but, despite it being a partnership of creative equals, Alvar invariably received top billing, while his wife's contribution was almost entirely overlooked – a situation that played out, time and again, over the following decades with couples who worked together in the design industry.

FEMINIZING DESIGN PRACTICE IN THE 1940S AND 1950S

The outbreak of World War II in 1939 witnessed once again the mass mobilization of women into different work roles, including that of military combatants, in some countries, and home-front workers. Indeed, the military of all countries involved in the conflict were reliant on the arms, munitions and machines, churned out by factories being 'manned' by women. The American wartime 'We Can Do It!' propaganda poster created by J. Howard Miller in 1943, featuring Rosie the Riveter with her hand raised in a fist, was the perfect symbol of women's can-do resolve during this period. As with the previous war, the immense wartime contribution made by women provoked a re-evaluation of their roles in society and, as a result, the postwar period witnessed a softening of gender-demarcation lines when it came to work. Even so, the few women working as professional designers often failed to receive the credit they deserved, despite that fact that the numbers entering the profession continued to build over the 1940s and 1950s.

The early 1940s saw the first infiltration of women designers into the automotive industry, which until then had been a bastion of masculinist design. In 1942 General Motors began hiring female stylists to create cars that would appeal to the increasingly important women's market. Helene Rother was the first female automotive-designer hire and one of her first tasks was the design of seating and wall-coverings for General Motors' Train of Tomorrow (1945–47) – a futurist demonstration locomotive intended to showcase state-of-the-art innovation. The fact that General Motors was employing women in their design department was, however, kept under wraps until the mid-1950s, when the company began promoting their 'Damsels of Design' for public-relations purposes.

During the postwar period, a number of media-friendly and super-talented design power couples emerged, which helped the growing professional recognition of women designers. The most notable of these were Ray and Charles Eames in America, and Lucienne and Robin Day in Britain. The latter worked separately from each other, but the former worked together and, as a result, Ray's contribution to the Eames oeuvre was often underestimated. A perfect example of this was when Arlene Francis, the host of NBC's Home television show introduced the couple to a live audience in 1956. Not only did Francis credit the design of their chairs solely to Charles, she patronizingly asked Ray how she 'helped' him design them, before observing that 'in

a working family' it was important to have 'a critical viewpoint of your husband's work so he can improve [...] it'.[11] This total disregard for Ray's contribution might seem, by today's standards, incredibly sexist, but most women were still consigned to the role of apron-clad homemakers, so the fact that Ray appeared at all, albeit as Charles's side-kick, marked a small step forward in raising consciousness that there was, in fact, such a thing as a female furniture designer. In contrast, Lucienne Day, having a design career that was entirely separate from her husband's, managed to achieve far better recognition for her own impressive body of work, albeit in a more female-centric discipline.

In Scandinavia, Nanna and Jørgen Ditzel were a notable design couple during the 1950s, jointly creating award-winning furniture and jewellery. When he died unexpectedly in 1961, his young widow, despite having three young daughters to look after, had forged a remarkable solo career as one of the leading Danish furniture designers of her generation. In Italy, the married furniture-design duo, Luisa and Ico Parisi, who cofounded their Como-based studio in 1948, likewise helped to bolster the idea of women being actively engaged in professional design practice.

In Italy, during the postwar era, high-quality design education was opened up to female students who, in turn, further elevated the status of women in design thanks to their sheer professionalism over the succeeding decades. Anna Castelli Ferrieri was the first woman to graduate as an architect from the

'We Can Do It!' poster by J. Howard Miller for Westinghouse, 1943.

Politecnico di Milano in 1945, and she was followed subsequently by Cini Boeri and Gae Aulenti who graduated in 1951 and 1954 respectively. This trio of stylish and creatively savvy women went on to demonstrate that female designers could be every bit as technically accomplished as their male peers by creating some of the most avant-garde furniture and lighting of the 1960s and 1970s. Indeed, our whole concept of progressive Milanese design from this period has been shaped by their contributions. Likewise, Lella Vignelli trained at the Università di Architettura in Venice during the 1950s and went on to introduce a distinctively Italian sophistication into the American corporate-design landscape during the 1960s and 1970s, and was hugely influential. Their breakthrough into the world stage of design was not, however, solely attributable to their first-class training, but the result of dramatic societal shifts that occurred during the 1960s and 1970s. It also helped that the highly intellectualized world of Milanese design provided these individuals with the most fertile design background of this period.

THE 1960S AND 1970S: CHANGING THE GENDERED DESIGN LANDSCAPE

Outside Milan, things were often very different. In America, July 1961, *Playboy* magazine published an article entitled 'Designs for Living' featuring the leading 'creators of contemporary American furniture' – all of whom were men. This was unremarkable, given the near-invisibility of female designers at this time. Despite the inauspicious start to this decade, the 1960s marked an era of seismic change when it came to gendered work roles, as younger women increasingly rejected the societal norms of the past. Many actively rebelled against the traditional homemaker role that had been their mothers' lot and, instead, sought greater emancipation by joining the workforce. For some, that meant training and then working as architects and designers. The launch of the first oral contraceptive pill in 1960 also meant that women were more in control of their biological destinies, and, therefore, their professional career choices. The career of the British fashion designer Mary Quant typified the growing sense of egalitarianism that emerged from 1960s Pop culture, her mini-dresses expressing the newfound freedoms of the period.

The full socio-cultural impact of the pill, however, was not realised until the late 1960s, when laws in both America and Britain extended its availability to include younger unmarried women. As economists Claudia Golding and Lawrence F. Katz, of Harvard University, explain, 'The pill had a direct positive effect on women's career investment by almost eliminating the chance of becoming pregnant and thus the cost of having sex. The pill also created a social multiplier effect by encouraging the delay of marriage generally and thus increasing a career woman's likelihood of finding an appropriate mate after professional school.'[12] There followed an upsurge of women taking university degrees and entering professional practice, including architecture and design. By the late 1960s and early 1970s, this shift could already be detected in the pages of design journals such as *Domus*, *Casabella* and *Mobilia*, which increasingly showcased the work of young, female rising stars.

The second wave of feminism that occurred in the late 1960s and early 1970s was prompted by the 're-discovery' of Simone de Beauvoir's *The Second Sex*, which had been published in 1949. Often cited as the catalyst for this new chapter of female activism, it questioned the existing perceptions of gender differences 'imposed' on women by the patriarchy rather than by biology. In 1970 Britain's first national Women's Liberation Conference was held at Ruskin College, Oxford, an event that for the first time brought together women's groups from across country. Similar 'Women's Lib' events were held in other countries around this time and they had a ripple effect across society, especially within the print media. In Britain, *Spare Rib* magazine, founded by Marsha Rowe and Rosie Boycott in 1972, became a feminist 'platform for issues that wouldn't often have a platform'.[13] Likewise, in America, *Cosmopolitan* magazine was transformed under the editorship of Helen Gurley Brown, who peddled sexually explicit content from a seemingly feminist perspective, promoting the idea of women being able to control their own destinies. Other controversial feminist publications that had a similarly galvanizing effect on women's attitudes during this era were Germaine Greer's *The Female Eunuch* (1970), Kate Millet's *Sexual Politics* (1970), Erica Jong's *Fear of Flying* (1973) and Shirley Conran's *Superwoman* (1975), all of which transformed their readers' views on the nuclear family, sex and patriarchy, no-strings-attached sex and the possibility of a have-it-all lifestyle. This wave of pro-feminist sentiment extended to all areas of life, including design practice.

In 1971 Sheila Levrant de Bretteville helped establish the first Women's Design Program at the California Institute of the Arts, which was one year in length and sought 'to embody feminist principles into a course of study'.[14] Some of the graphic artwork emanating from this programme was later showcased in *Icographic* magazine, along with an essay by Levrant de Bretteville entitled, 'Some Aspects of Design from the Perspective of a Women Designer'. This text asked for a re-examination of female values in design, which had always been denigrated for their very femininity. Levrant de Bretteville was also instrumental in staging the first Women in Design conference in Los Angeles, 1975, for which she designed an eye-catching poster featuring a field of eyebolts, representing the female Venus symbol. That same year, across the Atlantic, thanks to the endeavours of activists, the Sex Discrimination Act was passed in Britain making it illegal to discriminate against women in work, education and training – another leap forward for women in the workplace, or so it must have seemed at the time.

THE 1980S AND THE HADID EFFECT

The radical activism of the 1970s Women's Movement laid the societal groundwork for Margaret Thatcher to become Britain's first female prime minister in 1979. As the British feminist author, Natasha Walter points out, 'Women who complain that Margaret Thatcher was not a feminist because she didn't help other women or openly acknowledge her debt to feminism have a point, but they are also missing something vital. She normalized female success. She showed that although female power and masculine power may have different languages, different metaphors, different gestures, different traditions, different ways of being glamorous or nasty, they are equally strong, equally valid [...] No one can ever question whether women are capable of single-minded vigour, of efficient leadership, after Margaret Thatcher.'[15] Certainly, the steely resolve of the 'Iron Lady' – whether you agreed with her politics or not – and her powerful, different-yet-equal ethos made her a formidable role model for young women growing up in the 1980s. This generation of women were weaned on the belief that they could have it all and that virtually all professions were open to them. As a result, they tended to have self-confidence in their own abilities and a determination to make it in their chosen careers. In practice, however, the poor careers advice available in British schools at the time meant, all too often, that female students were pushed towards the more female-centric design disciplines – fashion, textile or graphic design – little realizing that there was a host of other design disciplines that they could have considered.

It was still enormously difficult for most women designers to sustain and build on any kind of success they enjoyed early in their careers unless they had supportive partners or eschewed marriage and motherhood completely. The 1980s saw the publication of two notable books that looked at the state of play for women in design, the first, Liz McQuiston's *Women in Design: A Contemporary View* (1988) showcased the work of 43 designers from Britain, America, Italy, Holland, India and Japan, and revealed the growing breadth of design practice in which women were actively engaged. Thirty years on, however, it is remarkable how few of the women featured remain well known for their contributions to the design world. The second, *A View from the Interior: Feminism, Women and Design* (1989) was a diverse collection of essays edited by Judy Attfield and Pat Kirkham that set out to re-examine design history from a feminist perspective and expose the pre-existing male-orientated social constructs that had governed it.

During the 1980s, there was a common belief among many career women that they needed to prove themselves men's equals in a man's world, with the padded shoulder-pads of power dressing being one of the most outward expressions. All too often, what this meant in practice was that they had to work harder and be significantly better at what they did, for the same amount (or less) of recognition and remuneration than their male counterparts. Elizabeth Wetzel, who began as an intern in the General Motors bus and truck division in 1983, and rose to become the company's first female Vehicle Chief Designer, has said of her career trajectory: 'To achieve this position, I had to work harder than the men to prove the legitimacy of my talents and skills,'[16] – a sentiment that has rung true, and no doubt continues to ring true, for many women working in design. In the 1980s, many found the notion of 'women designers' distasteful and believed that any woman working in design should be thought of simply as a 'designer'. But this meant that gender discrimination in the design industry was often not confronted. Both Nathalie du Pasquier and Martine Bedin, who achieved recognition for their work with the Memphis design group during the 1980s, still hold the belief that designers should not be categorized by their gender. This rather misses the point because, unless people speak out about 'women in design', the entrenched gender-biases that the vast majority of female designers still encounter will continue.

The best example of the struggle for equal recognition during the 1980s came when Zaha Hadid won a major competition to design the Peak Leisure Club in Hong Kong (1982–83), only for the project to be promptly shelved. It was widely felt at the time that this was because she was a woman. Whether this was actually true is a moot point, but certainly no one had counted on the tenacity of Hadid in the face of adversity. As she would later reflect, 'Women are always told, "You're not going to make it, it's too difficult, you can't do that, don't enter this competition, you'll never win it" – they need confidence in themselves and people around them to help them to get on',[17] which is exactly what she had, and did. It took nearly a decade of dogged determination for her first building to be built – the Vitra Fire Station (1993) – but, with its bold gestural concrete planes, it showed not only that her Neo-Suprematist drawings could be dramatically lifted off the paper and transformed into three-dimensional buildings, but also that the design world had a new female genius in its midst. Hadid became the first woman to be inducted into the 'starchitect' hall of fame. She had shattered the long-existing architectural glass ceiling on her own terms. Emboldened, she spread her creative wings beyond architecture during the late 1990s and early 2000s to encompass other areas of design, with spectacular results.

THE MILLENNIUM: A NEW DAWN

During this period Hella Jongerius, who trained at the Design Academy Eindhoven, began making waves as part of the New Dutch Design movement, while, in Italy, the critically acclaimed furniture manufacturer, Moroso (under the inspired female leadership of Patrizia Moroso), started working with Patricia Urquiola. The work of both Jongerius and Urquiola is significant in that it projected an unashamedly feminine aesthetic. This was something new and refreshing in the world of contemporary design, which, up to that point, had been dominated by a cabal of international design-superstars, all of whom were men – namely, Ron Arad, Tom Dixon, Ross Lovegrove, Jasper Morrison, Marc Newson and Philippe Starck. The work of this talented female duo also influenced a new handcrafted sensibility, which helped shape the direction of design practice over the following decade. It was the standout, international success of Hadid, Jongerius and Urquiola that paved the way for the next, and larger, generation of high-profile women designers, many of whom are featured in this book.

The profile of women in design was raised further in 2000 by the 'Women Designers in the USA' exhibition held at the Bard Graduate Center in New York. Since then, academic interest in women designers from the past has grown, as has recognition of their historic achievements in design-based organizations such as the Industrial Designers Society of America (ISDA). Indeed, the ISDA has been hugely instrumental in raising the profile of the ongoing women-in-design debate, dedicating an entire issue of its *Innovation* journal to the subject in 2016 and also, the following year, hosting the first Women+Design Summit. Definable progress is being made in America and Europe, although less perhaps than in Sweden, where White Arkitekter – the largest architecture practice in Scandinavia – has a female CEO and a board where over 50 per cent of its members are women. Certainly, most of the contemporary designers featured in this book, we suspect, would admit that being a successful woman in design has not been an easy journey. Many may only have been able to achieve what they have done through the help of supportive partners, many of them designers themselves. The main reason so many talented design-trained women do not enjoy stellar careers in their chosen field is because of lack of support. If they decide to have children, as many do, they often find it hard to sustain their career momentum due to a lack of practical help.

There have been numerous debates about bio-determinism versus cultural determinism when it comes to gender traits; differences obviously do exist and should probably be embraced for what they are. No one can deny that men and women's different physical characteristics lead to different interests and skills. But, in the end, what really matters is that, regardless of our gender and the male/female bio-cultural baggage associated with each sex, we are able as human beings to share equally in life's opportunities in education and careers. Nevertheless, all too many women designers still find it hard to follow their career dreams, so the obstacles they encounter need to be removed. Greater flexibility within the workplace, especially in relation to hours and location, being the primary need. But it is also down to women themselves, whenever they can, to fight for their rights, too. And, certainly, those who do have a voice in the design world are morally bound to speak out for those that do not. Despite all the obstacles and setbacks encountered over the decades, however, as this book shows, there have been many women designers who have with drive and determination used their creativity and female ingenuity to create innovative and, often, beautiful work, which in the long run has helped change the goals and focus of design. For far too long, the role of women has been a hidden history, though the legacy of female designers in the history of design is immense. By introducing a female sensibility to problem-solving, they have contributed to a psychologically broader and more humane understanding of design. And, as to the future, women designers will no doubt increasingly shape the course of design from a female perspective.

Above: Vitra Fire Station in Weil am Rhein, designed by Zaha Hadid for Vitra International, 1990–93.

Left: Pushed Washtub sink prototype by Hella Jongerius, 1996.

Right: Comback rocking chair designed by Patricia Urquiola for Kartell, 2012.

AINO AALTO

MODERNISM · FURNITURE · GLASSWARE

Finnish
b. and d. Helsinki, Finland,
1894–1949

Aino and Alvar Aalto were the most celebrated design couple of their generation, and together pioneered a new organic language of Modern design. Yet, for years after her death, Aino's contribution was largely overlooked.

Following high school, Aino studied architecture at Helsinki's Institute of Technology as one of only three girls on her course. On graduating in 1920, having neither the financial resources nor the social connections to establish her own office, she spent the next four years working for the architect Oiva Kallio in Helsinki. Eventually, she joined Alvar Aalto's practice in early 1924, and the couple got married six months later. Having given birth to their first child the following year and a second in 1927, Aino continued her career alongside her role as a wife and mother.

Except when her children were very small, Aino was responsible for overseeing the day-to-day administration of the design office, which involved managing client relationships, employee issues and finance. Despite her creative and logistical input, the office was always known as 'Alvar Aalto Architects' – for at this stage men were invariably seen as the lead partners in any male-female creative couplings. Yet Aino still managed to forge her own distinguished career as a designer and architect, while also working in partnership with her husband on certain projects. For instance, according to Alvar, she was responsible for 'the most beautiful staircase in the world',[1] designed for his Viipuri Library (1927–35). She also created a stool/table for his Paimio Sanatorium (1929–32) that was stridently modern.

It was, however, her Böljeblick glassware range (1932) created for the Karhula-Iittala Glass Competition of 1932 that brought her the greatest recognition as a design innovator in her own right. That same year prohibition in Finland had been lifted and as a result there was an increase in demand for drinking and entertaining glassware. The competition was divided into four categories, including one for a set of pressed tableware. Aino's Bölgeblick set won second prize in this category and was put into serial production two years later. Its title, meaning 'wave view', was a nod to Erik Gunnar Asplund's lakeside Böljeblick restaurant at the 1930 Stockholm Exhibition, while referencing the glassware's concentric pattern inspired by rippling water. Thanks to its stackable practicality and progressive Functionalist aesthetic, the range became so popular that over the years more pieces were added.

In 1935 the Aaltos, together with Maire Gullichesen and Nils-Gustav Hahl, established the furniture company Artek – its name being a contraction of 'art' and 'technology'. Aino played a significant role in this company's development and was its managing director from 1941 until 1949, when her life was cut tragically short from breast cancer. Indeed, much of the furniture produced by Artek must be considered a joint effort, for Aino helped develop the innovative laminated wood and plywood forming techniques that made its production possible. From existing documents, it is also clear that Aino was instrumental in laying the aesthetic foundations of Artek. In many ways, Aino was more of a modernist than her husband, and their work both together and separately was based on complete creative equality.

Opposite: 606 side table/stool for Artek, 1932 (originally designed for the Paimio Sanatorium).

This page, clockwise from top left: Side chair for Artek, 1938; Ama 500 pendant light for Valaistustyöky, 1940s; Böljeblick bowl for Karhula Glasfabrik (later Iittala), 1932.

ANNI ALBERS

MODERNISM · TEXTILES

German (active USA)
b. Berlin, Germany, 1899
d. Orange, CT, USA, 1994

Below: Woven mercerized
cotton and silk wall
hanging, 1926.

Opposite: Gouache
study for unexecuted
wallhanging, 1926.

Among the best-known textile designers of the twentieth century, Anni Albers's trailblazing work led to a major re-evaluation of the status of textiles. Some of her exquisitely composed woven wall-hangings should be viewed as works of art as readily as any painting or sculpture. Along with her husband, artist Josef Albers, she was also an influential educator. Throughout her long career, the Bauhaus-trained Albers tirelessly experimented with printing and weaving techniques, pushing their technical boundaries in the pursuit of innovation.

Born and raised in Berlin, Albers was encouraged by her parents to study drawing and painting, although it was never expected that she would pursue art or design seriously. But Albers had other ideas and, rebelling against her privileged Jewish background, went to an art school that had already achieved notoriety for embracing Modernism, and where the living conditions were pretty rough and ready. She enrolled at the Bauhaus in Weimar in 1922 and began its one-year preliminary course. Shortly after arriving, she met Josef Albers, eleven years her senior and a tutor of stained glass. A relationship soon ensued. After completing her first year, Albers trained in the weaving workshop, headed by Georg Muche. She chose this because, although the Bauhaus's director, Walter Gropius, had insisted that there would be 'no difference between the beautiful and the strong sex',[1] when it came to it, female students had very little choice as to what they studied. Most women who trained at the Bauhaus had to be content with weaving because it was regarded as a more feminine pursuit than, say, metalworking, carpentry or woodcarving. The school's hands-on teaching methods, based on learning-through-experimentation, was, however, completely revolutionary and Albers embraced it wholeheartedly under the tutelage of Gunta Stölzl (see pages 216–17). Approaching textiles from an artisanal

standpoint, she used hand-weaving techniques as a medium of expression.

In 1925 the Bauhaus moved to Dessau and the couple relocated with it, marrying that same year. They moved into one of the newly built masters' houses, which had been designed by Gropius. In accordance with the Bauhaus's desire to forge better links with manufacturing industries, Albers developed a sound-absorbing furnishing fabric, devised to improve the acoustics of an auditorium designed by Hannes Meyer for the ADGB Trade Union School. When Stölzl departed the Bauhaus in 1931, Albers replaced her as the master of the weaving workshop, reflecting the esteem in which she was now held at the school. The National Socialists, however, shut the school down in 1933, which prompted Albers's decision to emigrate to the United States.

Josef had been invited by the newly founded Black Mountain College in North Carolina to set up its visual arts programme, and Albers was subsequently hired to teach weaving and textile design there. They remained at Black Mountain until 1949, during which period she busied herself with not only teaching, but also creating innovative textiles, which incorporated, among other things, Lurex and cellophane. Her textiles were influenced by her husband's optical-illusion-based colour theories; so, although carefully plotted on a grid and invariably featuring a geometric pattern, they possessed a distinct visual spontaneity and tonal vibrancy. For Albers, the act of creativity was all about 'listening' to materials, but she also had an encyclopaedic knowledge of weaving from different cultures and historical timeframes, as demonstrated in her seminal book *On Weaving* (1965). It was this in-depth technical and cultural understanding of textile design that shaped Albers's work and imbued it with a unique artistic quality.

D 25   Anni Albers

LAURA ASHLEY

1960S–1980S · FASHION · TEXTILES

British
b. Dowlais, Merthyr Tydfil, UK, 1925
d. Coventry, UK, 1985

Laura Ashley was a Welsh-born textile and print designer, whose Victorian-inspired patterns became synonymous with British good taste, while enjoying international commercial success. She was born to a strict Baptist family in Wales and attended schools in Wales and England until the outbreak of World War II, when she was evacuated back home and went to secretarial school. In 1942, at the age of 16, she joined the Women's Royal Naval Service. It was during this wartime service that she met Bernard Ashley, whom she married in 1949 and with whom she had two children. Ashley took a secretarial role with the Women's Institute – a bastion of Middle England, which was formed to revitalise local communities by encouraging women to develop new skills and produce their own food. Inspiration struck in 1953 when the Ashleys visited a Women's Institute-sponsored exhibition on traditional crafts at the Victoria and Albert Museum in London. Frustrated that she was unable to purchase contemporary equivalents of the complex, figurative fabrics she had seen at the show, Ashley set about producing her own using natural materials.

Bernard put his wartime engineering skills to good use, building a mechanical printer and oven in order to produce Ashley's textiles in their tiny Pimlico flat. A distinctive range of headscarves resulted, which, like many of the designs she produced over her career, bore the influence of her idyllic pastoral childhood in the Welsh hills. This natural, yet whimsical, look was a refreshing change from the seriousness of pre-war Modernist textiles and pre-empted the nostalgic Arts and Crafts revival of the coming decade. The designs became an unexpected hit and, such was the demand, that the retail giant John Lewis began stocking them and the

pair were able to quit their jobs to develop the business.

In 1961 the Ashley family moved to a Surrey cottage and the business to nearby Kent. This allowed the Laura Ashley brand to grow, gaining such popularity that its designs were sold in Europe, America and Australia. Bolstered by this success, the couple moved their production facility further afield to Montgomeryshire in Wales, where they produced humble milkmaid-style dresses and other garments in classic styles from Ashley's own textiles. As the business expanded and her creative scope widened, they manufactured not just outfits, but a whole world of Laura Ashley domestic items, from oven gloves to aprons and gardening smocks. She drew inspiration from the hands-on agricultural environment of her youth and, in fact, the whole enterprise was an early and influential progenitor of lifestyle design.

The unassuming simplicity of the firm's designs, however, belied the Ashleys' creative ambitions and business acumen that led them to open their first shop in South Kensington, London, in 1968. This prominent metropolitan storefront ensured that Laura Ashley fast became a household name. The 1970s witnessed the opening of 70 international stores, including a flagship shop in every fashion capital. Throughout, Ashley was unerring in the application of her signature

silhouette – pinned bodices, full skirts and high necklines. But she also researched continuously and painstakingly, hunting scarcely seen historic textiles in archives and private residences for fresh inspiration.

Commercial success rendered the Ashleys fantastically wealthy. In the late 1970s the family moved to Château de Remaisnil, an eighteenth-century Baroque edifice in Picardy, France. They renovated the dilapidated interior with touches of their own style and Ashley, herself, designed an English garden for the grounds. From this stately residence, they monitored their vast global retail empire, which by 1985 comprised 220 shops in 12 countries.

That same year, Ashley fell down the stairs of her daughter's Cotswold home. She suffered a brain haemorrhage and died, at the age of 60. Two months later, her namesake company was publicly floated and, as its CEO, Bernard continued to run the business according to the design principles established by his wife. Overall control of the company has since passed to the Malaysian Chinese businessman, Khoo Kay Peng, who has overseen the expansion of Laura Ashley's worldwide franchise operation and encouraged more licensing projects. These have helped perpetuate Ashley's remarkable design legacy and brought her quintessentially British 'heritage' prints to a new global audience.

Opposite: Rolls of Laura
Ashley wallpaper in the
Laura Ashley shop in
Llanidloes, Wales, 1970s.

Clockwise from right:
Laura Ashley publicity
photograph, *c.* 1975;
advertisement for the
USA market, 1970s;
Victorian Revival long
dress, *c.* 1974.

Overleaf, left to right:
Gothic Neo-Revival
printed textile, 1970s;
Art Nouveau style
printed textile, early
1970s.

GAE AULENTI

1960S–2000S · FURNITURE · LIGHTING · ARCHITECTURE

Italian
b. Palazzolo Della Stella, Italy, 1927
d. Milan, Italy, 2012

Gae Aulenti enjoyed a long career designing innovative furniture and lighting, alongside her work as one of Milan's foremost architects. She was a leading proponent of the postwar Neo-Liberty movement in Italy, which rejected the Modernist International Style in favour of a more experimental and creatively expressive approach to design. She was internationally renowned for her bold and playful product designs during the 1970s and 1980s, while the latter part of her career was marked by her skilful and imaginative renovation of public spaces, including the Musée d'Orsay in Paris and Milan's Piazzale Cadorna.

Having studied architecture at the Politecnico di Milano, Aulenti graduated in 1954 and established her own Milanese practice, also joining the editorial team of the journal *Casabella*, then under the editorship of the architect Ernesto Rogers. She remained on the staff until 1965 and, during this time, became well versed in the debate surrounding the need for a more culturally inclusive approach to design

that embraced the continuity of history, which was what the Neo-Liberty movement stood for. During the 1960s, she assisted Giuseppe Samonà in teaching architectural composition at the University of Venice, and later fulfilled a similar role for Rogers at her alma mater. It was, however, her early Neo-Liberty designs that first brought her widespread attention, most notably her Sgarsul rocking chair designed for the manufacturer Poltronova in 1961. This remarkable composition in bent wood was followed by a plethora of lighting designs that were both technically and formally inventive: notably, her Pipistrello light (1965) with its curious bat-shaped shade; her King Sun lamp, designed for the Olivetti Showroom in Buenos Aires; her Rimorchiatore combined light, candleholder, vase and ashtray (1967) with its strong architectonic feel; and her Mezzo Pileo floor lamp (1972) with its visor-like adjustable shade.

Aulenti also began making a name in the field of interior design with a number of showroom schemes for Olivetti, commencing in 1966, as well as showrooms for Fiat and Knoll. The latter went on to manufacture her imposing marble Jumbo table (1965) in 1972, and introduced her Aulenti collection of lounge seating, side chair and tables in 1974 – thereby cementing her international design reputation. Aulenti also created a similarly innovative furniture group for Kartell, which included her amply proportioned 4794 lounge chair. During the 1980s, her work possessed a playful poetic quality that flirted with Postmodernism, such as the portable and multifunctional Mini Box table light (1981), co-designed with architect Pier Giacomo Castiglioni, or her ready-made Tavolo con Ruote (1980) for FontanaArte, comprising a square of glass raised on four gigantic castor wheels.

It was, however, her clever remodelling of existing public spaces that brought her the greatest recognition,

beginning in 1980 with her interiors for the Musée d'Orsay. The critical success of this project prompted other museum interior-design and remodelling commissions, including the Georges Pompidou Centre's Museé d'Art Moderne, the Museu Nacional d'Art de Catalunya in Barcelona and San Francisco's Museum of Asian Art. Aulenti approached the design of these public spaces within the context of their architectural surroundings, and did not let the objects exhibited in them dictate the style of the schemes. This understanding of context is what ultimately gave these examples of Aulenti's work their all-important sense of place. While her oeuvre largely fell within the Modernist canon, she was not a dogmatic Modernist, but rather a pragmatic one, whose work always displayed a cultural sensitivity and left-field originality. In tribute to her immense contribution to design and urban planning, Aulenti received the prestigious French award, Légion d'honneur, in 1987 and the Praemium Imperiale in Japan in 1991. In 2012 she was the recipient of the Milan Triennale career award and that same year a Milanese piazza was renamed after her.

LINA
BO BARDI

POST-WAR–1980S · FURNITURE · ARCHITECTURE

Italian/Brazilian
b. Rome, Italy, 1914
d. São Paulo, Brazil, 1992

Among the most important Latin American architects of her generation, Lina Bo Bardi designed buildings and furniture that were startlingly avant-garde. Over her long career she consistently brought a Milanese creative sensibility to the Brazilian design landscape.

Born in Rome to a Genoese family with limited financial resources, Bo Bardi was nevertheless able to study fine art at secondary school and then, unusually for the time, trained as an architect at the newly established University of Rome. She flourished in the mostly male teaching environment. The teaching was more traditional than in the architecture schools of Milan and Turin, but its students were well aware of the battle of styles raging between the progressive Rationalists and adherents of the historicizing Novecento style. And so, in 1940, Bo Bardi moved to Milan, to set up an architecture practice with her fellow classmate and boyfriend, Carlo Pagani.

The same year, their designs for a seaside house in Sicily were featured in *Domus* magazine by Gio Ponti, who later asked the couple to act as contributors to *Lo Stile*. In 1943 Bo Bardi was sent to Rome to interview another contributor, Pietro Maria Bardi. A romance ensued and they married in 1946. A month later, the couple travelled to Rio de Janeiro, where Pietro staged three exhibitions and met all the prominent members of the Brazilian artistic avant-garde. The following year, he was asked to establish the São Paulo Museum of Modern Art, for which Bo Bardi later designed the building.

In 1951 Bo Bardi became a Brazilian citizen and completed her first architectural project, the Glass House, made of concrete and glass as a residence for herself and her husband that was a daring exercise in modern living. Encircled by the Atlantic Forest that surrounds the city, the house accommodated a full-grown tree at its centre. Also in 1951, she designed her famous Bowl chair, which was widely publicized with her sitting in it. This low-tech yet ingenious design, which was used in the Glass House, had different seating positions depending on how the hemispherical seat shell was placed on its simple metal-ringed base.

In 1958 Bo Bardi became director of the Museum of Modern Art of Bahia, for which she skilfully restored the seventeenth-century Solar do Unhão sugar mill as its headquarters. In 1966 she returned to São Paulo and resumed work on her design for the Museum of Modern Art building, which was completed two years later and is now regarded as one of the great landmarks of Brazilian Modernism. Two notable renovation projects followed: the Centro de Lazer Fábrica da Pompéia, completed in 1982, a Brutalist tour de force that converted a drum factory into a leisure centre, and the Teatro Oficina, which transformed a burnt-out office into an experimental theatre space with a creative use of internal scaffolding.

Throughout her career, she was interested in sustainable architecture as well as the social and cultural potential of design. As early as 1958, she published a 90-page thesis intended as a manifesto for building sustainability, writing that architecture was 'an art that must seriously take into account the land in which it takes place'.[1] Crucially, with her various historical building preservation projects, she demonstrated how it was possible to create an utterly modern architectural statement that worked in harmony with traditional restoration principles. She undoubtedly had an enhanced sensitivity to both function and context, which made this possible, and which ultimately enabled her to imbue her buildings with a strong sense of identity, community and place.

Opposite: Centro de Lazer
Fábrica da Pompéia
(now SESC Pompéia),
São Paulo, 1982.

This page, top to bottom:
São Paulo Museum of
Modern Art, completed
1968; Bowl chairs (reissued
by Arper), 1951.

CINI BOERI

Italian
b. Milan, Italy, 1924

Cini Boeri was once described as 'female emancipation in the shape of an architect, a woman of other times, past and future'.[1] Certainly, she possesses a tireless energy that is sustained by what she describes as the feeling of renewal that comes from 'always creating something new'.[2] Regarding design as both a creative joy and a social mission, she has, during her long career, always paid particular attention to the functional aspects of architecture and focused on the psychological relationships we have with our domestic environments. In the field of industrial design her work has long been driven by the search for innovative, functionally adaptive solutions that will simplify and thereby improve our ways of living.

After graduating from the Politecnico di Milano in 1951, Boeri interned with architect and designer Gio Ponti before commencing a long period of collaboration with Marco Zanuso, who also combined architecture with furniture design. In 1963 she founded her own studio specializing in civil architecture and industrial design. Her reputation

as a progressive designer was firmly established with her sculptural Bobo chaise longue (1967) and her continuously snaking, modular Serpentone seating system (1971), both utilizing state-of-the-art polyurethane-foam moulding technology and put into production by the furniture group Arflex. Inspired by the 'wrapped' artworks of the artist Christo, she later created the Strips range (1972) for Arflex, which comprised beds, armchairs and sofas. Made from blocks of polyurethane foam without any rigid structure, the pieces were fixed onto plywood bases with castors and came with zipped, padded slipcovers, which were easy to remove and completely washable. Hugely influential, these designs went on to win a Compasso d'Oro award in 1979.

Boeri also created innovative and highly sculptural furniture designs that pushed the physical limits and aesthetic boundaries of glass, most notably, the Lunario (1970) desk and table for Knoll and the transparent, seemingly gravity-defying, Ghost chair (1987) for FIAM. Additionally, she designed a number of interesting lights for Artemide, Arteluce and Stilnovo that possessed a bold architectonic aesthetic,

including her Brontes lamp (1981), which incorporated a pivoting pressed-glass headlamp-like diffuser that delivered a low-tech yet highly efficient level of lighting control.

What is so striking about Boeri's portfolio of work is its technical persuasiveness and bold sculptural bravado. And, although when she is designing she never thinks 'about being either a woman or a man', she does believe that being a woman allows one to think 'about design with a female sensibility'[3] with regard to aesthetics and functionality. She also believes that women bring a uniquely feminine perspective to the experience of design and have an enhanced ability to understand how design requirements can change over time. Certainly, throughout her career spanning five decades, she has never deviated from the belief that although there might be art in design, as a discipline it is principally about logic and the search for rational solutions. It is Boeri's analytical approach to problem solving, born of in-depth knowledge of materials and processes as well as usability, that has always set her work apart and also enabled her to become such an influential educator.

Opposite: Lunario tables
for Knoll, 1970.

Left: Serpentone seating
system for Arflex, 1971;
below: Bobo chaise longue
for Arflex, 1967.

IRMA BOOM

CONTEMPORARY · GRAPHICS

Dutch
b. Lochem, The Netherlands, 1960

In today's world of increasingly tight publishing deadlines, Irma Boom is an anomaly, for she thinks nothing of taking years to lay out a book. Her experimental approach has produced remarkable results that have pushed the boundaries of book design and won her numerous awards.

Irma Boom studied at AKI ArtEZ Academy for Art and Design in Enschede, which was founded on the principle of nurturing creative individuality. For her third-year internship, one of her tutors suggested approaching the design department of Staatsdrukkerij, the Dutch government's publishing and printing office. As Boom recalls, 'It turned out to be the best place for me … [because] they trained me in making books and identities.'[1] It was the 1980s, a financially golden period for art-book publishing, and Boom was offered much creative freedom there and was actively encouraged to use expensive 'special' treatments such as foiling. On graduating, she returned to the office and designed, among other publications, a book on the history of Dutch postage stamps, which established her reputation as an innovative designer, albeit by accident. As a young and inexperienced practitioner, Boom had incorrectly calculated the book's imposition, so when it was printed its pages were completely out of sync. The left-hand pages were on the right, and vice versa, but this proved a fortuitous mistake because it gave the book a strong and seemingly experimental dynamism. This publication, unsurprisingly, polarized the graphic-design community when it went on to win a Best Book award, with the jury noting that it represented 'a brilliant failure'. The book led to Boom's reputation as an eccentric-yet-gifted designer, which was underscored by her subsequent award-winning books for Staatsdrukkerij.

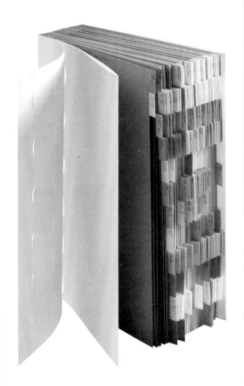

In 1991 Boom founded her own design practice in Amsterdam and has since worked on hundreds of book projects, each with its own distinct and highly considered identity. At the start of any commission Boom conducts meticulous research into the book's subject-matter, involving in-depth discussions with its subjects, editors and authors. She then painstakingly transforms this research into a very personalized graphic expression of the book's content. One of her best-known projects was created for the centenary of SHV, a Dutch trading company, and took five years to design. Boom spent three and a half years on preliminary research and it was only when she felt fully immersed in the company's corporate mentality that she began designing the *SHV Think Book* (1996). It was a very unconventional publication, running to 2,136 pages and incorporating various printing techniques. It had no pagination and was laid out in a non-chronological order because Boom wanted it to take the reader on a voyage of coincidental discoveries. It is this type of iconoclastic approach that gives Boom's work such a refreshing originality and such a strong 'book as object' presence. Her book designs often have a noteworthy textural quality that helps enhance their physicality – for example, the embossed cover and irregular rough-edge pages of her matte-white monograph, *Sheila Hicks: Weaving as Metaphor* (2006), cleverly convey the handcrafted nature of the woven textile pieces shown inside.

Today, Boom enjoys the patronage of a variety of clients who understand that when they commission her to design a publication they are commissioning a bespoke graphic artwork. She is a remarkable one-of-a-kind designer and is widely recognized as such. In 2001 she became the youngest-ever recipient of the Gutenberg Prize for outstanding technical and artistic achievement in printing and in 2014 received the Johannes Vermeer Award – the Dutch state prize for the arts – for her 'unparalleled achievements in the field of graphic design'.

Opposite: Dai Fujiwara's *The Sky Diary*, book design made for 21_21 Design Sight/Issey Miyake Foundation, 2013.

Right: *Sheila Hicks, Weaving as Metaphor*, book design for Bard Graduate Center for Studies in the Decorative Arts, 2006; below: Jennifer Butler's *James Jennifer Georgina*, book design for Erasmus Publishing, 2010.

SHEILA HICKS

MARIANNE BRANDT

MODERNISM · METALWARE · LIGHTING

German
b. Chemnitz, Germany, 1893
d. Kirchberg, Germany, 1983

Of all the women who studied at the Bauhaus, it was Marianne Brandt who undoubtedly had the greatest impact on the development of Modernist design. Unlike many of her female peers at this experimental teaching establishment, she avoided being drawn into the weaving department, instead managing to get herself into the metal workshop, where she created pioneering designs. She was also one of the very few Bauhaus designers who was able to create designs for industrial mass production that went on to become commercially successful.

Brandt began her studies in 1911 at the Grossherzogliche Sächsische Hochschule für bildende Kunst (Saxon Grand Ducal Art School) in Weimar, under Fritz Mackensen. From 1917, she worked as an independent artist in her own studio, creating paintings that fell within the Expressionist school. After her marriage in 1919 to the Norwegian painter Erik Brandt, she lived in Norway and France, before returning to Weimar in 1921. Three years later, at the age of 31, she enrolled at the Bauhaus in Weimar, where she undertook the school's famous foundation course. This course had just been taken over by the artists László Moholy-Nagy and Josef Albers, who introduced a more rational Constructivist agenda to its teaching than Johannes Itten's earlier art-for-art's-sake Expressionist approach.

This change of teaching emphasis no doubt benefitted Brandt who, after completing the course and acting on the advice of Moholy-Nagy, was apprenticed in the Bauhaus's metal workshop. As the sole woman, she was initially given subordinate tasks. However, she soon adopted Moholy-Nagy's Constructivist approach to problem-solving and created innovative prototypes and models for everyday household objects,

including her famous Model No. MT49 teapot (1924). This diminutive design was a masterpiece of geometric simplification, which revealed Brandt's interest in basic shapes that were perfectly suited for machine production.

After receiving her journeyman's certificate, Brandt spent six months in Paris before returning to the Bauhaus as deputy director of its metal workshop. She began collaborating with two lighting manufacturers, Kandem (short for Körting & Mathiesen) in Leipzig and Schwintzer & Graff, Berlin. In 1926 Brandt also co-designed, with Hans Przyrembel, a number of utilitarian lights for the new Bauhaus building in Dessau, which underscored the institution's increasing focus on designs intended for industrial production. In 1928 she co-designed, with Hin Bredendieck, the no-nonsense No. 679 desk lamp and the diminutive Model 680 bedside lamp, both produced by Kandem. The latter is now regarded as one of the great icons of German design.

Between 1929 and 1932, Brandt was director of Dessau Bauhaus's metal workshop, a remarkable accomplishment in a male-dominated design discipline. During this period, she also headed the design department at the Ruppelwerk metalware

factory in Gotha. There, she designed strikingly modern homewares, including a triangular napkin holder, tray, clock, ashtray and spherical liquor-set holder.

In 1933, with Germany's economy floundering and few design commissions in the offing, Brandt returned to Chemnitz and took up painting, weaving and photography. After World War II, she taught at the Dresden Academy of Fine Arts (1949–50) and the Institute of Applied Arts in East Berlin (1951–54), and also curated a major exhibition entitled 'Deutsche Angewandte Kunst' ('German Applied Art') held in Beijing and Shanghai (1953–54). Countering the prevailing belief that 'a woman's place is not in the metal workshop', Brandt proved unequivocally that women were as able as men in designing products for industrial mass production. She was a truly inspirational role model for all the female designers who followed in her wake.

Opposite: Ashtray for Bauhaus Metal Workshops (reissued by Alessi), 1924.

This page, clockwise from left: Kandem No. 679 lamp for Körtingen & Mathiesen, *c.* 1928 (co-designed with Hin Bredendieck); Table Clock for Ruppelwerk GmbH, *c.* 1930; MT49 Teapot for Bauhaus Metal Workshops, 1924.

MARGARET CALVERT

British
b. Pretoria, South Africa, 1936

Margaret Calvert was responsible for the design of some of the world's most influential signage systems. Born in South Africa, she was schooled in Pretoria and London, and then trained as a graphic designer at Chelsea College of Art, London. While there, her tutor Jock Kinneir asked her to assist him with a major commission: public display signs for the new Gatwick Airport (1957–58). The resulting signage system was notable for its strikingly modern clarity and formal consistency.

This job, along with a baggage labelling system Kinneir had created for P&O Orient Line prompted Sir Colin Anderson, who was the chairman of the new Ministry of Transport's Advisory Committee on Traffic Signs for Motorways, to ask Kinneir to design a new motorway signage system. Kinneir was given a completely open brief, except for one notable stipulation, which was that lowercase lettering should be used on a blue background, as was being used for Germany's autobahn signage.

Employing a research-based approach, Calvert assisted Kinneir in the development of this new motorway signage system, which was cleverly devised using separate letter tiles laid out on a grid in order to determine their overall size and spacing. In fact, Calvert and Kinneir ingeniously designed the signage family using a system of proportional relationships that was mathematically guided by the top and bottom strokes of the letter 'I' from their specially designed 'Transport' sans-serif typeface. This typeface had been developed to maximize legibility so it could be read at high driving speeds. They also adopted a mixture of upper case and lower case letters, despite the original brief's typographic guidelines, as it was found likewise to be easier to read.

Calvert and Kinneir's revolutionary signage was trialled on Britain's first stretch of motorway, the Preston bypass, in 1958 and then installed on the M1 the following year. Yet, despite its design being a joint effort, Kinneir was for many years credited as its sole creator. Thanks to its success, the Government subsequently asked Sir Walter Worboys to set up a new committee in 1961 'to review traffic signs on all-purpose roads, as distinct from motorways, including roads in urban areas, and to recommend what changes should be made'. This led to Kinneir and Calvert being commissioned to develop another comprehensive system of lettering and graphics, this time for all primary and non-primary roads in the UK. Introduced on 1 January 1965, this new signage won a CoID Design Award in 1967. The same year, *Design* magazine attributed its development only to Kinneir even though the duo's office had now been renamed Kinneir, Calvert and Associates to reflect Calvert's equality of input. Among these new traffic signs was one for 'children crossing', based on a childhood photograph of Calvert, which, with its big sister and small brother

pairing, subtly reflected the shifting sands of gender equality in 1960s Britain. As Calvert later noted of the pictograms she created for the signage system, 'I wanted them to be more human, figurative ... have more personality'.[1] It was this intuitive touch that ultimately made Calvert-Kinneir signage systems so engaging and impactful. The pair later created the Rail Alphabet typeface for British Railways, which was central to its rebranding by the DRU in 1965. Calvert also taught at the Royal College of Art, eventually heading its department of graphic arts and design from 1987 to 1991. It was not until 2016, however, that Calvert's enormous contribution to the typographic and signage landscape of Britain was recognized with an OBE.

28 The NORTH
Leeds
Sheffield

Mansfield

A 38

Matlock
(A 615)

Opposite top: Quayside/ river bank road signage for the Department of Transport, 1965; opposite bottom: children crossing road signage for the Department of Transport, 1965.

Above: Motorway junction signage for the Department of Transport, 1958.

LOUISE CAMPBELL

CONTEMPORARY · FURNITURE · LIGHTING · PRODUCT DESIGN

Danish
b. Copenhagen, Denmark, 1970

Louise Campbell is one of the Nordic region's pre-eminent designers and works for a roster of manufacturing companies. Born to a Danish father and an English mother, her dual heritage has led to a synthesis in her work of the best of two design cultures – a strong arts-and-crafts sensibility on the Danish side, with a delight in innovative, hands-on experimentation emanating from the British side.

She graduated from the London College of Furniture in 1992 and then completed her training at The Royal Danish Academy of Fine Arts. In 1996 she set up a Copenhagen-based studio, but it was not until she won a competition to design a chair for the Danish crown prince, Frederik, that Campbell began enjoying recognition among the international design community. The Prince chair, which embodied an unashamedly feminine aspect, reflected the contrasts within the prince's own life, who, though bounded by historic traditions, was also a young man in touch with his own generation. As Campbell explains, 'On one level it illustrates a motif resembling fine old lace (there is a point to the transparency of the chair – it is hard for a prince to hide from the public eye), on the other level the chair is produced using visibly high technology methods.'[1] Its perforated seat shell was made from laser-cut steel onto which a thick layer of water-cut neoprene was glued. By using high-tech CAD cutting techniques, Campbell was able to replicate precisely the perforated motif of abstracted butterflies, flowers and leaves across two very different materials – steel and neoprene – the latter providing a comfortable softness, as well as being 'a refreshing alternative to upholstery'.[2]

The Prince chair was also a forthright rejection of an obsession in Danish design with design archetypes and the quest for ideal forms. The Prince chair was put into production by HAY in 2005, and the following year Campbell created

another chair that generated a similar level of publicity – the Veryround chair for Zanotta. As she observes of this unusual design, 'it doesn't care much about what other chairs look like'[3] and, certainly, its delicate-looking, shadow-casting structure made of two layers of three-dimensionally laser-cut sheet steel looks more like an Op art sculpture than a practical seating design. This seemingly complex, yet actually quite simple, bowl-like design was based on an interlinking pattern of 240 circles, with the inner layer being exactly the same as the outer layer, only 20 per cent smaller. The visual lightness of this chair, which has none of the elements normally associated with seating – no legs, no joints, no upholstery – belies the fact that it is strong enough to support a seated adult. It can even be rocked gently from side to side.

Campbell's playful and experimental approach, pushing materials and production technologies in new creative directions, soon caught the attention of other leading manufacturers, including two of Denmark's most famous design brands: Louis Poulsen and Georg Jensen. For the former, Campbell has created a number of innovative lighting designs, including her Collage (2005) and Shutters (2012) pendant lamps, which use light-filtering perforated shades made of laser-cut matt acrylic and die-cast aluminium respectively. Campbell's stainless-steel cutlery (2014) for Georg Jensen was likewise designed from a functional perspective and, in this case, all ornamentation was eliminated, in order not to detract from the aesthetics of the food being eaten. It is this consideration of function and her judicious use of decoration that makes Campbell's work so captivating. It has allowed her to work across a spectrum of projects, from design– art installations to her simple Flora vases (2007) for Holmegaard and The More, The Merrier modular system of candleholders (2007) for Muuto.

Opposite: Veryround chair
for Zanotta, 2006.

This page, right: Cutlery
for Georg Jensen, 2014;
below: Prince chair for
HAY, 2005.

ANNA CASTELLI FERRIERI

Italian
b. and d. Milan, Italy, 1918–2006

Anna Castelli Ferrieri was the leading female industrial designer in Italy for nearly three decades. Her career spanned the so-called golden period of Italian design, from the early 1960s to the late 1980s, and she contributed much to this phenomenon both as a designer in her own right and as the influential art director of Kartell.

Born and raised in Milan, Castelli Ferrieri was the daughter of a renowned journalist, film director and screenwriter, and so grew up in the midst of Italy's progressive cultural community. Not surprisingly given her background, she opted to study architecture at the Politecnico di Milano, which was then already at the forefront of design teaching in Italy. In 1943 she became its first female architecture graduate and the same year married the chemical engineer Giulio Castelli. He went on to establish his own plastics manufacturing firm, Kartell, in 1949, which from the start was very much a design-led enterprise. From its founding, Ferrieri was greatly involved in the development of the firm's high-quality products. Initially, however, she chose to pursue an independent career of her own practising architecture. With this aim, she participated in the Congrès Internationale d'Architecture Moderne (CIAM) in 1949, and three years later became a member of the Istituto Nazionale di Urbanistica, the national body for city planning. Between 1955 and 1960, she was also a correspondent for *Architectural Digest*.

During the 1960s, Castelli Ferrieri collaborated with the architect Ignazio Gardella on a number of interesting building projects and urban plans, including Alfa Romeo's headquarters in Arese (1968–74) and Kartell's own manufacturing and administration complex in Noviglio (completed 1967). The pair also co-designed some innovative furniture, including the Model 4991 table (1964), which was Castelli Ferrieri's first design for Kartell. Three years later, she designed two revolutionary

storage systems – the first being the square-sectioned Multi-Box system, which was shortly followed by the cylindrical Model 4965-6-7 Componibili stacking storage units. Both of these systems comprised injection-moulded acrylonitrile butadiene styrene (known as ABS) modular units, available in two sizes, which stacked one on top of another with a tray-like top. These units also came with optional hinged or sliding doors and could also be mounted on castors for enhanced manoeuvrability. Functionally flexible, lightweight and colourful, these designs were perfectly in tune with the more informal lifestyles of young people in the 1960s and, to this day, are among Kartell's bestsellers.

From 1976 to 1987, Castelli Ferrieri was Kartell's art director and continued to design furniture for the company, as well as smaller household items. Her designs were always technically advanced and rationally conceived, yet also infused with a distinctly Milanese neo-Modernist stylishness. As her obituary in *The New York Times* observed, she was, 'an emblematic member of a generation of Italian designers that … energetically transformed the world of design with their interest in using new technologies and materials'.[1] Indeed, she was not only instrumental in the development of Kartell's remarkable product line and enduring design-led culture, but also, by default, helped to shape the whole notion of 'Made in Italy' with her own stylish, practical and affordable designs.

Opposite: 4965-6-7
Componibili storage
units for Kartell, 1967.

This page, clockwise
from right: Model 4814
armchair for Kartell, 1988;
4970/4979/4978/4972
Multi-Box storage units
for Kartell, 1967.

COCO CHANEL

1920S–1960S · FASHION

French
b. Saumur, France, 1883
d. Paris, France, 1971

There is perhaps no more iconic twentieth-century fashion designer than Coco Chanel. Yet at birth, she did not seem particularly fated for success. Gabrielle Bonheur 'Coco' Chanel was born in a workhouse in 1883. As her mother was unmarried, she was soon taken to an orphanage, which was attached to the Cistercian Monastery of Aubazine in Corrèze. There, she learnt her trade as a seamstress, becoming skilled enough to take up work aged 18 with a local tailor.

Fuelled by a desire to prove herself legitimate to French society, Chanel moved to Paris at the turn of the century. By 1910, she had opened the doors of her first boutique at 21 Rue Cambon, selling fine hats to a glamorous clique of actresses and socialites under the brand Chanel Modes. Her personal style became a sensation, too, causing much of Parisian society to imitate her elegant, unfussy and modern dress.

Within three years, she was able to expand her enterprise with a new boutique in fashionable seaside Deauville, where she introduced a revolutionary line of casual garments and sportswear made from stretch jerseys. Dynamic, minimal and famously comfortable, these pieces drew inspiration from the traditional masculine workwear of the French coast. Chanel set about defining an entirely new approach to womenswear that chimed perfectly with the bold sensibilities of the Jazz Age. Within a decade, the 'Chanel look' cleared away the physically restrictive corsetry, pomp and formality of the Belle Époque before it. Soon, modern, monochromatic Chanel awnings were put up above the windows of couture houses in Biarritz and Paris.

In 1921 Chanel's star rose even further, with the launch of Chanel No. 5 – a scent created with Ernest Beaux, former perfumer at Rallet, supplier to the Russian

Above: Model wearing beaded cocktail dress, 1926.

Opposite, left: Metal embroidered silk coat, c. 1927; right: Gabrielle winter suit, 1963–64.

imperial family. Initially given as a gift to preferred clients, distribution of the perfume was expanded by her business partner, Pierre Wertheimer. Chanel worked through the mid 1920s producing garments for which she would be internationally celebrated. The cardigan jacket (1925) and 'little black dress' (1926) have become archetypes of sleek sophistication, often imitated nearly a century later. Such was her international reputation, Chanel was invited to Hollywood by movie mogul Samuel Goldwyn in 1931 to style his silver-screen stars in the latest on-trend fashions from Paris, before they reached American shores via sea-bound importation.

At the outbreak of World War II, Chanel closed her shop and stepped away from the world of fashion. With Paris under strict German occupation, she lived in close proximity to Nazi officers in the Hotel Ritz and her seeming involvement with this enemy elite became such a subject of speculation that Chanel moved to neutral Switzerland, returning only in 1944 to stand trial for collaboration. She was cleared thanks to lack of evidence and, reputedly, a 'good word' having been put in by Winston Churchill.

In 1954 Chanel judged that enough time had passed since liberation, and returned to the helm of her company. However, she soon found her spare, androgynous style in stark contrast to the overtly feminine excesses of Christian Dior's now-popular 'New Look'. Despite this, Chanel remained firm in her aesthetic convictions, spending the next two decades elaborating on her singular and stylish vision. The label went on to huge international commercial success, especially in the American market. When she died in her luxurious Ritz suite in 1971, Chanel left behind a globally renowned fashion empire, which has since grown into one of the world's greatest luxury fashion brands.

LOUISE CHÉRUIT

BELLE ÉPOQUE · FASHION

French
b. and d. France, 1866–1955

One of the great fashion innovators of the Belle Époque era, Louise Chéruit went on to become the first woman to establish and run a significant French fashion house. Born in 1866, she was the daughter of a seamstress. Fascinated by her mother's trade, she took up professional training at the earliest opportunity with Parisian dressmakers, Raudnitz & Cie. It was found that she had an affinity with fine fabrics and elegant, flowing forms. Alongside her sister, Marie, she quickly rose to the top of the company, so much so that, before the turn of the century, labels bore her name above those of the proprietors.

In 1895 she married her lover, Prosper Chéruit, whose wealth gave her real purchase in the elite world of Parisian fashion. By 1906 she had acquired the company and renamed it Chéruit. Aided by the prominent position of her premises at the Hôtel de Fontpertuis in the elegant Place Vendôme, Chéruit quickly gained the rapt attention of the Parisian fashion press.

Her early work typified the late Belle Époque era – elaborate evening dresses that allowed light to play through complex layers of taffeta, lamé and gauze. In 1911 she produced ankle-length pannier (hooped) gowns, delighting her aristocratic clientele with their allusions to court fashions of centuries gone by. However, Chéruit was not blind to the nascent power of Modernism as it blossomed in pre-war Paris. She began experimenting with streetwear – walking suits and afternoon gowns that presaged the ready-to-wear culture of later decades.

Keen to express this modern mood further, in 1912 Chéruit took a position with Lucien Vogel at the influential illustrated fashion magazine, the *Gazette du Bon Ton*. There, she collaborated closely with fellow couturier Paul Poiret, of whom she had been an early champion. The epitome of opulence, the *Gazette* commissioned delicate pochoir prints by the most sought-after French Art Déco illustrators – Pierre

Brissaud being Chéruit's favourite. The waifish, slightly androgynous figures that graced the *Gazette*'s pages served to infuse the Chéruit brand with the Spirit of the Age.

Even a World War I scandal relating to her then lover, an Austrian nobleman and military officer accused of espionage, was not enough to compromise her position in the Parisian fashion world. Though socially excluded as a result of this turn of events, she was still able to maintain influence on the direction of her company. In particular, her hand-painted experimentation with Cubist designs drew some notable critical acclaim.

Unfortunately, however, this was not enough to secure her position in the mood of post-Chanel minimalism, which soon came to dominate the fashion scene in interwar Paris. In 1923 Chéruit retired. Her studio survived without her at the helm for a further ten years, before being bought and transformed a few months after Chéruit's death, in 1935, by the avant-garde Surrealist Elsa Schiaparelli (see pages 198–99). Although Chéruit's contribution to fashion history was overlooked for many decades, it could reasonably be argued that no fashion designer captured the spirit of the pre-war Gilded Age better than she did. Her feminine gowns of soft, figure-draping fabrics had such distinctive and innovative silhouettes that were so absolutely of their time.

Opposite, far left: Metal-embroidered silk evening wrap, 1902-4; left: inside the Maison de Chéruit, c. 1900.

This page, clockwise from left: Silk tea gown, 1922; taffeta afternoon dress with beaded bodice, 1916; fashion plate from *Les Élègances Parisiennes* showing three Chéruit daytime ensembles, 1910s.

KIM COLIN

CONTEMPORARY · FURNITURE · PRODUCT DESIGN

American/British
b. Los Angeles, USA, 1969

This page, below: Radice stool for Mattiazzi, 2013; above: Tumbler outdoor lighting for Santa & Cole, 2018.

Opposite, from top to bottom: Formwork desk accessories for Herman Miller, 2014; Wireframe sofa for Herman Miller, 2014.

Although the Royal Society of Arts in London first introduced the Royal Design for Industry (RDI) award in 1936, it took nearly 80 years for Kim Colin to become, in 2015, the first female product designer recipient.[1] It was an honour long overdue on various fronts, but especially given that her life and business partner, Sam Hecht, had received an RDI seven years earlier, despite their joint partnership as founders of the highly respected Industrial Facility design consultancy in London. Hecht's design work had already achieved considerable recognition prior to the establishment of Industrial Facility, but even so, it is indicative of the difficulty women face in gaining professional recognition in certain male-dominated fields of design.

Born and raised in Los Angeles, Colin studied art history and architecture there at the Southern Californian Institute of Architecture. Her first practice, Secret Studio, focused on working with fine artists and included assisting Mike Kelley with the execution of his seminal *Educational Complex* (1995). Her work with contemporary artists prompted a move to London in 1997, where she became an editor for the art-book publisher Phaidon Press. In 2002 she met Hecht at an exhibition in London while he was working for IDEO in Japan, and they instantly hit it off. At the time, Hecht felt that industrial design was lacking a sense of responsibility and direction but could see that this was not the case in architecture and he 'wanted to bring Colin's dialogue to design'.[2] With this aim, the pair established Industrial Facility that same year. The central idea behind the studio's founding was 'to explore the junction between industrial design and the world around us'.[3]

By pooling their talents, they aimed to create product designs that were more research-driven and, ultimately, more meaningful. As Colin explains, 'Product designers are typically thinking about the object: the surface of the object, the edges of the object and that's where it stops. They're not thinking about context so much and architecture is all about context.'[4] Initially, Hecht served as the face of the practice because he was better known within the design world, but from day one they worked collaboratively. The couple became retained designers to Muji in 2002 and worked on the development of various homewares, which went on to receive a G-mark (Japan Good Design Award) in 2006, when they also received an iF Hanover gold award for a series of knives and a knife sharpener that they designed for the Sheffield firm Taylor's Eye Witness. They were subsequently retained in 2007 as design advisors to Herman Miller, for whom they have designed not only various innovative ranges of office furniture and desk accessories, but also the Wireframe Sofa group for the company's relaunched Collection range, which won a Design Guild award in 2014.

The couple have also amassed their remarkable Under a Fiver collection of everyday consumer products from around the world, which they have exhibited at various venues and which formed the basis of a book entitled *Usefulness in Small Things* (2011). Indeed, it is their interest in enhancing the functionality of everyday things from a holistic viewpoint that makes their work so interesting, and which has made Industrial Facility one of the world's most progressive and respected design studios.

COLLIER CAMPBELL

1960S–1980S · TEXTILES

Susan Collier; British
b. Manchester, UK, 1938
d. London, UK, 2011

Sarah Campbell; British
b. Hertford, UK, 1945

Sisters Susan Collier and Sarah Campbell designed dazzling textiles during the late 1970s and 1980s, notable for their vibrant colours and bold patterning. Their hand-painted patterns gave their work a definable signature, though their sources of inspiration were highly diverse, from the canvases of Henri Matisse and the woven Bauhaus tapestries of Gunta Stölzl (see pages 216–17) to traditional English floral chintzes, Indian paisleys and North African geometric carpet weaves. One of their great strengths as designers was their ability to create a stylistically broad range of textiles, but still infuse each pattern with their distinctive design flair.

The elder of the two sisters, Susan Collier, had been utterly captivated as a child by a book on Henri Matisse, who she referred to as her 'lifelong friend',[1] such was the influence of his work on her own designs. Having decided she was no artist herself and having been completely underwhelmed by the textiles then being sold in British department stores, she turned her hand to textile design. Although completely self-taught, she possessed a natural talent for colour and composition and her earliest designs were used on scarves manufactured by Richard Allan and Jacqmar.

In 1961, armed with a portfolio of colourful and painterly textile designs, Collier approached London's Liberty & Co., promising herself that if the company bought just two of these patterns she would fully commit to a career in textile design. Liberty acquired six of them and commissioned her to produce more of the same and, in 1968, employed her on a retainer. At this stage, she was mainly creating fresh-looking floral prints for Liberty's line of fine cotton Tana Lawn fabrics.

Campbell, meanwhile, had been training as Collier's assistant and began working with her for Liberty. In 1971, Collier became Liberty's main design consultant and the following year the two siblings issued what would become one of their most famous furnishing textile designs, Bauhaus (1972), which was jointly credited under the Collier Campbell name. This best-selling Liberty textile was a vibrant homage to an earlier woven wall tapestry created by Stölzl at the Bauhaus in 1927–28 (see page 217), and perfectly captured the renewed interest in Modernism during the early 1970s – as Pop gave way to a neo-Modernist aesthetic. This design was a perfect example of how the sisters were able to 'cheat the repeat', as Collier put it – meaning that their patterns were so fluid that the borders of their repeats were virtually impossible to detect. Like most of their patterns, Bauhaus came in a range of beautiful hues, from a vibrant primary

colourway of blue, scarlet and yellow, which was stylistically attuned to the architectural and industrial High-Tech style, to a subtler earth-toned colourway better suited to the more restrained neo-Modernist interiors of the time.

Other well-known textiles produced for Liberty included Kasbah (1983) and Cottage Garden (1974), both of which were richly polychromatic. In 1977 the sisters left Liberty and set up an independent Collier Campbell label, while continuing to produce designs for Liberty as well as Habitat, Yves Saint Laurent, Cacharel, Marks & Spencer and Jaeger. One of the best-known designs from this period was Cote d'Azure (1975), a glorious homage to Matisse that reflected the sisters' passion for bold and colourful patterning and went on to become one of the most popular textiles of the early 1980s. Around this time, they cleverly diversified into homewares and all kinds of accessories, and Collier Campbell make-up cases, shower caps and spectacle holders became a ubiquitous feature of the early 1980s, both in Britain and abroad. Their international success in this area undoubtedly served as an inspirational catalyst for later female designers to set up their own textile-led brands.

In 1984 the sisters were awarded the Prince Philip Designers Prize for their Six Views collection and, in 1988, the Conran Design Group commissioned them to create carpets for the new North Terminal at Gatwick Airport. Collier died of cancer in 2011, just weeks before a major retrospective exhibition of Collier Campbell work was held at the National Theatre in London. Today, Campbell continues to work as a designer, though their eponymous label has long since passed into external ownership.

This page: Detail of Bauhaus textile for Liberty, 1972; opposite: Cote d'Azure textile for Collier Campbell, 1975.

Overleaf, left: Sakkara textile for Habitat, 1983; right: Cottage Garden textile for Liberty, 1974.

MURIEL COOPER

American
b. Brookline, MA, USA, 1925
d. Boston, MA, USA, 1994

Fondly remembered by people who knew her as 'simply a great person',[1] Muriel Cooper was a pioneering visual communicator as well as a prophetic researcher and inspirational educator who believed, fundamentally, that 'information is only useful when it can be understood'.[2] In line with this credo, she was, ostensibly, 'an architect of information,'[3] whose process-driven approach to graphic design was enormously influential, especially on her students at the Massachusetts Institute of Technology (MIT), many of whom went on to enjoy illustrious careers in the design and digital worlds. Crucially, from the mid-1970s to the early 1990s, her work spanned graphic design's monumental transition from the static, analogue world of pens, paper, Letraset and print into the digital realm, which gave her increasing scope for movement, layering and interactivity. During this period, she was at the vanguard of software interface design, helping to shape its early development through her visionary leadership of MIT's Visible Language Workshop.

Born in Massachusetts, Cooper obtained a degree in education from Ohio State University in 1944, before gaining another undergraduate degree in design and an additional one in education from the Massachusetts College of Art, in 1948 and 1951 respectively. After completing her studies, she began working in MIT's recently established Office of Publications, in 1952. She left there in 1958 to take up a Fulbright scholarship in Milan and, on her return to Boston, established her own graphic-design practice, with one of her most important clients being the MIT Press. In 1962 Cooper created a new colophon for the imprint, which cleverly took the form of seven vertical bars that not only abstractly spelled out 'MITP' in lower-

case lettering, but also visually evoked a line of books on a shelf.

In 1967 Cooper was appointed MIT Press's first art director and, subsequently, became internationally renowned for her eye-catching book designs. Among her most notable was *Bauhaus* (1969), a major survey of the German design school, the cover of which she emblazoned with optically distorting typography in offset CMYK colours. Her book cover for *Learning from Las Vegas* (1972), with its translucent glassine wrap, was similarly hailed as a design masterpiece when first published, despite that fact that its authors, Robert Venturi and Denise Scott Brown, had reservations, fearing it was too monumental for a publication that was essentially all about 'ugly and ordinary architecture'.

In 1974 Cooper began teaching a course at MIT entitled 'Messages and Meanings', exploring the relationship between graphic design and emerging technologies. This eventually led to her co-founding the Visible Language

Workshop at MIT's world-famous Media Lab in 1984, which embodied the institute's interdisciplinary ethos by bringing students with design and computing backgrounds together to explore the potential of intelligent design applications.

Throughout her four-decade long career at MIT, Cooper produced work that had a strong sense of dynamism, whether it was in a static traditional medium – such as a book or a poster – or conceived as a multi-layered digital animation. But then, she was herself a dynamic personality who was, as Nicholas Negroponte, chairman emeritus of MIT Media Lab, observed, 'deep, funny, fearless and willing to try anything'.[4] A truly visionary designer, Cooper died unexpectedly of an apparent heart attack in 1994 while still an active professor at MIT Media Lab. A major retrospective of her groundbreaking work was held the following year, but it is only recently that her significance as one of the great pioneers of digital design has become more widely acknowledged.

BAUHAUS

Opposite: MIT Press colophon, 1962.

This page, clockwise from left: Book design for Hans Wingler's *Bauhaus*, 1969; book design for Robert Venturi and Denise Scott Brown's *Learning from Las Vegas*, 1972; Visible Language Workshop computer paint software, 1974; screen from Information Landscapes, 1994.

A Significance for A&P Parking Lots, or Learning from Las Vegas. Commercial Values and Commercial Methods. Billboards Are Almost All Right. Architecture as Space. Architecture as Symbol. Symbol in Space before Form in Space: Las Vegas as a Communication System. The Architecture of Persuasion. Vast Space in the Historical Tradition and at the A&P. From Rome to Las Vegas. Maps of Las Vegas: Las Vegas as a Pattern of Activities. Main Street and the Strip. System and Order on the Strip, and "Twin Phenomena." Change and Permanence on the

Technique Function and Formal Design are ideas which are quite inseparable

MATALI CRASSET

CONTEMPORARY · FURNITURE · LIGHTING · PRODUCT

**French
b. Châlons-en-Champagne,
France, 1965**

The French industrial designer Matali Crasset has always viewed design as an act of research and, as a consequence, throughout her career has enjoyed experimenting with materials and technologies as well as playing with form and function. She has an open-minded approach to design, questioning obvious design solutions and seeking to construct alternative answers that are often based on the concepts of modularity, networks and interdisciplinary convergence. As she notes, she starts any project 'from a position on the outer periphery looking in, a perspective that allows me access to everyday life and also gives me the ability to imagine future scenarios'.[1]

She grew up on a farm in a small village, which she credits for keeping her ideas fresh. During these formative years, design was not part of her life and, as a result, she has always felt somewhat alien in the design world. But this outsider position means she has found it easier to break the rules in design, giving her work a refreshing originality. She trained as an industrial designer at the École Nationale Supérieure de Création Industrielle in Paris, graduating in 1991. She moved to Milan, where she worked for the architect–designer, Denis Santachiara. Returning to Paris in 1993, she headed up Philippe Starck's design studio before working as a designer for the consumer electronics group Thomson Multimedia. In 1998 she founded her own design agency, Matali Crasset Productions. In the early 2000s she converted an old printing house into a dedicated design studio adjacent to her house, in the popular Belleville region of Paris, and has been working out of there ever since.

Many of her designs have an endearing quirkiness, such as her When Jim Comes to Paris bed roll (1995) for Domeau & Peres, which was intended to function as a guest room in a bag and which, like much of her work, sought to investigate the customs and rituals surrounding daily life.

A strong graphic quality, as well as a bright and colourful palette, also distinguishes Crasset's work, which is often related to concepts of hospitality or domesticity. Another feature of her career is her frequent collaboration with creatives working in other fields: the famed French pastry chef, Pierre Hermé, helped her develop a clever cake knife that also functions as a server, and a mixing bowl that has a secondary, bowl-like depression in which smaller quantities of ingredients can be mixed. She has also worked with filmmakers and musicians, and the breadth of her design projects is vast, from exhibition installations to interiors, eyewear and chandeliers. For IKEA's progressive annual PS collections, she designed both an eye-catching wire cabinet that can be easily customized with coloured elements and an intriguing, handled tray that can be stacked. In 2017 she contributed a portable caged light that harks back to the railway lamps of yesteryear.

As Crasset notes, the profession of design is becoming increasingly about being a 'midwife of ideas'. It is 'less about creating material and aesthetic forms than about teasing out and bringing into high relief the common interests and shared values of society, as well as responding to the movements in these vast networks of exchange'[2] that result from working collaboratively, as she invariably does. She is a one-of-a-kind designer, who has a singular vision of what design can be and the creative wherewithal to transform her innovative ideas into realities. To put it simply, she designs outside the box, and that is what makes her work so thought-provoking and so compelling.

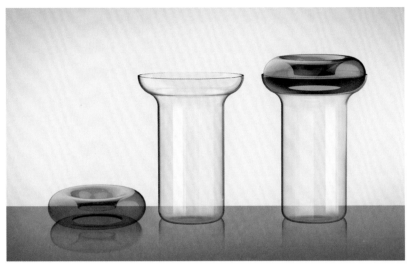

Opposite: Extension de générosité armchair for Campeggi, 2017.

This page, clockwise from left: Ring vase for Danese, 2015; PS 2014 armoire for IKEA, 2014; Reflexcity installation at the Asia Cultural Centre (ACC) in Gwangju, South Korea, 2016.

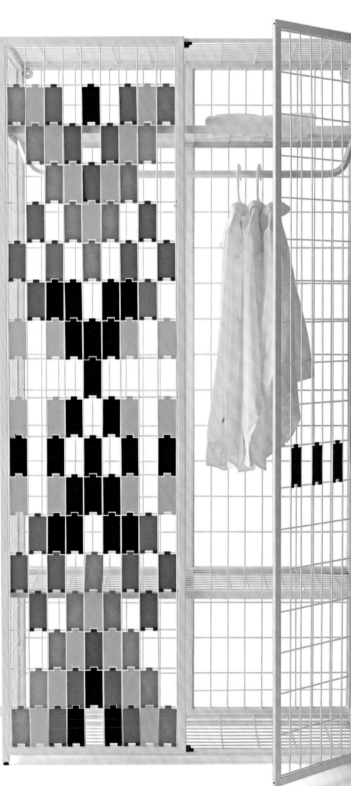

LUCIENNE DAY

British
b. Coulsdon, UK, 1917
d. Chichester, UK, 2010

During the postwar period, Lucienne and Robin Day were Britain's most high-profile design power couple, yet, unlike Ray and Charles Eames in America (see pages 84–85), they always kept their careers separate, despite working out of the same office. Recognized as an influential creative in her own right, it is difficult to imagine the domestic landscape of postwar Britain without Day's vibrant Modernist textiles, which so perfectly captured the optimistic, youthful spirit that was emerging.

Day grew up in prosperous London suburbs to a Belgian father and an English mother; and she had always been interested in fashion as well as art and design. She studied at Croydon School of Art, where Peter Werner introduced her to the Bauhaus and Swedish Modernism. She went on to train as a textile designer at the Royal College of Art in London in 1937. Three years later, at a college dance, she met the furniture designer Robin Day, who had previously studied there. They instantly hit it off and married in 1942. They shared a passion for Modernist design and went on to transform contemporary British design, espousing the belief that good design should always be affordable.

During World War II, they both taught at Beckenham School of Art. After the war she began designing dress fabrics, because rationing on other types of textiles was still in force. She became a member of the Society of Industrial Artists (SIA) in 1946, and established the organization's Textile Group. It was through the SIA that she met Alistair Morton, director of Edinburgh Weavers, who encouraged her to become more business-like in her approach to design.

In 1948 the Days set up their own design office and Morton commissioned her to design two furnishing textiles,

Above: Apex furnishing textile for Heal's, 1967.

Opposite: Larch furnishing textile for Heal's, 1961.

Overleaf: Calyx furnishing textile for Heal's, 1951.

Florimel and Elysian (1949). These screen-printed patterns acted as a career springboard, catching the eye of Anthony Heal, who asked Day to design some similarly Modernist-style textiles for Heal & Son in 1950. This was the beginning of a fruitful creative collaboration spanning many years. An early design, Calyx (1951), was inspired by forms found in nature, as well as contemporary abstract art by the likes of Paul Klee, Wassily Kandinsky, Joan Miró and Alexander Calder. With its free-floating pattern of abstract flower buds, Calyx had a refreshingly contemporary visual rhythm and marked a radical departure in British textile design. It was one of a number of Day's textile and wallpaper designs that were exhibited in two room-settings created by her husband for the Homes and Gardens Pavilion at the Festival of Britain (1951) and evoked the spirit of new growth and optimism characterized by the festival. Confounding the cautious expectations of Heal's managing director, Tom Worthington, Calyx went on to become a bestselling design. It became Day's most famous pattern and helped define the 'New Look' of British postwar design.

Throughout her life, Day was a keen gardener, and this interest in horticulture inspired the linear representations of flowers, herbs and trees found on her other textiles from the 1950s. From the mid 1960s onwards, however, her patterns became compositionally bolder and more brightly coloured, in accordance with the fashions of the day. In 1962 the Days became design consultants to the John Lewis Partnership and, over the next 25 years, they jointly helped establish the company's very distinctive house style, which was tastefully understated, practical and contemporary. From the 1980s Day shifted her focus towards art textiles, creating silk mosaic wall-hangings that demonstrated exquisitely her remarkable talent for both colour and composition.

CARLOTTA DE BEVILACQUA

Italian
b. Milan, Italy, 1957

One of the leading lights in the world of Italian design, Carlotta de Bevilacqua skilfully balances, like so many women who have found success in their chosen careers, a number of diverse roles. As she notes, 'I am an architect, a designer, a professor, a wife, a mother, [a rescuer of] animals and so on, [but] my main role in life is to design.'[1] De Bevilacqua is probably known as much for her entrepreneurial role as vice president and CEO of the world-renowned Artemide Group as she is for the numerous innovative lighting designs she has designed for the company over the years.

Having studied architecture at the Politecnico di Milano, de Bevilacqua graduated in 1983. Between 1989 and 1993, she was the art director of both Memphis and Alias. During the early 1990s she also began conducting research into artificial lighting and developing state-of-the-art LED lighting solutions for Artemide – the company having been founded by her husband, Ernesto Gismondi, in 1960. Around this time, she also became involved with the Italian design-led company Danese, which she later went on to acquire in 1999, subsequently reviving its profile and fortunes.

In 1996 de Bevilacqua spearheaded a design initiative for Artemide known as the Human Light, which is based on the idea that the design of lighting should be informed fundamentally by what people's lighting needs actually are at any given moment in time. Key to this concept is the belief that lighting must have an inherent flexibility and adaptability in order to respond to changing individual needs, according to the different stages of life and within different interior and exterior contexts. This human-centric approach to lighting design was totally revolutionary at the time, as were the resulting products, notably her Metamorfosi range that

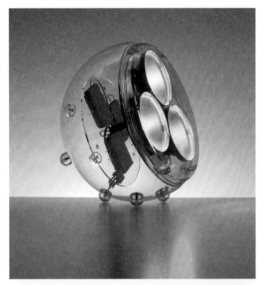

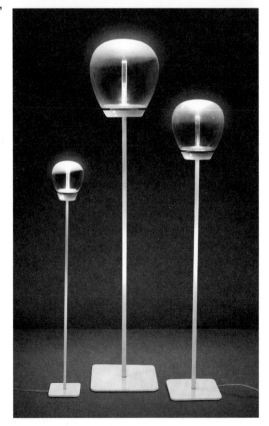

includes the Yang (2000) floor light, which features a remote-control system that enables the user to change the luminosity and colour of the light being emitted.

Despite the common understanding now, back then de Bevilacqua was one of the first contemporary lighting designers to properly grasp the relationship between light and mood and to realise that good lighting can promote a sense of wellbeing. Indeed, her early Human Light designs functioned ostensibly as polychromatic light-therapy units, which could be used to create sensory environments that were conducive to relaxation and, ultimately, more healthful living. The Human Light project represented a new way of looking at the design of lighting and it went on to shape Artemide's philosophy for the development of all its products. This human-first approach to lighting design also involves keeping the consumption of environmental resources to a minimum because that affects people, too.

Since the early 2000s, de Bevilacqua has continued to investigate the multifaceted nature of lighting and how it connects with people's physiological and psychological wellbeing, and, through her research, has set new benchmarks in both lighting performance and energy-consumption. Her numerous product solutions are the physical outcome of her relentless, frontier-pushing research into photonics and the possibilities offered by emerging technologies, such as IoT (Internet of Things) connectivity. A passionate animal rights activist and vegetarian, de Bevilacqua blends her interests in humanism and science to originate designs that are not only exquisitely functional, but also quite literally easy on the eye.

Opposite: Yang (LED) multi-coloured floor light for Artemide, 2000; Emaptia floor lights for Artemide, 2014 (co-designed with Paola di Arianello).

This page, clockwise from right: Copernico suspension light for Artemide, 2012 (co-designed with Paola Dell'Elce); Algoritmo floor/wall lighting system for Artemide, 2010 (co-designed with Paola di Arianello); Ina task light for Artemide, 2007.

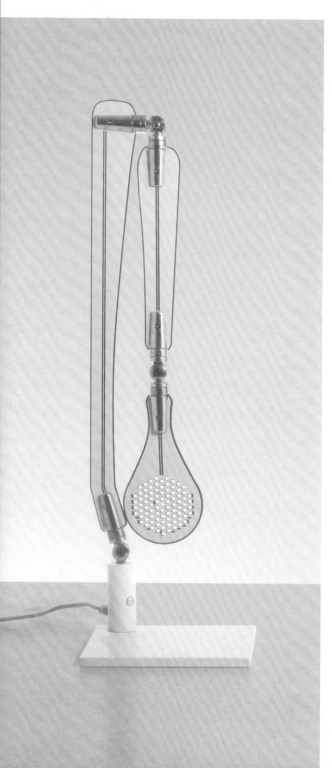

SONIA DELAUNAY

ART DECO · MODERNISM · FASHION · TEXTILES

Ukrainian/French
b. Odessa, Ukraine, 1885
d. Paris, France, 1979

Sonia Delaunay was born into a middle-class Ukrainian family, but was adopted as a teenager by a well-heeled branch of the family in St Petersburg and, accordingly, changed her name from Sarah Stern to Sonia Terk. With her adoptive aunt and uncle, she toured the art galleries and museums of western Europe and took to drawing with a passion. She attended both the State Academy of Fine Arts in Karlsruhe, Germany, and the Académie de La Palette, a private art school in the bohemian district of Montparnasse, Paris.

In Paris, she met and married the noted gallerist, Wilhelm Uhde. This union gave Delaunay access to Parisian art and social circles, and she quickly fell under the influence of the Post-Impressionists and Fauvists. In 1909 Sonia met the abstract artist Robert Delaunay at an event at Uhde's gallery and fell in love. By 1910, she had divorced Wilhelm, married Robert and was pregnant with his child. The couple developed Robert's form of abstract art known as Orphism – painting that explored the harmonies, contrasts and juxtapositions of colour fields. Within their paintings, forms gained meaning not through their figurative content, but from their chromatic relationships with each other. The Delaunays referred to this effect as 'simultaneous contrast'. During this period, Delaunay created hugely influential large-scale Orphist works, such as her dynamic *Le Bal Bullier* oil painting of 1913.

In 1911 she produced a patchwork quilt for her son, an appliqué assemblage of textiles in the colloquial Ukrainian style. The quilt inspired her to take her colour language beyond paint into the wider applied arts and to apply the near-mystic rhetoric of Orphism to a range of media, including stage sets, pottery and illustration. She illustrated the work

of poet Blaise Cendrars on one huge concertina-folded sheet, expressing her ideas of simultaneity by breaking from the traditional linearity of literature. Through her experimentation with 'craft' forms, Orphism acquired a utopian totality – a universe of intricately harmonized hues.

When the Russian Revolution struck in 1917, the couple's financial link to Delaunay's uncle was severed. By then in Madrid, she founded Casa Sonia – a boutique selling her patterns for interior design and dressmaking. The couple also designed densely symbolic costumes and sets for the ballet impresario Sergei Diaghilev and his prestigious staging of the ballet Cleopatra.

In 1921, back in Paris, Delaunay struck a deal to produce 50 textile designs for a major manufacturer in Lyons and adopted the Orphist term, Simultané, as her trademark. The couple regularly opened their home as a salon for artists, including Dadaist poets such as Tristan Tzara. Delaunay incorporated their words into avant-garde garments for private clients and friends. She also designed geometrically shaped, angular costumes for Tzara's play, *The Gas Heart*. For Delaunay, the process of garment design was an expression of simultaneity: producing the print and fitting it, simultaneously, to suit the form of her client.

In 1924 Delaunay set up a studio with the noted fashion designer Jacques Heim, and the following year they co-created the Boutique Simultané pavilion at the 'Exposition Internationale des Arts Décoratifs et Industriels Modernes' ('International Exhibition of Decorative and Industrial Arts'). In 1927 she delivered a lecture at the Sorbonne entitled 'The Influence of Painting on the Art of Clothes', highlighting the emancipatory power of casual women's ready-to-wear.

The 1930s Great Depression saw a downturn in the Delaunays' business activities and a return to painting. Together, the couple joined the Abstraction-Création association, which led them to create public works, including large-scale murals. After Robert died of cancer in 1941, Delaunay dedicated the next decade to championing the Orphist cause to preserve her husband's legacy. She returned to painting in the 1950s and, in 1964, became the first living female artist to be given a solo exhibition at the Louvre. Continuing to work until her death at the age of 94, this restless creative spirit once noted, 'I always changed everything around me ... I have done everything. I have lived my art.'[1]

Opposite: Tissu Simultané
no. 46 silk textile, 1924.

This page, clockwise
from left: Diagonale wool
tapestry for Ateliers Pinton
à Aubusson, *c.* 1970, after
Delaunay's painting, entitled
Rhythm couleur, from 1967;
textile design pochoir print
in Compostions portfolio,
plate 24, published by
Éditions d'Art Charles
Moureau, 1930; models
wearing fur coats designed
by Delaunay with a Citroën
B12 Coupé with body paint
scheme by Delaunay,
c. 1925.

ELSIE DE WOLFE

BELLE ÉPOQUE · INTERIORS

American
b. New York, USA, 1865
d. Versailles, France, 1950

As a self-professed 'rebel in an ugly world',[1] legendary tastemaker, society celebrity, ardent Francophile, yoga devotee and lifestyle icon, Elsie de Wolfe is often cited as being 'America's first interior designer'.[2] While this is not wholly correct, she certainly did much to popularize the profession. She once declared, 'I'm going to make everything around me beautiful – that will be my life',[3] and she certainly helped promote the notion of design as lifestyle. As the first woman to make her mark in the field of interior design, she brought a much-needed woman's touch to the art of decorating. She introduced, for instance, the idea that interiors should reflect 'the personality of the mistress of the house'[4] rather than the husband's financial status – revealing a much more individualistic approach to the design of domestic interiors than had been practised hitherto.

The daughter of a Canadian doctor, de Wolfe was highly sensitive to her surroundings: as a child, she became inconsolable when her parents' drawing room was redecorated with an 'ugly' Morris & Co. wallpaper (see pages 168–71). Throughout her career, she strove to banish the Victorian look, which she absolutely detested, perhaps because it reminded her of her less-than-happy childhood. She was 40 years old before she embarked on a career in interior design. When her father died in 1890, leaving the family penniless, de Wolfe became an actress as a means of supporting herself and spent the first half of her adult life on the stage. Her agent was Elisabeth 'Bessy' Marbury with whom she enjoyed a close personal relationship: they lived together and shared a passion for antiques collecting. During the fin de siècle period, she became well known, though more for her fashionable wardrobe and her beautiful homes on East 17th Street, New York, and in Versailles, France, than for her beauty or acting talents.

As she aged, her theatrical reviews became progressively worse, so she cast around for an alternative career. In 1905, de Wolfe announced in *Vanity Fair*: 'I am going in now for interior decoration. By that I mean supplying *objets d'art* and giving advice regarding the decoration of their houses to wealthy persons who do not have the time, inclination nor culture to do such work for themselves. It is nothing new. Women have done the same thing before.'[5] And so they had, but never with as much theatrical bravado or market shrewdness. That same year, she received her first commission from the publisher John R. McLean for a games room, and then landed the most significant project of her career, the creation of interiors for the Colony Club in New York.[6] It was the city's first all-female members club and de Wolfe broke radically with the established convention of what a club should look like. Instead of wood panelling and buttoned-leather chairs, she went for a casual and airy look, which was unashamedly feminine. Opting for a light palette of greens and yellows, she designed an influential indoor pavilion room furnished with wicker furniture and adorned with trellised wallpaper, which, like glazed chintz, became a signature of her interiors. At a stroke, this career-changing project established her professionally and, over the next three decades or so, her business, Elsie de Wolfe Inc., undertook hundreds of commissions, many for the most famous families in America, including the Whitneys, Vanderbilts, Fricks and Morgans.

But de Wolfe's reputation as a design tastemaker was really made through her book, *The House in Good Taste*, first published in 1913 and aimed at a female readership. This room-by-room, how-to guide stressed the importance of 'suitability, simplicity and proportion'[7] and gave advice on all manner of decor, including colour choices, soft furnishings and artificial lighting. Having been in a relationship with Elisabeth Marbury for decades, she rather surprisingly married British diplomat Sir Charles Mendl in 1926. A purely platonic affair, this marriage of convenience must have been advantageous to both parties in disguising the true nature of their respective sexualities and, thereby, helping to avoid scandal. With the marriage came the title Lady Mendl, which de Wolfe adopted to her advantage. Her trailblazing success established the notion of women as interior designers and she inspired a generation of women to follow in her footsteps. The interwar period was marked by an overtly feminine interior look that is largely attributable to de Wolfe's lead. In the postwar period, Modernism's more masculine aesthetic largely supplanted this trend and it is only recently that de Wolfe's warm, inimitable interior style has enjoyed a revival.

Opposite: Illustration from *The House in Good Taste,* 1913.

This page, clockwise from below left: The Trellis Room at the Colony Club in New York, 1905; watercolour by William Rankin of Elsie de Wolfe's Music Room at the Villa Trianon, her residence in Versailles, France, c. 1920s; limed oak, glass and brass dining table, c. 1945.

ELIZABETH DILLER

CONTEMPORARY · ARCHITECTURE

American
b. Lodz, Poland, 1954

A visionary architect, Elizabeth Diller has twice made it onto *Time* magazine's annual list of 100 Most Influential People in the World – first in 2009 and more recently in 2018. She has also scooped an impressive number of honours and awards over her five-decade long career, notably a Lifetime Achievement award from the National Academy of Design, the Arnold W. Brunner Memorial Prize from the American Academy of Arts and Letters and the Barnard Medal of Distinction. Entrepreneur and philanthropist, Eli Broad, perfectly sums up her achievements: 'She imagines things the rest of us have to see to believe. She can turn a metaphor into brick and mortar.'[1] This rare ability stems from Diller's early career as a conceptual architect, which gave her a hardwired mental capacity to think, quite literally, outside the traditional building box.

Born in Poland to a Holocaust-surviving family, Diller emigrated to the United States as a young child. She graduated from the Cooper Union School of Architecture in 1979, where she was influenced by the rise of the Radical Architecture movement. That same year,

she began working with fellow architect, Ricardo Scofidio, who had previously been her tutor and whom she married, after her graduation. She was an associate professor at her alma mater from 1981 to 1990 and then, in 1990, was appointed an associate professor of architecture at Princeton University.[2]

During the 1980s, working as Diller + Scofidio, the couple became well known for creating thought-provoking installations and experimental performance pieces, which explored the tensions between art and architecture, form and function. As Diller later recalled in an interview with Edwin Heathcote in 2017, 'I was a rebel. I never wanted to build. We thought of architecture as intellectually bankrupt and slightly corrupt and I was always more interested in other forms of discourse. We were trying to be academics practising in a more dissident form.'[3] But build these architectural renegades eventually did, after they won the commission to redesign the public spaces of the vast and sprawling Lincoln Center in New York in the late 1990s. The scheme intelligently stitched together this performing arts centre's disparate buildings designed by, among others, Philip Johnson

and Eero Saarinen, and also added a visually dynamic prow-like extension to the Alice Tully Hall, thereby giving the existing, rather staid, Modernist building a revitalizing architectural face lift.

Around this time, Diller + Scofidio were awarded the MacArthur Fellowship (1999–2004), known as the 'Genius Grant'; this was the first time it had been given in the field of architecture, which testified to the esteem in which the practice was now held. The duo went on to create the Blur Building pavilion on Lake Neuchâtel for the Swiss Expo 2002, which comprised a tensile-structured open-air platform enveloped in a man-made cloud of water vapour that was generated by 31,500 high-pressure mist nozzles. Beautiful and poetic, this temporary structure allowed visitors to experience being in a 'white out' and drew critical acclaim for the way it altered sensorial perceptions.

It was, however, the High Line (2009), a disused piece of railway infrastructure transformed into a much-loved green public space – an elevated, linear public park running through Manhattan – that really propelled the office[4] into a whole new league, professionally. Since then, the practice has been involved in numerous high-profile projects, with highlights including The Broad museum in Los Angeles, The Shed arts centre in New York and the Berkeley Art Museum and Pacific Film Archive. More than anything, Diller's work is about convergence – the melding of design, performance and electronic media with architectural theory and practice – and the exploration of how spaces of all kinds can encourage social relationships, something that is all too often forgotten in large-scale architectural schemes.

NANNA DITZEL

Danish
b. and d. Copenhagen, Denmark,
1923–2005

Denmark's first lady of furniture design, Nanna Ditzel helped shape Scandinavian Modernism with her progressive and beautifully sculptural vocabulary of form. She studied cabinetmaking at Richard's School in Copenhagen and trained in the furniture department of the Kunsthandvaerkskolen (Arts and Crafts School) from 1943 to 1946, where she was taught by, among others, Kaare Klint, Orla Mølgaard-Nielsen and Peter Hvidt.

In her first year at the school, she met her future husband, Jørgen Ditzel, also studying to be a furniture designer. She later recalled that it was love at first sight. In 1944 they jointly exhibited some living-room furniture at the Cabinetmakers' Annual Exhibition in Copenhagen. The following year, they won second prize – no mean feat considering how young they were, and the technical accomplishments of some of the other exhibitors. In 1946, with Ditzel having just graduated, they married and established their own design studio in Copenhagen. For the next 15 years, they worked together designing jewellery, as well as furniture. Initially, the duo focused on furnishing solutions for smaller postwar living spaces, which led Ditzel to come up with the novel idea of using kitchen units as room dividers. In 1950, their first daughter was born, followed four years later by twin girls, and parenthood prompted the design of a range of plywood children's furniture in 1952.

The manufacturer Poul Kold asked the pair to develop some furniture pieces for his company. Among the resulting designs was one of the Ditzels' most successful, the Ring chair (1958), which incorporated state-of-the-art, latex foam upholstery. By using this new material, they were able to create seating designs with a far stronger sculptural quality than with traditional sprung upholstery.

In 1956 the couple was awarded the Lunning Prize, ostensibly for their children's highchair designed the previous year. Using the prize money, they funded study trips to Greece, Mexico and the USA. The duo's career highpoint came when they won a gold medal at the 1960 Milan Triennale for a silver bracelet they had designed for Georg Jensen. In 1961 Jørgen died unexpectedly after a stomach operation, leaving Ditzel with no other option than to pursue a solo design career. As a young widow looking after her daughters, her attention turned again to children's furniture, resulting in the creation of her charming Toadstool (1962), inspired by her observation that 'children never sit still for two minutes; they get up, stand on the chair and subsequently it tips'.[1] That same year, her work was the subject of a one-woman show in London, and subsequent exhibitions were held in New York, Berlin and Vienna – all of which helped to secure her reputation as a formidable designer in her own right. In 1965 she made waves in the field of textile design, creating the ever-popular Hallingdal furnishing fabric, which is still produced by Kvadrat in an astonishing 58 colourways.

In 1968 she remarried and moved to London. With her new husband, Kurt Heine, she established the Interspace furniture showroom in Hampstead and, from 1970, also ran her own design studio. After Kurt's death in 1985, she returned to Denmark where she created a number of notable seating designs including the Bench for Two (1989) and the Trinidad stacking chair (1993), which was awarded an ID Prize in 1995. Always pushing the boundaries in material, technology and aesthetics, Ditzel forged a truly significant career over the course of six decades that places her, uniquely as a woman, in the rarefied echelons of acknowledged Danish design masters.

Opposite: Ring lounge chair
for Kold Savvaerk, 1958 (co-
designed with Jørgen Ditzel).

This page, clockwise from
above: Egg hanging chair for
Wengler, 1959 (co-designed
with Jørgen Ditzel); stack
of Toadstools for Kold
Savvaerk, 1962; Highchair
for Kold Savvaerk, 1955 (co-
designed with Jørgen Ditzel).

MARION DORN

ART DECO · TEXTILES

American
b. Menlo Park, CA, USA, 1896
d. Tangier, Morocco, 1964

Best known for her vibrant textile and carpet designs, Marion Dorn studied graphic design at Stanford University. She married her tutor, painter Henry Varnum Poor, and moved with him to New York. In 1923, however, a series of chance encounters in Paris changed her life completely. With fellow designer, Ruth Reeves (see pages 188–89), she met the Fauvist painter Raoul Dufy, who had expanded his practice into textiles. Inspired by his work, Dorn resolved to apply her Art Deco-infused illustrative style to fabrics. She also encountered Edward McKnight Kauffer, a talented American-born graphic artist who became her lover and lifelong partner. Together they moved to London and began to establish themselves professionally.

Dorn's first recognition came in 1925, when her batik designs were featured in *Vogue* magazine. These embodied the spirit of Art Deco, merging machine-age angularity with a symmetrical glamour redolent of Graeco-Roman designs. This distinctive neoclassicizing Modernity struck a chord with the affluent youth of 1920s London, and Dorn's textiles were soon stocked in stores across the city. Wilton Royal Carpets exhibited her rugs at the Arthur Tooth & Sons Gallery, Bond Street, and her avant-garde credentials led to coverage in *The Studio Yearbook of Decorative Art* and participation at the 1927 International Exhibition of Arts and Crafts in Leipzig. That year, Dorn designed the rug for the first of the 'white rooms' by interior decorator Syrie Maugham. It was Dorn's most overtly Modernist design yet: a complex of thick, intersecting shag strips on a field of clean ivory, demonstrating her genius for 'sculpting' the surface of a rug into a terrain of harmonized relief.

Her work for luxury hotels in London was also much acclaimed. In 1931 she produced room carpets for the Berkeley Hotel, followed by a series of monumental floor coverings for Claridge's. This was swiftly followed by similarly scaled work for the Savoy – a total of 369 sumptuous rugs in various geometric configurations. The peak of her interaction with England's moneyed elite, however, came in 1933, when the millionaire Stephen Courtauld and his wife, Virginia, commissioned a Dorn rug as the focal point for the entrance hall of their glamorous Art Deco extension at Eltham Place, designed by Rolf Engströmer and Peter Malacrida. Upon the concentric, semi-circular sweeps of this rug, the cream of British society were entertained.

Dorn's waveform rugs also acted as a centrepiece for the central foyer of the Midland Hotel in Morecambe. As was the fashion, the hotel was awash with aquatic allusions to the sleek, hydrodynamic lines of modern steamships. Perhaps as a result, Dorn was subsequently commissioned to

design carpets and textiles for ocean liners, including *Orion* (1934), *Queen Mary* (1936) and *Orcades* (1937).

She founded her own company in 1934 and, in 1938, transformed the seating of London Underground carriages with a beautifully executed moquette fabric, christened Colindale after the recently opened Northern Line station. The influence of this design, with its formalized leaf motif and pared-back colour palette, can still be spotted on transport seating across the world.

Dorn's love affair with London ended abruptly with the outbreak of World War II, when she and her husband heeded advice and left for New York. She worked as a commercial designer, producing myriad wallpaper and textile prints for companies such as Schumacher and Greeff Fabrics throughout the 1940s. But Dorn struggled to maintain the same level of high-end commissions as in England. After Kauffer died in 1954, she began winding down her creative practice. She signed off her career, however, with one last great achievement: a large carpet for the Diplomatic Reception Room at the White House (1960). On retiring, she decamped to Morocco in 1962, where she died two years later.

Left: Geometric carpets designed for the lobby at Claridge's Hotel in London, 1931.

Opposite: Entrance hall of Eltham Palace, London, with Dorn's circular, geometric rug, 1933.

Overleaf, left: Barley motif carpet designed for Bryan and Diana Guiness, c. 1935; right: Avis furnishing textile for Edinburgh Weavers, c. 1939.

NIPA DOSHI

CONTEMPORARY • FURNITURE • PRODUCT

Indian/British
b. Bombay (Mumbai), India, 1971

Nipa Doshi is one half of the acclaimed London-based design duo Doshi Levien, which she runs with her husband, Jonathan Levien. With her Indian background, Doshi brings a polyethnic awareness to the studio's work, as well as all-important feminine sensitivity. Her strength as a designer lies in her international outlook and her perceptive understanding of visual culture – both of the East and West – and she perfectly compliments the skill set of her life and business partner, who comes from a more industrial design and craft-making background.

Having spent most of her childhood in New Delhi, Doshi later spent six years studying at the renowned National Institute of Design (NID) in Ahmedabad, which had been established in 1961 as a result of recommendations put forward in *The India Report* (1958) drafted by Charles and Ray Eames (see pages 84–85). While still a student at this 'Institution of National Importance', Doshi visited London in 1994 where she met Tom Dixon. Through him, she became acquainted with Jasper Morrison, who inspired her to apply to do an MA in furniture design at the Royal College of Art (RCA), London, and kindly wrote her an academic recommendation to support her application. She got onto the course the following year and initially studied under Professor Floris van den Broecke, who was instrumental in helping Doshi obtain a RCA scholarship. It was at the RCA that she also met Levien. After graduating together in 1997, Doshi spent some time working with craftspeople in India, before returning to London to work in David Chipperfield's architecture practice.

In 2000 she married Levien and they established their own studio. Their first commission came the following year from Tom Dixon, then Creative Director of Habitat, to design some drinking glasses and cutlery. The resulting designs revealed a strong sculptural confidence as well as a solid understanding of functional utility. It was, however, the duo's Mosaic cookware range (2003) for Tefal that firmly established their design profile. This innovative range of non-stick cookware was inspired by the different culinary cultures around the world and comprised modern interpretations of vernacular cooking pots – the Moroccan tagine pot, the Chinese wok, the Indian karhai pot, the Spanish paella pan and Mexican fajita pan. Rethought into modern materials and form, the Mosiac range intentionally expressed the identity of each pot's origin with culturally specific patterns specially devised by Doshi for their bases. The Mosaic collection perfectly expressed the globalization of modern design, and went on to win an FX design award's 'Best Furnishing or Accessory for Residential Interiors' category in 2003. Since then Doshi Levien have created numerous designs for a host of design-led manufacturers, including Moroso, Kvadrat, B&B Italia, Cappellini, Camper and Swarovski. Among their most notable designs are the Charpoy range (2007), referencing traditional Indian daybeds, and the My Beautiful Backside sofa (2008) inspired by an Indian painting of a princess surrounded by a multitude of cushions. By infusing their designs with a handcrafted sensibility, Doshi creates objects that are not only thought provoking and eye-catching but also have a poetic resonance and a charming multicultural originality.

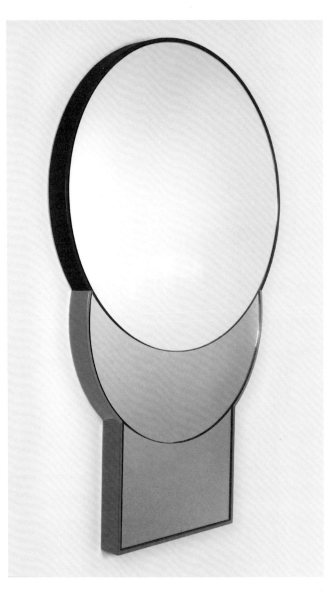

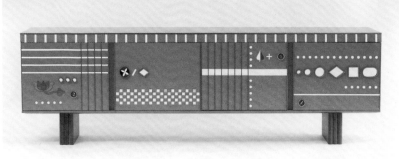

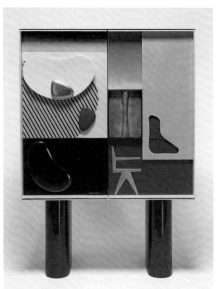

Opposite: Regionally specific pattern design for the Mosaic cookware range for Tefal, 2003.

This page, clockwise from far left: Squarable Lune mirror for Galerie Kreo, 2013; Kundan cabinet for Galerie Kreo, 2015; Le Cabinet, 2017 (made in collaboration with Manufacture nationale de Sèvres); My Beautiful Backside sofa for Moroso, 2008.

DOROTHY DRAPER

1930S–1950S · INTERIORS

American
b. Tuxedo Park, NY, USA, 1889
d. Cleveland, OH, USA, 1969

Dorothy Draper was an enormously influential figure who helped professionalize the field of interior design by establishing her own high-profile decorating company in 1925. As her interior-design protégé, Carleton Varney, notes, 'Dorothy Draper was to decorating what Chanel was to fashion. The woman was a genius; there'd be no professional decorating business without her.'[1]

Born into a wealthy family, Draper enjoyed a privileged childhood in Tuxedo Park – a swanky high-society community in Orange County, New York. Her family owned multiple homes and they went on regular trips to Europe.

Like so many women of her generation, Draper fell into her profession thanks to sheer talent over any formal training. Having been a debutante, in 1912 she married Dr George Draper, who later became President Franklin Delano Roosevelt's personal physician, and she continued to enjoy a glamorous lifestyle, which involved redecorating her various homes.

Her financially charmed circles not only provided Draper with a network of well-heeled potential clients, but also the necessary confidence to believe she could set up her own decorating company – something that was practically unheard of for women of the time.[2] It also, crucially, gave her 'a first-hand acquaintance with historical styles that she would freely interpret and transform'[3] into her own, very distinctive, signature look. Such was her obvious skill in this field, that her wealthy friends soon asked her to decorate their homes, too. Eventually Draper opened her own decorating firm, the Architectural Clearing House, in 1925. Four years later it was renamed Dorothy Draper & Company.

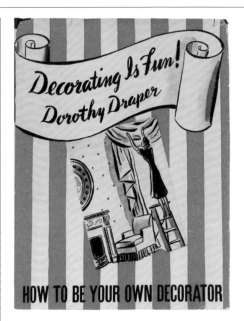

Draper's language of design eschewed minimalistic Modernism in favour of a flamboyant and glamorous look, inspired by historical styles such as Baroque and Rococo, and her deluxe look epitomized what has become known as the Hollywood Regency style. After divorcing her husband in 1930, her professional ambition moved up a notch and she began to receive increasingly important commissions. Her first major break came in 1933, when she was asked to design the lobby of the Carlyle Hotel on Madison Avenue, New York – the success of this project led to numerous other hotel commissions. Indeed, it is not particularly surprising that she was at ease in this lucrative sector, being part of the very demographic that these upmarket hotels hoped to attract. It could be said she understood what her 'tribe' needed and desired – which in the 1930s, against the backdrop of the Depression, was a playful touch of theatrical glamour and high-style panache. Her interiors featured dramatic colour contrasts, bright colours set against

black and white and, often, the combination of bold stripes and oversized chintzy florals.

By the late 1930s, Draper had become a celebrated authority on interior design matters and capitalized on this renown by publishing a book, *Decorating Is Fun! How to be Your Own Decorator* (1939). It provided a host of practical decorating tips, such as how to avoid being swayed by 'fads in colours' or paying 'too much for your rugs or carpets unless you really have money to burn'.[4] In 1941 she also published *Entertaining is Fun! How to be a Popular Hostess*, also a bestseller. That same year, in an interview, Draper noted, 'A great deal of superfluous nonsense is talked about women combining careers with a normal home life. The way to combine the two is to combine the two and not dramatize them.'[5] It was this can-do approach that established her as an extraordinary style guru, who empowered countless ordinary American women to experiment with design themselves.

Opposite: Cover of
Decorating is Fun!, 1939.

This page, clockwise from
above: Lobby lounge at
the Greenbrier resort in
West Virginia, USA, 1948;
Rhododendron wallpaper
for Dorothy Draper & Co.
Inc., 1948; Spiral staircase
at the Greenbrier resort,
1948.

Overleaf: Lobby mezzanine
at the Greenbrier resort,
1948.

CLARA DRISCOLL

American
b. Tallmadge, OH, USA, 1861
d. Austin, TX, USA, 1944

The story of Clara Driscoll is a good example of how, historically, women working in the field of design have not been properly credited for their work.

The creative input of women designers was invariably overlooked – even if their work had been truly impressive, as in Driscoll's case. Her considerable contribution to the output of Tiffany Studios was fully revealed in 2006, only due to investigative research undertaken by the design historian Martin Eidelberg in conjunction with New-York Historical Society curators, Nina Gray and Margaret Hofer.[1] For decades, the design authorship of some of Tiffany's most famous leaded glass lamps – including Dragonfly, Wisteria, Daffodil and Peony – had been mistakenly credited to Louis Comfort Tiffany himself whereas, in actuality, Driscoll was responsible for their design.

Born in Ohio, Driscoll lost her father when she was only twelve years old. Despite this setback, she was encouraged to pursue higher education and, having displayed an obvious talent for art, studied at the Western Reserve School of Design for Women (later the Cleveland Institute of Art). This recently founded institution was guided by a progressive Arts and Crafts outlook that sought to teach young women the practical skills that would allow them to pursue careers in the burgeoning design industry. After briefly working for a local furniture manufacture, Driscoll moved to New York where she resumed her vocational training at the new Metropolitan Museum of Art School.

In 1888 Driscoll was hired by Louis Comfort Tiffany to work at his Tiffany

Glass Company (later renamed Tiffany Studios). Over the next two decades she worked there, on-and-off, as a designer of lighting and other decorative objects, as well as supervising the firm's women's glass cutting department. The reason for the intermittency of her employment was that engaged or married women were forbidden to work at the company and so she left for the duration of her first marriage, from 1889 to 1892. She returned to the studios after the death of her husband and remained there more or less continuously until 1909,[2] when she remarried and left again for good. During her time at Tiffany, she worked closely with other women in the studio who became collectively known as the 'Tiffany Girls' and included, among others, Alice Carmen Gouvy and Lillian Palmié. Thanks to the discovery by Nina Gray of a cache of letters written by Driscoll to her mother and sister, it has now been irrefutably proved that she and the women who worked under her designed many of the lamps previously ascribed to Louis Comfort Tiffany or to his team of male designers. These letters also revealed that Driscoll's very first lighting design was the Daffodil, with its stunning cascading composition of leaves, stems and flowers in subtly hued light-filtering opalescent glass.

The Tiffany Studios headed by Driscoll functioned as a sort of quasi-sorority of gifted designer–artisans who, under almost complete anonymity, designed the wonderful leaded lamps, stained-glass windows and other objets d'art that made Tiffany and his company famous throughout the world. Indeed, during the fin de siècle era, Driscoll's lighting designs for Tiffany marked the apotheosis of American design – their excellence was on a par with the highest quality work then coming out of Europe. Yet, it is only belatedly that Driscoll and her band of highly talented women have emerged from the historical shadows and shed new light not only on Tiffany's oeuvre but also, perhaps even more importantly, on the wider historical context of women working in the design industry.

LUCILE, LADY DUFF-GORDON

British
b. and d. London, England, 1863–1935

Lady Duff-Gordon, also known as 'Lucile', was an influential British couturier in the late nineteenth and early twentieth centuries and one of the first female designers to find international success in the fashion world. Her father, a Scottish civil engineer, died of typhoid fever when she was only two and, reeling from the shock, her mother moved the young family from London to their grandparents' farm in Guelph, Ontario. In these remote Canadian surroundings, the future Lady Duff-Gordon kept herself busy by making clothes for her dolls. In 1871 her mother remarried and they returned to Britain – settling in Saint Helier, Jersey, where Duff-Gordon lived a rather provincial, island-bound life.

Aged 21, she married James Stuart Wallace, a known alcoholic and womanizer. They had a child, Esme, in 1885, but their marriage soon collapsed. Duff-Gordon was now a divorcée, which was a source of great shame at that time. She was also penniless, so began making clothes in her mother's flat. Building a network of society friends, she was able to sell enough to support herself and her daughter.

In 1894 she took a great leap by opening Maison Lucile, a workspace and shop in Burlington Lane, west London. The store, stocked with elegant and expressive dresses, soon became a hit with the capital's social elite. Often utilizing flowing chiffon and lace, her elegant, draped designs were less stuffy than the contemporary Victorian style. They stood out through their candid exploration of sensuality – even her tea dresses, in which nude tones and low necklines teased the eye. She even marketed seductive silk lingerie, and her designs were a harbinger of the new Edwardian age. She was perhaps best known for her 'personality dresses', one-off pieces created for wealthy clients. Every detail was considered, including

matching accessories ranging from bags to parasols. She also found success designing costumes for well-known theatrical productions, dressing acclaimed actresses, including Ellen Terry.

Duff-Gordon gained access to this elite clientele in no small part due to an easy social grace, which belied her humble beginnings. For an Edwardian divorcée, this degree of social mobility was highly unusual. However, social success did not guarantee financial buoyancy. Often unable to recover money owed to her by clients for fear of severing relationships, she fell into bankruptcy. She turned to her friend, Sir Cosmo Duff-Gordon, initially for financial advice, but their relationship deepened and the pair married in 1900, although they lived separately. This vital bond allowed her both aristocratic status and financial stability.

Buoyed by this new social standing, she opened a prestigious Hanover Square shop, where she hosted theatrical displays of her new designs. These turn-of-the-century soirées are considered some of

the earliest fashion shows. Staged for elite crowds of industry and Court insiders, they even featured a 'mannequin parade' of young models walking a runway. This exposed her work to the press and Duff-Gordon quickly gained international attention. In 1909 she opened a boutique in New York (specializing in opulent 'Money Dresses', so named because they cost so much), and, in 1911, a boutique in Paris. She licensed her name to prêt-à-porter lines and various merchandising concerns, extending the Duff-Gordon brand far beyond couture.

However, this international expansion contributed to her downfall – for it was to keep an urgent appointment at her New York salon that she booked a ticket on the *Titanic*'s fateful maiden voyage. When the ship struck an iceberg and began to sink, Duff-Gordon found a place with her husband on the captain's life raft. Complaining that her kimono was ruined, she and her husband urged the lifeboat's crew to leave immediately, thereby saving only twelve people in a vessel designed for forty. The incident became known as the 'Millionaire's Lifeboat' in the international press, with Sir Cosmo branded a despicable coward. The scandal left Duff-Gordon's professional reputation in tatters, and both she and her husband faced cross-examination at the official Court of Inquiry.

Caught in the glare of public disapproval and the deprivations of World War I, Duff-Gordon was forced to close many of her boutiques. During this period, she resided mainly in New York. When peace was achieved in Europe, another challenge arose: the new generation of socialites considered her designs a bit passé, aspiring as they did to the sleek, boyish modernity of the Jazz Age. In 1923 Duff-Gordon found herself bankrupted once again and took work as a fashion columnist. She never designed again although her remarkable contribution to the story of fashion design has not been forgotten.

Opposite: Lucile dress, 1920.

This page, left: Silk, fur and metallic thread evening dress, *c.* 1920; right: silk, cotton and lace evening dress, *c.* 1916.

RAY EAMES

MID-CENTURY · FURNITURE · TEXTILES · EXHIBITIONS

American
b. Sacramento, USA, 1912
d. Los Angeles County, USA, 1988

Ray Eames is one of the best-known woman designers of all time, having been half of the most famous design power-couple of the twentieth century. Yet, during their shared career, all too often her husband, Charles, received far more of the limelight and, as a consequence, much greater recognition professionally – despite the fact that virtually all Eames designs were joint efforts, to a greater or lesser extent.

As with any working partnership, it is difficult to unpick exactly who did what, but in the case of Ray and Charles Eames, their individual abilities so complemented each other that their creative whole was assuredly greater than the sum of its individual parts. Having studied architecture, Charles understood the rules of construction and was entranced by new technologies and materials, whereas Eames had trained as a fine artist and had an intuitive eye for colour, form and detail. They also shared a love of the whimsical and, by pooling their talents, created furniture, toys, films and exhibitions that had a rare functional and aesthetic originality but which were also emotionally engaging. It was this ability to make connections on all sorts of levels that set their work apart and it is the reason behind its enduring appeal.

Born in California, Eames studied painting under Hans Hofmann at the renowned Art Students League, New York. She went on to study fine art at the Cranbrook Academy of Art in Michigan and there met Charles in 1940, while he was working as an industrial design tutor. Charles divorced his first wife and married Eames the following year. The newlyweds moved to California and developed innovative plywood-moulding techniques in the spare room of their apartment. This early hands-on research won them

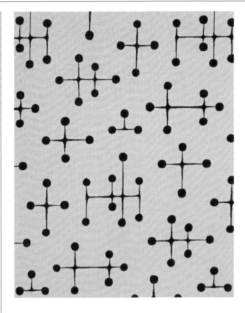

a major contract in 1942 from the US Navy, supplying ergonomically moulded plywood leg splints and litters. After the war, they applied this hard-won technical knowledge to the development of their seminal moulded Plywood Group of seating (1945), which included the iconic Lounge Chair Wood (LCW) with its 'potato-chip' seat and back made of compound-moulded plywood. This seating range was put into production by Herman Miller, which manufactured all their subsequent furniture designs, including the revolutionary Plastic Shell Group (1948–50) that cleverly utilized a universal seat shell made of fibreglass which could be used in conjunction with eleven different bases according to functional requirement. These included a rocking sled base, designed specifically for nursing mothers.

They also designed children's furniture and numerous innovative toys and puzzles, revealing Eames's intuitive understanding of the needs and requirements of the customer/user and the potential of her designs. She also designed a number of textiles – the only

designs specifically ascribed to her alone – that give us an insight into her abilities as a patternmaker and colourist. Among these is Crosspatch, originally designed for a competition for printed fabrics held by MoMA, New York, in 1947, and then put into production by Schiffer Prints. Its lively non-representational pattern of squares, triangles and circles was perfectly in tune with the cool 'New Look' interiors of the postwar era that were characterized by a refreshing, artistic informality.

Eames's playful Sea Things pattern was designed for the same competition and was, likewise, turned into a screen-printed textile by Schiffer. This *faux*-naïve hand-drawn pattern of swirling seaweeds, seashells, starfish, crabs and other aquatic life proved so popular that it was later used on transfer-printed plastic trays. It was, however, her Dot Pattern (1947) that was her most accomplished textile design, with its beautiful rhythmic pattern of molecular-like forms.

Only in the last thirty or so years has Eames begun to receive widespread recognition as a truly equal design partner to her husband. Perhaps the most poignant reflection of how much her contribution was undervalued came in 1967, when the British Society of Industrial Artists and Designers awarded Charles their design medal and then, as a token gesture, presented Eames with a red rose. This simple, unthinking act sums up the enormous gender prejudice women designers have had to put up with and – even now – still have to fight against.

Opposite, from left: Dot Pattern textile, 1947 (not realized during Eames's lifetime, but later produced by Maharam); House Bird, original created for the Eameses' house and later reissued by Vitra, c. 1950 (co-designed with Charles).

This page, right: Hang-It-All coat rack for Tigrett Enterprises (later Herman Miller), 1953 (co-designed with Charles); below: Child's Chair for Evans Products Company, c. 1940 (co-designed with Charles).

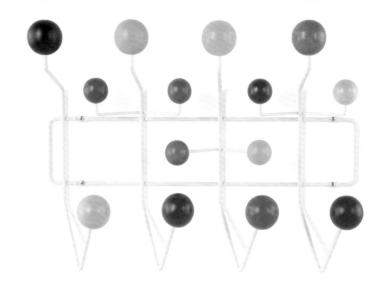

ESTRID ERICSON

MID-CENTURY · INTERIORS · TEXTILES · PRODUCT

Swedish
b. Öregrund, Sweden, 1894
d. Stockholm, Sweden, 1981

Estrid Ericson was not only a gifted designer, but also a formidable entrepreneur who founded Sweden's leading interior design business. Her collaboration with Josef Frank, the Austrian émigré architect, redefined the Scandinavian interior, and it is a tribute to her remarkable legacy that her company, Svenskt Tenn, continues to flourish and is still seen as the epitome of good taste in Sweden. Many of her product designs remain in production, testifying to their timeless appeal.

Ericson started her career as an art teacher, but when she was left a small inheritance by her father she set up her own company in 1924 with the designer Nils Fougstedt, who was already well-known for his metalware designs. Her business, based in Stockholm, comprised a showroom with an adjoining workshop. She called it Svenskt Tenn, meaning 'Swedish Pewter'.

Pewter was then a fashionable alternative to silver and silver plate and the firm soon made a name for itself through the high quality of its wares – in both their design and manufacture. Ericson is known to have designed some of the pieces herself, while some were produced by Fougstedt and other Swedish designers. Only a year after its founding, the company received a gold medal at the landmark 'Exposition Internationale des Arts Décoratifs et Industriels Modernes' ('International Exhibition of Decorative and Industrial Arts') in Paris, 1925 – with the British journalist Philip Morton Shand coining the phrase 'Swedish Grace' to describe the Art Deco Neoclassicism of the designs on show in the Swedish pavilion. Certainly, the firm's products from this period epitomized this very distinctive Nordic style and many of Ericson's later metalware designs continued to reference classical motifs, but in a thoroughly contemporary way. In 1928 Svenskt Tenn received a royal warrant and relocated to larger premises on Strandvägen, where it remains today.

By the early 1930s, the firm was at the vanguard of Swedish Modernism, with Ericson commissioning designs from the Functionalist architects Uno Åhrén and Björn Trägårdh. In 1933 the renowned Austrian architect–designer, Josef Frank, who had previously designed for the Wiener Werkstätte, fled to Sweden to escape Nazi persecution and the following year began working as a designer for Svenskt Tenn. It was the start of a lifelong collaboration between Ericson and Frank. His influence not only changed the stylistic direction of Svenskt Tenn but

also Ericson's role within the company. While he became the firm's chief designer, creating furniture, lighting and textiles, she concentrated on the interior design side. Incorporating Frank's designs, she produced interior schemes that came to define the Svenskt Tenn look – comfortable, bright and cheerful spaces with a strong sense of domesticity. Rejecting the increasingly puritanical doctrine of the Modernist movement, Svenskt Tenn produced designs that could be easily mixed and matched, enabling the realization of visually interesting spaces with a relaxing ambience.

During her many trips abroad, Ericson was always on the lookout for interesting and beautiful things that she could sell in her store. One trip to Africa inspired her iconic Elephant textile, based on a cloth pattern from the then Belgian Congo. This cheerful design was first printed in the late 1930s and remains a popular and much-loved mainstay of the Svenskt Tenn range. In many ways, this simple print reflects the forward-looking eclecticism of Erisons's approach to interior design. Indeed, throughout her life, Ericson's wanderlust helped to inform her constantly evolving sense of beauty. Combining artistry with entrepreneurship above all, she demonstrated that the Modernist interior need not be severely ascetic but could be joyfully aesthetic, if a human-centric approach to design was taken.

Opposite: Schnapps
Fish decanter for
Svenskt Tenn, 1920s.

This page, clockwise
from left: Acorn vase
for Svenskt Tenn, 1930s;
Elefant (Elephant) textile
for Svenskt Tenn, late
1930s; Svenskt Tenn
interior at the New York
World's Fair, 1939.

VUOKKO ESKOLIN-NURMESNIEMI

Finnish
b. Helsinki, Finland, 1930

Vuokko Eskolin-Nurmesniemi is one of Finland's most famed designers, whose textiles and fashions epitomized the fresh and youthful confidence of Nordic design of the 1950s and beyond.

Intellectually curious and highly creative from a young age, she undertook a summer apprenticeship with the Helsinki-based ceramics firm, Arabia, when she was 15 years old. Suspecting that it was in the field of ceramics that her main creative talents lay, she enrolled at the Centralskolan för konstflit (Central School of Arts and Crafts) in Helsinki to train as a ceramist. Upon graduating, in the early 1950s, she secured a position in the art department at Arabia, where she designed marketing materials. It was during this period that her interest shifted towards two-dimensional print design.

In 1953 Eskolin-Nurmesniemi joined Marimekko, established the previous year as a fashion-led sister company of the furnishing textile company, Printex. This new venture was seeking to create ready-made garments from their growing library of hand-produced, screen-printed textiles. Her visual sensibilities were a perfect fit for the company's aesthetic approach – interested as she was in a simple, playful and humanized interpretation of Pop-inspired Modernism. She set about collaborating with Marimekko's founder, Armi Ratia, on a raft of distinctly Scandinavian prints that gracefully walked the line between geometric rigour and organic naivety, and this ethos was carried into her experimentation with the printing process itself. Making a feature of the notoriously difficult task of precise screen registration, she intentionally offset and overlaid colour-blocks on top of each other. Where two hues were overprinted, they created subtle colour variations, bestowing her apparently simple designs

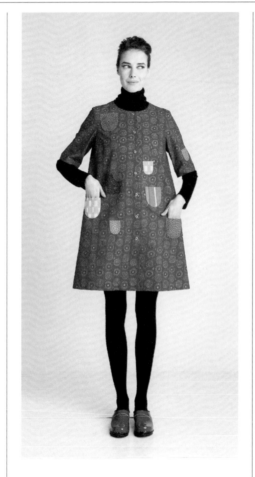

with a visual complexity and tonal depth that drew the viewer's attention to the craft processes used to produce them.

Thanks to her university training in three-dimensional design, she also commanded a genius for innovative garment patterns. The casual, tent-like trapeze dresses she pioneered for Marimekko were a perfect celebration of the new freedoms women were enjoying in liberalized mid-century Finland. The design for which she is best known, however, was a much more structured affair – the Jokapoika (Every Boy) shirt of 1953, produced in the painterly stripes of her Piccolo print (1953). True to its name,

this design proved universal, becoming as it did a sort of quasi-uniform for creative professionals – and, to this day, it remains a bestseller.

Eskolin-Nurmesniemi's garments from the postwar period helped to pioneer a new folk-craft tradition. She injected an unmistakable sense of joy and humanity into her textiles and clothing, which set her work apart from many of her European Modernist contemporaries. In 1960, during her final year of working at Marimekko, she married the architect and furniture designer, Antti Nurmesniemi. Keen to carry tokens of his affection wherever she went, she designed a smock-like dress upon which were haphazardly stitched a multitude of small pockets. Each was intended to hold a note or trinket from her beloved Antti. Named the Happy Jacket, it was soon worn by fashionable women across the Western world.

Upon leaving Marimekko, she founded her own signature label, Vuokko Oy. Carrying an increasingly bold range of ready-to-wear garments and printed homewares, in its first year the company was awarded the prestigious Lunning Prize for design. The company closed briefly in 1988, only to reopen in 1990 under the name, Vuokko Nurmesniemi Oy. Throughout this period, she continued to be fascinated by the manufacturing processes used to make her garments and, in accordance with her deep respect for the natural world, she sought to reduce their impact on the environment. A truly modern Scandinavian, her mission is to design a totally coherent way of life, in which ethics, emotion and aesthetics are inseparably entwined.

Opposite: Happy Jacket
dress for Marimekko, 1960.

Left: Velvet coat for Vuokko
Oy, late 1970s/early 1980s.

FRONT

CONTEMPORARY · FURNITURE · LIGHTING · PRODUCT

Stockholm, Sweden, est. 2004
Anna Lindgren / Sofia Lagerkvist /
Katja Pettersson (left 2009) /
Charlotte von der Lancken (left 2014)

It was in the Nordic countries, specifically Sweden, that women first achieved widespread prominence in the field of professional design practice. Indeed, one of the great founding texts of modern Scandinavian design was written in 1898 by the Swedish feminist writer, Ellen Key, who penned a small but hugely influential pamphlet entitled *Beauty for All*. This publication explored the ethics of aesthetics and can be seen as the primary seed from which Scandinavian design has since grown and flourished. Certainly, throughout the twentieth century, women designers in Scandinavia enjoyed far greater parity with their male counterparts than those working outside the Nordic region, thanks, in large part, to these countries' more progressive and socially inclusive societies.

It is not surprising, therefore, that it was in Stockholm that the first high-profile all-women design group, Front, was founded in 2004. It originally had four members – Sofia Lagerkvist, Anna Lindgren, Katja Pettersson and Charlotte von der Lancken – who met while studying at the Konstfack (University College of Arts, Crafts and Design) in Stockholm. After graduating, they collectively showed their work at the Milan Salone and soon began attracting attention from the international design press for their provocative work. These early designs led Moooi's co-founder, Marcel Wanders, to ask them to make a lamp that even his grandmother would like. This made them think of making 'something that is taken from nature and presented as a piece of furniture'.[1] Featuring life-sized models of a rabbit, a horse and a pig turned respectively into two lamps and a side table, their Animal Thing range (2006) perfectly channelled the off-the-wall quirkiness of the New Dutch Design movement, which Moooi had come to represent. It was also a highly confrontational statement of intent given that these were Swedish designers

effectively trashing the legacy of Swedish Modernism, which, for so long, had been associated with thoughtfully and rationally conceived design solutions and, essentially, 'good taste'. The Horse lamp, in particular, sharply divided opinion, with people either loving or hating it. For some interior designers, who were furnishing hotel foyers and the like, it did strike a chord for it provided a strong Neo-Postmodern ironic focal point. The design press, always looking for something controversial and eye-catching to feature, also rather predictably latched on to it, with it even gracing the cover of *Time* magazine.

Since creating waves with their Animal Thing collection, Front has generated a variety of designs for a host of manufacturers, all of which possess a strong poetic quality, from their Melt lamp for Tom Dixon to their Blow Away vase for Moooi. Pettersson left the group in 2009 and, six years later, von der Lancken also moved on to pursue a solo career. Today, Lagerkvist and Lindgren remain at the helm of this celebrated practice, which continues to communicate stories about design matters through its creation of objects that frequently challenge design and manufacturing conventions. Above all, their work is, according to Front themselves, 'inspired by their fascination with magic'[2] – meaning, the alchemy of materials and technologies. It is their playful subversion of form, function and materials that has brought them respect among their peers, for they have dared to break the rules and, in so doing, have produced designs that have an undeniable emotional resonance.

Opposite, far left: Rabbit
Lamp for Moooi, 2006;
left: Blow Away Vase for
Moooi, 2008.

This page, clockwise from
above: Melt pendant lights
for Tom Dixon, 2015; Füria
rocking horse for Gebruder
Thonet, 2016; Horse lamp
for Moooi, 2006.

'GEORGIE'
GEORGINA
GASKIN

ARTS AND CRAFTS · JEWELLERY

British
b. Shrewsbury, UK, 1866
d. West Malling, UK, 1934

Georgie Gaskin was a high-profile proponent of the British Arts and Crafts Movement, who forged a reputation as a talented jewellery designer and illustrator. She left a remarkable body of work that testifies to her gift for composition and patternmaking and today, her exquisitely executed gem-encrusted pieces are highly sought after by collectors as representing the apotheosis of British Arts and Crafts jewellery design.

Gaskin studied at the Birmingham School of Art, which was then under the enlightened headmastership of Edward R. Taylor, a champion of the Arts and Crafts Movement. While studying there she met fellow student Arthur Gaskin whom she married in 1894. Crucially, during the mid to late nineteenth century, Birmingham, with its burgeoning Jewellery Quarter, was one of the great centres of excellence for silver- and goldsmithing. It is reckoned that by 1850 the city's manufacturers were responsible for around half the gold and silver items sold in London alone. As a result, by the 1890s, Birmingham School of Art had become one of the country's most important art-and-design teaching institutions, especially in the teaching of metalware design. Certainly, the Gaskins both received the highest level of artistic and technical training at the college, at which Arthur later taught.

In 1899 the couple began producing jewellery under the joint authorship of Mr and Mrs Arthur Gaskin. It would appear, however, that Georgie took the lead role in the actual design of the pieces. In 1929 she described their roles thus: 'In the jewellery I did all the designing and he did all the enamel, and we both executed the work with our assistants.'[1] Various family friends who knew the couple well later confirmed this division of creative roles. Given this, it is safe to assume that most of the jewellery attributed to the Gaskins was designed solely by her, albeit strongly inspired by Arthur's interest in medieval metalwork.

Initially, their jewellery designs were quite simple, often featuring semiprecious stones and mother-of-pearl set within intricate, scrolling silver wirework mounts that were exquisitely executed. Over the years, however, their designs became increasingly elaborate and pictorial, often incorporating densely set floral clusters of precious and semiprecious stones. Echoing the exquisite detailing and beautifully stylized compositions of medieval manuscripts, these later designs had a distinctive resplendence that revealed both the Arts and Crafts Movement's reverence for the past and its worship of nature in all its bountiful glory.

In 1901 their jewellery was exhibited at the Glasgow International Exhibition, and at this show Georgie was identified as a jewellery designer in her own right. Her credits continued in the pages of *The Studio* magazine, in which pieces were sometimes attributed jointly to the couple or individually, depending on their specific personal involvement. Although the Gaskins spent the majority of their working lives in Birmingham and were actively involved with the so-called Birmingham Group of designers and artists, they were also frequent visitors to Chipping Campden in the Gloucestershire Cotswolds. They eventually relocated there in 1924 and carried on designing silver and enamel work, executing jewellery and creating book illustrations. Although widowed in 1928, Georgie continued to work as a designer in her own right until shortly before her death in 1934.

Opposite: Rose Lattice
brooch, 1912 (co-designed
with Arthur Joseph Gaskin);
Emerald, sapphire and
seed pearl ring, c. 1930
(co-designed with Arthur
Joseph).

This page, clockwise
from right: Gem-encrusted
openwork silver demi-parure
set consisting of a matching
necklace and brooch,
c. 1914 (co-designed with
Arthur Joseph); Loves
Garland brooch, 1912
(co-designed with Arthur
Joseph Gaskin); Pink
tourmaline, emerald paste
and mother-of-pearl set
silver openwork necklace,
c. 1907 (co-designed with
Arthur Joseph).

GENERAL MOTORS' 'DAMSELS OF DESIGN'

American, active 1950s
Dagmar Arnold / Marjorie Ford,
Ruth Glennie / Gere Kavanaugh /
Jan Krebs / Jeanette Linder
Sandra Longyear / Helene Pollins /
Margaret 'Peggy' Sauer /
Jayne Van Alstyne /
Suzanne Vanderbilt

Harley Earl, arguably the most influential automotive designer of all time, as head of the Art and Color Section of General Motors (GM) famously introduced the game-changing concept of the stylistically driven 'annual model change' – and, in so doing, transformed the automotive industry forever. What is less well known is that, in this capacity, he was also an early and influential champion of professional women designers working in the automotive sector during the 1940s and 1950s, something virtually unheard of before then. It was at his personal behest that the first prominent all-female design team in America, known as the 'Damsels of Design', was formed.

Over the years, Earl had observed that it was invariably wives who had the final say in the purchasing decision of a family car, and so it followed that it was important to design cars that would appeal to women. But, more than this, increasingly during the postwar era, women were learning to drive and, as a consequence, had their own cars. In order to produce cars that were more appealing to female consumers, Earl began hiring female designers, notably Helene Rother in 1943 and Amy Stanley in 1945, but the involvement of these first female designers at GM was not widely publicized.

In the mid 1950s Earl ramped up the recruitment of women to his design team, many of them having previously trained as industrial designers under Alexander Kostellow at the Pratt Institute in New York. These new recruits were assembled into a high-profile all-women team, which was heavily promoted by GM's PR department. As Earl would later note in a press release in 1958, 'The skilled feminine hands helping to shape our cars of tomorrow are worthy representatives of American women, who today cast the final vote in the purchase of three out of four automobiles.'[1]

The team was christened GM's 'Damsels of Design', much to their personal chagrin for they felt that the title, though catchy, detracted from their professional credentials. The group designed every kind of automotive interior element imaginable (apart from instrument panels, which were still deemed a male preserve) as well as related displays and exhibits. The ten-member team included four industrial designers, Dagmar Arnold, Gere Kavanaugh, Jan Krebs and Jayne Van Alstyne. Prior to this, Van Alstyne had been involved in the creation of Frigidaire's Kitchen of the Future project,[2] which was included in the short promotional film *Design for Dreaming* (1956) produced by GM. The team's six remaining designers, Marjorie Ford, Ruth Glennie, Jeanette Linder, Sandra Longyear, Peggy Sauer and Suzanne Vanderbilt, were mainly industrial design graduates from the Pratt Institute, although Sauer, for example, had trained as a sculptor at Cranbrook Academy of Art, where she gained extremely useful form-giving skills.

This remarkably talented team provided an all-important women's touch to GM's range in the mid to late 1950s, with more female-friendly features that went on to become standard items in later cars, such as illuminated make-up mirrors, child-proof door locks, handy storage consoles and retractable seat-belts. They also helped to shape a much softer feminine aesthetic that took on board the latest colour trends. To further promote their work in this field, Earl organized the 'Feminine Auto Show' in 1958, which was held at the GM Technical Center's Styling Dome in Warren, Michigan.

Earl retired shortly after the exhibition and his successor, Bill Mitchell, was not nearly as enthusiastic about working with women designers. As a result, the 'Damsels of Design' team dispersed, most of its members moving to design jobs at other companies. That said, both Vanderbilt and Van Alstyne remained at GM for many years and, through their work, continued to challenge the male bias traditionally found in automotive design. Short-lived but influential, the 'Damsels of Design' team was important, for it demonstrated that areas of design that were traditionally male-dominated could be significantly improved with female ingenuity and creativity.

Opposite: Jeanette Linder with a luggage set and matching 'trunk textile' she designed for the Chevrolet Impala Martinique concept car, 1958.

SOPHIE GIMBEL

MID-CENTURY · FASHION

American
b. Houston, USA, 1898
d. New York, USA, 1981

Sophie Gimbel famously introduced the 'New Look' to America and, in 1947, became the first American fashion designer to feature on the cover of *Time* magazine. She summed up her style thus: 'I try to make a woman look as sexy as possible and yet look like the perfect lady.'[1] This proved to be a winning formula, and propelled Gimbel and her employer, Saks Fifth Avenue, to ever-greater commercial and critical success over the succeeding decades.

Like so many pioneering women in design, Texas-born Gimbel did not have a particularly easy childhood. Her tobacco-merchant father died when she was four, her mother remarried the following year and the family had to move to Atlanta, Georgia. There, the young Gimbel entertained herself by making clothes for her dolls. Brought up in a family that espoused traditional southern values, Gimbel was married at 19 to Jay Harry Rossbach, a member of the wealthy Bache family, owners of a successful leather business. For a while, she fulfilled the conventional role of an affluent homemaker – her only creative outlet being the making of costumes for local theatrical productions. When her marriage collapsed in 1926, she left this safe and comfortable lifestyle to pursue adventure in New York.

In 1929 she met Adam Gimbel, president of the Saks Fifth Avenue department store. He was concerned about the financial decline and critical reception of the company's Salon Moderne, which offered custom-made gowns to New York's elite, and asked Gimbel to oversee the design direction of that department. Aware that Paris was still considered by many as the unassailable capital of fashion, she undertook a string of trips across the Atlantic. She returned with designs from rising stars such as Coco Chanel and Elsa Schiaparelli, introducing them to the nascent American luxury market. She is credited as the first to sell culottes – the French split skirt – in America. On one of these voyages, via a ship-to-shore telephone, Adam Gimbel proposed and they married in 1931.

Alongside European pieces, Gimbel introduced a modest selection of her own creations. With no training or formal background in design, she hired sketchers and draftsmen to bring her ideas to life. Her concepts were often carefully studied modifications of existing patterns, gently modernizing and 'Americanizing' looks with which her buyers would be familiar. She often borrowed classic pieces of historic importance from the Brooklyn Museum for this very purpose and her work displayed a far greater continuity with the past than her counterparts in the radical Parisian ateliers. The value of her work lay more in the quality of the handiwork and the sumptuousness of the materials than in the novelty of the silhouette. Her conservative approach was also reflected in the hemlines and necklines of her designs, always modestly concealing while still flattering their wearer.

Gimbel also took on costume design commissions for a variety of Broadway musical productions – some 50 in total across her career. These generated valuable publicity for the original design output of the Salon Moderne and Gimbel's custom work soon outsold and overshadowed French couture, tripling overall sales for the department. The shift in emphasis away from Europe was aided, in part, by the outbreak of World War II, which saw most French fashion houses closed under the Nazi occupation. Gimbel's success was symbolic of a wider cultural shift that occurred when America emerged as the great cultural and economic powerhouse in the postwar era.

This trend started when Gimbel's American-made designs featured on the cover of *Vogue*'s first US fashion edition, in 1940. Three years later, she played a key role in establishing the first 'combined showing of American fashion'[2] – an event that later morphed into New York Fashion Week. In 1947, the cover of *Time* displayed an illustration of Gimbel alongside the caption, 'Who Wants the New Look?', which effectively pitted her against Christian Dior as the arbiter of mid-century style. This status allowed her to dress many of the matriarchs of the American establishment, including Rose Kennedy and the president's wife, 'Lady Bird' Johnson. Gimbel maintained her role at the Salon Moderne until its closure in 1969 and, throughout her career, was known professionally as 'Sophie of Saks Fifth Avenue'. Her success lay largely in her uncanny ability to predict fashion trends, as she once noted: 'The trick is timing. You must pick the right idea from the past and use it at the right time in the present.'[3] Much of her fortune was donated during her lifetime to philanthropic projects, notably the Adam and Sophie Gimbel Design Library at The New School University in New York City.

Opposite: *Time* magazine cover featuring Gimbel with the byline 'Who Wears the New Look?', 5 September 1947.

Clockwise from top right: Embroidered pink satin cocktail dress for Saks Fifth Avenue, 1954; silk chiffon sequined dress for Saks Fifth Avenue, c. 1962; blue and green gauze cocktail dress for Saks Fifth Avenue, 1954.

THE GLASGOW GIRLS

ARTS AND CRAFTS • TEXTILES • GRAPHICS • METALWARE

British, active 1890s–1920s
Margaret Macdonald Mackintosh /
Frances Macdonald MacNair /
Jessie Marion King / Ann Macbeth /
Jessie Newbery

During the *fin de siècle* period many women were actively involved in the British Arts and Crafts Movement, which had at its core a socially progressive agenda. In Scotland, a group of very gifted female artist–designers was integral to the development of the so-called Glasgow School – a regionally specific expression of the Arts and Crafts Movement. All of these women had trained at the Glasgow School of Art, from 1885 to 1917, under the enlightened directorship of Francis 'Fra' Newbery. They later became known as the Glasgow Girls.

Foremost among their ranks were the Macdonald sisters, Margaret and Frances, who opened their own studio in Glasgow in the 1890s. They achieved international acclaim together with their respective husbands, Charles Rennie Mackintosh and Herbert MacNair, when they exhibited together as 'The Four' at

the 1900 Secessionist exhibition in Vienna. Of the two, Margaret was the better known thanks to her collaborations with her more famous husband, whose furniture and interior schemes often incorporated her own figurative gesso panels. She also produced several textile panels of note, typified by their swirling floral motifs and highly stylized figures. Her sister Frances produced designs for posters, metalwork and textiles that possessed a similarly strong graphic stylization and incorporated subject matter that tended towards an otherworldly ethereality.[1]

Jessie Marion King enjoyed a career as a successful illustrator while also designing books, jewellery and textiles. Having studied at the Glasgow School of Art, she taught book decoration and design there from 1899 to 1908 and married the gifted furniture designer, E.A. Taylor. Ann Macbeth worked across a number of disciplines and, after the Glasgow School of Art, became an assistant to Jessie Newbery, talented wife of the school's director and head of its needlework and embroidery department. Macbeth succeeded her in this position in 1908 and published a book entitled *Educational Needlecraft* (1911) that was used to teach sewing skills in Scottish schools until the 1950s. Through her teaching and publications, she helped to perpetuate the Arts and Crafts Movement's goal of empowering women creatively and financially by teaching them vocational design and craft skills. Macbeth also encouraged ordinary women to make clothing to their own designs using, as she put it, 'humble materials'.[2] As a militant member[3] of the suffrage movement – which was strongly aligned to the Arts and Crafts Movement's social-equality agenda – Macbeth produced two embroidered banners for the cause. She also designed books, metalwork and carpets, while Liberty & Co. sold a number of her embroidery patterns as iron-on transfers.

Others who studied at the Glasgow School of Art included Eleanor Allen Moore, Agnes Banks Harvey, Dorothy Carleton Smyth, Stansmore Dean Stevenson, Christian Jane Fergusson, Annie French, De Courcy Lewthwaite Dewar, Bessie MacNicol and Norah Neilson Gray – and, while most of them worked as fine artists and illustrators, some also turned their hands to product design, often to spectacular ends. The reason behind this crossover between the fine and applied arts was that one of the Arts and Crafts Movement's key aims was to infuse objects with an artistic aesthetic as well as a craft sensibility in order to raise standards of both design and manufacture.

In comparison to their female peers, these women, like others associated with the Arts and Crafts Movement, managed to achieve a far greater degree of personal liberation. This was largely thanks to the socially progressive ethos of the movement, which promoted the cause of female design education in the knowledge that, if women were able to earn a living for themselves, they were more likely to enjoy a higher degree of emancipation.

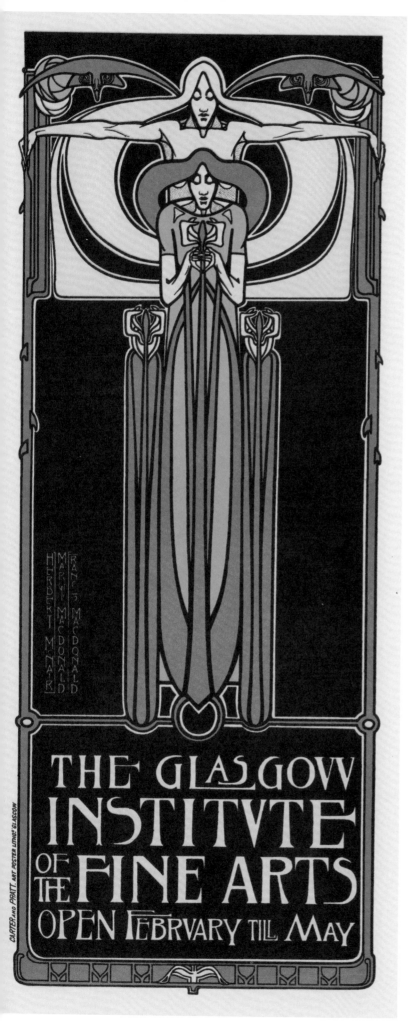

HERBEKT MCNAIR
MARY MACDONALD
FRANCES MACDONALD

THE GLASGOW
INSTITVTE
OF THE FINE ARTS
OPEN FEBRVARY TILL MAY

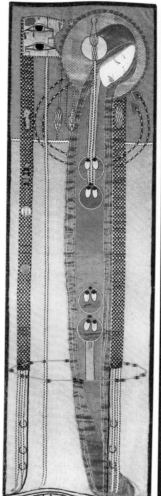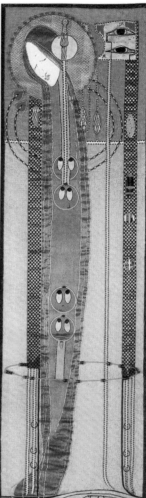

Opposite top, clockwise from top left: Margaret Macdonald Mackintosh, Jessie Marion King, Anne Macbeth and Jessie Newbury.

Opposite bottom: Jessie M. King, cover design for Thomas Lodge's *The Story of Rosalynd*, 1902.

This page, clockwise from left: Margaret Macdonald Mackintosh, Frances Macdonald Macnair and Herbert MacNair, The Glasgow Institute of the Fine Arts poster, 1897; Margaret Macdonald Mackintosh, embroidered panels, *c.* 1902–4; Jessie M. King, silver and enamel buckle, 1906.

LONNEKE GORDIJN

CONTEMPORARY · ART · INSTALLATION

Dutch
b. Alkmaar, The Netherlands, 1980

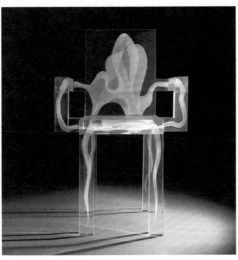

Lonneke Gordijn, together with Ralph Nauta, founded the boundary-pushing practice Studio Drift in 2007, which is internationally renowned for its thought-provoking blurring of art and design. The Dutch design duo not only represent a marriage of curious minds but also a partnership of creative equals, using design as a form of metaphorical discourse in order to explore the synergetic relationship that exists between humans, nature and technology. The pair's experimental works have a captivating, poetic sci-fi quality that is otherworldly in aspect and, for this reason, they are keenly sought by design–art collectors.

Born in North Holland, Gordijn studied at the renowned Design Academy Eindhoven from 1999 to 2005, where she met British-born Nauta. Her training there included a year-long work placement in London, as an intern in Tord Boontje's studio. The delightful charm and visual lyricism of Boontje's work, which is often inspired by nature, undoubtedly had a strong influence upon Gordijn as her later work for Studio Drift possesses a similar ethereality. She graduated *cum laude* from the Eindhoven academy, honoured by the Man and Well-Being design department for her thoughtful psychological approach to design.

In many ways, the Studio Drift partnership represents 'New Dutch Design 2.0', or, in other words, the post-Droog (the influential conceptual design company) generation. This generation emerged in the wake of the first successful breakout of Eindhoven graduates onto the international design stage in the early to mid 1990s, which witnessed the likes of Marcel Wanders and Hella Jongerius (see pages 126–27) achieving superstar designer status. This post-millenium wave of New Dutch Design practitioners are more digitally savvy and more conceptually based, preferring high-tech to low-tech means of construction and embracing

a blend of creative disciplines. In Studio Drift's case, the focus is on creating site-specific interactive installations that seamlessly merge design and art. These mix advanced technologies with beautiful thought-provoking imagery and often poetically reference nature, be it the flight pattern of birds or the colours found in a rainbow's spectrum.

Studio Drift's work also frequently explores light and movement. Its Ghost Collection of 2008, for instance, consists of four chairs that contain wispy 'organic and elusive' spectral elements within their hard-edged graphic profiles, which give the optical illusion of frozen smoke. When placed under certain light conditions, these encased ethereal elements glow like some spooky ectoplasm and, as one moves around the chairs, they appear to shape shift.

In contrast, the *Fragile Future III* installation incorporates real dandelion heads, which were laboriously picked apart and then glued onto tiny LED bulbs, shedding light, quite literally, on the precious transience of nature, while also making reference to the fact that light is fundamental to virtually all biological life. As Gordijn thoughtfully observes, 'People find the time to look at art within a gallery setting but the world is one big exhibition if you only care to look.'[1] And that is what her works ultimately highlight: the beautiful preciousness of the natural world – no more, no less.

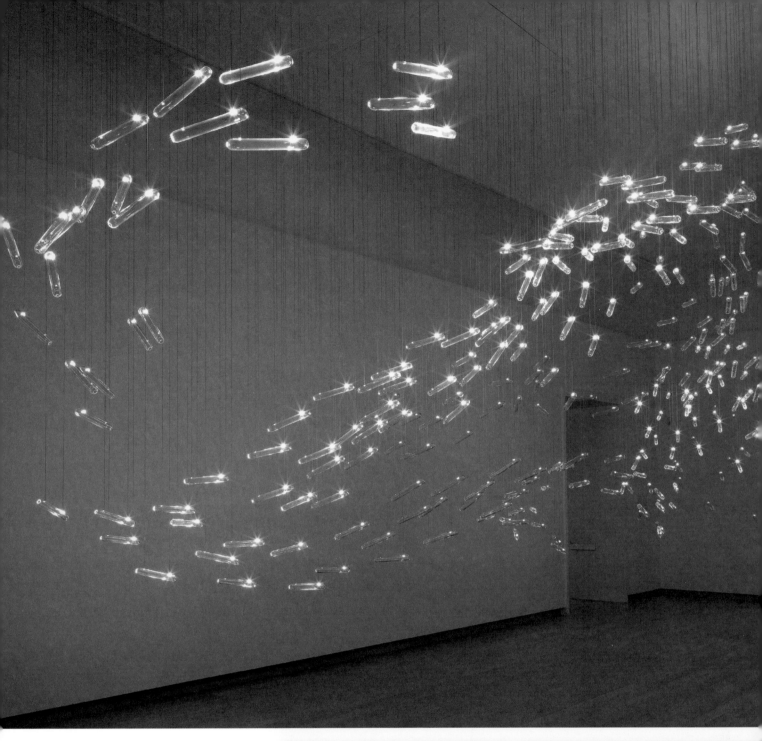

Opposite, above:
Dandelight, 2018 (co-
curated with Ralph Nauta);
below: Queen chair from
the Ghost Collection, 2008
(co-curated with Nauta).

This page, above: Flylight
installation at the Stedlijk
Museum, 2018 (co-curated
with Nauta); right: Nola
colour-mixing LED lights for
Buhtiq31, 2015 (co-curated
with Nauta).

EILEEN GRAY

ART DECO/MODERNISM · FURNITURE · LIGHTING · INTERIORS

Irish/France
b. Enniscorthy, Ireland, 1878
d. Paris, France, 1976

Eileen Gray, through sheer persistence, 'outlier' opportunity and prodigious talent, managed to forge an international reputation in the early twentieth century. She was especially notable because her designs bridged the ideological transition from sumptuous French Art Deco to full-blown steel-and-glass Modernism.

Her parents were the Scottish painter James McLaren Smith and Eveleen Pounden, who inherited a title, to become the 19th Baroness Gray and changed the family name from Smith to Gray. In 1897 Gray moved to London to study painting at the Slade School of Art, one of the first women to be admitted there. She visited Paris with her mother to see the 1900 Exposition Universelle and, falling in love with the city, relocated there in 1902 to continue her artistic training at the Académie Colarossi and the Académie Julian. In 1905 she returned to London to look after her ailing mother and began learning lacquering techniques from a Soho-based antiques restorer. Returning to Paris the following year, she met Seizo Sugawara, a Japanese lacquerware master, under whose guidance she became one of the first noteworthy Western practitioners of Japanese lacquering, a time-consuming art involving hazardous materials.

In 1907 Gray furnished her apartment with Art Deco pieces of her own design. The interiors of this stylish apartment were published in a number of journals, publicizing her talent as an innovative designer. She set up a studio with Sugawara and, over the next two decades, they collaborated on the design and execution of landmark furniture pieces, including her Serpent armchair (1917–19). In 1913 she exhibited some of her lacquer pieces at the Salon des Artistes Décorateurs and received her

first significant furniture commission from the art-collecting couturier, Jacques Doucet. Her first major interior design commission, to redecorate and furnish an apartment, came from the wealthy milliner Madame Mathieu-Lévy of the boutique J. Suzanne Talbot. Inspired by African tribal art as well as by Modernism and Japanese aestheticism, Gray created a suite of rooms that featured some of her key designs, including her Brick screen, and a remarkably elegant lacquered daybed. These interiors were updated in 1933 to include her iconic Bibendum chair, reflecting a maturing of Gray's Art Deco style and epitomized her distinctive East-meets-West look.

In 1922 she opened her own showroom, Galerie Jean Désert, and took part in an exhibition of French artists in Amsterdam. She attracted the attention of members of the De Stijl movement, including architect Jan Wils, and an issue of the Dutch architecture journal *Wendingen* was dedicated to her work, securing her international reputation. In 1923 her stark Bedroom-boudoir for Monte Carlo caused quite a stir at the Salon des Artistes Décorateurs. With its bold palette and abstraction, reflecting the influence of

De Stijl, one critic described it as a 'room of horror', but Gray became increasingly aligned with Modernism and exhibited a group of chromed steel, tubular metal and glass furniture designs in 1925, showing just how avant-garde she was.

Architect Jean Badovici urged Gray to try her hand at architecture and the result was two remarkable Modernist houses in the Alpes Maritimes. The first, E1027 (1926–29), was a summerhouse she shared with Badovici, overlooking the sea at Roquebrune. Le Corbusier visited and, outraged a woman had created such a significant work in a style he considered his own, desecrated the walls with garish murals, which Gray described as 'an act of vandalism'. The second project, the Tempe à Pailla in Castellar, was also designed and built for her personal use, but was sadly ransacked during the war. Having fallen into disrepair, E1027 has recently been restored to its former glory. Today, it is considered Gray's Modernist masterwork and serves as an impressive testament to her pioneering credentials, which ultimately made her one of the most progressive female designers of her generation.

Opposite: Salon de Verre (Glass Room) for Madame Mathieu-Levy, designed by Paul Ruand and furnished with designs by Gray, 1933.

Clockwise from right: Brick screen for Galerie Jean Désert (later Aram Designs), 1922–25; Tube light for Galerie Jean Désert (later Aram Designs), 1927; Bibendum chair for Galerie Jean Désert (later Aram Designs), 1926.

APRIL GREIMAN

1970S–CONTEMPORARY · GRAPHICS

American
b. New York, USA, 1948

April Greiman helped pioneer digitally based graphic-design practice during the early 1980s. She was one of the earliest designers to grasp that computers could be powerful design tools and possessed the crucial technical wherewithal to fully exploit their creative potential. Since then, Greiman has continued to refine her approach, which seeks to unite the visual arts with digital technology in order to produce visually compelling and thought-provoking experimental work that is often of a multi-sensorial nature.

Having studied graphic design and ceramics at the Kansas City Art Institute (1966–70), she trained at the renowned Allgemeine Kunstgewerbeshule (School of Arts and Crafts) in Basel, Switzerland. She studied under Armin Hofmann and Wolfgang Weingart – trailblazers of 'new' Swiss graphic design and typography. In the summer of 1971, while staying with Hofmann and his wife, Greiman received a telegram about her new teaching position at the Philadelphia College of Art, which came as a bit of a surprise to her as she had not applied for it. Hofmann, however, knew all about it, saying, 'There is no more I can teach you. You just have to get out there and start doing it.'[1] Following her tutor's advice, Greiman headed back to America to take up the post and at the same time set herself up as a graphic designer in New York.

In 1976 she became an instructor at the California Institute of the Arts (CalArts) and it was there that she began to develop her own distinctive postmodern graphic style that mixed her 'new' Swiss School training with an altogether freer New Wave sensibility. At CalArts she met the photographer Jayme Odgers and they worked together as Visual Energy from 1978 to 1981. They created numerous graphic artworks that were pasted up as traditional collages, then airbrushed and rephotographed. By combining original and found imagery with painting and

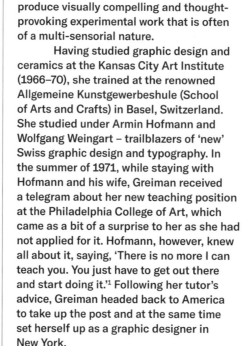

typography, the pair built up graphic landscapes with 'the elements interacting, seemingly spontaneously, to create a space of their own'.[2] Included in this body of work were two icons of Californian New Wave graphic design: a poster for CalArts (1977) and the cover of *WET* magazine (1979).

In 1982 Greiman was appointed head of design at CalArts and, at her instigation, the graphic design department's name was changed to 'visual communications' to reflect the widening remit of the course. She studied the effect that emerging technologies might have on her own work and, in 1985, returned to full-time practice. Having bought her first Macintosh computer, she began to experiment creatively, exploiting pixellation effects and other digital 'mistakes' to create compositions with a postmodern aesthetic. One such work was her fold-out poster Does It Make Sense? for issue 133 of *Design Quarterly* in 1986, which featured a life-sized representation of her naked body and was entirely executed on her 512k MacPlus computer, which was hooked up to a video camera. This memorable artwork forced the graphic-design community to acknowledge that the digital age had arrived, and that with computers came new, exciting creative possibilities. In 1990 she published her first book, *Hybrid Imagery: The Fusion of Technology and Graphic Design*, in which she wrote, 'Design must seduce, shape, and perhaps more importantly, evoke an emotional response.'[3] This has effectively been her modus operandi always, with her aptly named LA-based consultancy Made in Space specializing in what she terms 'transmedia' communications design intended to enhance environmental spaces.

Opposite: Mural above Wilshire/Vermont Metro Station in Los Angeles, 2007.

This page, left: Cover design for *WET* magazine, September/October 1979 (co-created with the photographer Jayme Odgers); Does It Make Sense? pull-out poster for *Design Quarterly*, issue 133, 1986.

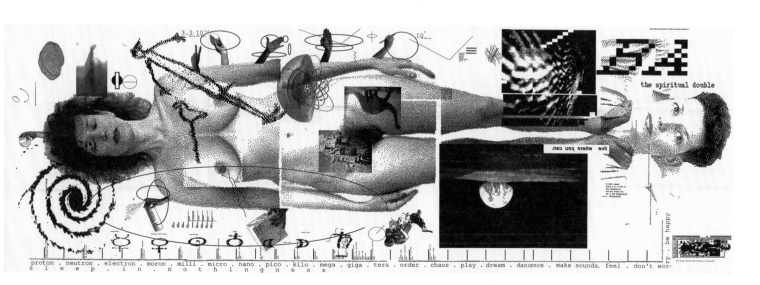

MAIJA GROTELL

MID-CENTURY · CERAMICS

Finnish/American
b. Helsinki, Finland 1899
d. Pontiac, Michigan, 1973

The renowned Finnish-American studio potter Maija Grotell has often been referred to as the 'mother of American ceramics' thanks to her long teaching tenure at the Cranbrook Academy of Art, which was a crucible of design talent during the interwar period and instrumental to the formation of postwar design practice in the USA. Set up as America's answer to the Bauhaus, the teachers at Cranbrook – Grotell among them – actively encouraged the exchange of ideas between different studios and workshops. During her career as both a designer and educator, Grotell won numerous awards for her ceramics and was an influential force in the world of studio pottery, bringing a refined Scandinavian Arts and Crafts sensibility to postwar American ceramics.

Grotell studied at The Ateneum (Central School of Arts and Crafts) in Helsinki, under the Belgian-born British ceramicist Alfred William Finch. After graduating in 1920, she worked for a textile firm while continuing her study of ceramics. Eventually in 1927, she emigrated to the United States and during her first year there attended a summer course taught by the English-born potter Charles Fergus Binns at the New York State School of Clayworking and Ceramics at Alfred University. Grotell subsequently became an instructor at the Inwood Pottery Studio in Manhattan, from 1927 to 1928. Over the following decade she held various teaching positions in New York City at Union Settlement (1928–29), Henry Street Craft School (1929–1938) and Rutgers University (1936–38). Having become an American citizen in 1934, Grotell took up a teaching post at the Cranbrook Academy of Art in Bloomfield Hills, Michigan in 1938. This august educational establishment had been founded six years earlier, and the architect Eliel Saarinen, who like Grotell was Finnish-born, was its first president. Indeed, many of Grotell's fellow teachers at Cranbrook had a Scandinavian background,

such as Swedish Carl Milles, the school's sculptor in residence, and Finnish Marianne Strengell, who headed its textile department. As head of the academy's ceramics department, Grotell remained at Cranbrook for the next 28 years, until 1966, teaching scores of students to explore the practical and creative uses of clay. She acted as a mentor to many of her students, most notably the Hawaiian-born Japanese ceramicist Toshiko Takaezu, and she was keen for them to develop their own creative autonomy, as she once remarked: 'If you help a student too much they are lost when they leave or you leave. The best thing you can do for students is to make them independent so they do not miss you.'

With her own work, she loved experimenting with form and decoration and her vessels often incorporated interesting slips and glazes. During this period she helped perpetuate the use of clay as a medium for personal expression, which influenced the emergence of a more creatively experimental approach to ceramics design. At the behest of Eero Saarinen (Eliel Saarinen's son) she also conducted extensive research into new glazing techniques for architectural bricks, the results of which were put to spectacular use on his General Motors Technical Center in Warren, Michigan (1965). Throughout her career Grotell was fascinated by the creative possibilities of materials and it was her standout ability to synthesize form and decoration into single wheel-turned vessels embellished with rich glazes that ultimately set her work apart.

Opposite: Glazed
earthernware vase,
c. 1940.

This page, left: Charger,
c. 1945; below left: glazed
stoneware vase, *c.* 1950;
below right: glazed
stoneware vase, *c.* 1940.

ZAHA HADID

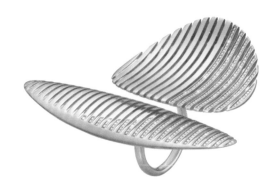

1990S–2010S · ARCHITECTURE · FURNITURE · PRODUCT

Iraqi/British
b. Baghdad, Iraq, 1950
d. Miami, FL, USA, 2016

Zaha Hadid, the first female 'solo' architect to be internationally acclaimed, was awarded the Pritzker Architecture Prize in 2004. The sculptural dynamism of her radical architecture and design work was an expression of her feisty personality, which emboldened her to challenge the design status quo and relentlessly push the boundaries of both form and function. Her early career, however, highlighted the difficulties women faced professionally in the realms of architecture and design. But her headstrong determination and remarkable creative talents could not be stifled and, ultimately, she succeeded spectacularly.

Hadid spent her early childhood in Iraq, which, during the 1950s and early 1960s, was a liberal, secular society with a burgeoning economy. Her father was leader of the country's Progressive Democratic Party and his strong sense of liberalism meant that Hadid was encouraged to think independently. Having attended Catholic school in Baghdad and an independent boarding school in England, she read mathematics at the American University of Beirut, before moving to London in 1972 to train at the Architectural Association – one of the most progressive architectural teaching institutions at the time.

After graduating in 1977, Hadid began working for the Office of Metropolitan Architecture (OMA), established a couple of years earlier by her former tutor, the Dutch architect Rem Koolhaas.[1] The following year, she started teaching at the Architectural Association, eventually leading her own studio there. In 1980 she founded her own architecture practice, though she continued to teach. Hadid won a prestigious competition for the design of a cliff-top resort, The Peak Leisure Club (1982–83) in Hong Kong, which, with its bold layering of horizontal planes and daring spatial dynamism, reflected the influence of Russian Suprematism and was intended to look like 'a man-made polished granite mountain'.[2] This progressive building was never built. Controversially, it transpired that at least one of the judges had not realized that she was a woman and some in the architecture community believed she was sidelined for that very reason. The difficulty of translating Hadid's daring plans into a physical reality must also have contributed to its abandonment, but the various pieces of furniture designed for the building gave a tantalizing insight into Hadid's architectural ambitions and helped to raise her profile.

A decade later, the first of her buildings was finally constructed: the Vitra Fire Station in Weil am Rhein (1990–93) was a daring architectural exercise intended to represent 'frozen movement'.[3] It was instantly iconic and, by the early 2000s, Hadid's international reputation as an avant-garde architect and innovative product designer had been well and truly forged. Her successes in the design field included dynamic Z-Play modular seating units (2002) for Sawaya & Moroni and the spiralling VorteXX chandelier (2005) for Zumtobel. She created exhibitions, interiors, products, fashion and furniture for an impressive roster of design-led companies, including Alessi, Artemide,

Melissa, Serralunga and Swarovski. In the mid 2000s, Hadid also achieved remarkable success in the lucrative design–art market, notably with her Aqua table (2005) for Established & Sons.

From the early 2000s, the use of highly sophisticated CAD software programmes by Hadid and her team enabled the creation of a host of seemingly gravity-defying buildings based on parametric algorithms and a plethora of innovative designs with a very distinctive 'signature' sculptural bravado. At the zenith of her career Hadid died unexpectedly of a heart attack in 2016. Tributes poured in for this acknowledged 'Queen of the Curve',[4] whose singular creative vision had done so much to alter the design and architecture landscape. More than this, she had shown by example how a woman could conquer the upper echelons of those worlds on her own terms.

Opposite, from far left: Mesa table for Vitra, 2007; Lamellae Twin gold ring for Georg Jensen, 2016.

This page, clockwise from left: Phaeno Science Centre in Wolfsburg, Germany, 2000–5; VorteXX Chandelier for Zumtobel, 2005; Heydar Aliyev Center in Baku, Azerbaijan, 2007–12.

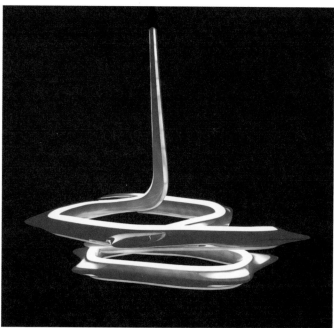

KATHARINE HAMNETT

1980S–CONTEMPORARY · FASHION

British
b. Gravesend, UK, 1947

Known for her bold, political slogan-led T-shirts, Katharine Hamnett has never been afraid of making a statement. The daughter of a socialite and an RAF defence attaché, Hamnett was raised within the British establishment. She received an education at Cheltenham Ladies' College, but soon fell out of love with the control and structure of such traditional and privileged institutions.

As soon as she was able, Hamnett applied to study fashion at Central Saint Martins in London. There, she developed an aptitude for material experimentation – helping to pioneer the stonewashing, stretching and distressing of denim. Upon graduating, Hamnett formed her first company, Tuttabankem, with former classmate Anne Buck. Though a successful venture, selling to the likes of Browns and Saks, it was short-lived. In 1979 Hamnett went her own way, founding her eponymous label. This was an even greater commercial success – soon selling in Joseph and other key retailers across the globe. Her garments ranged from beautifully tailored 1950s-inspired Capri pants and rockabilly pinch-waisted skirts in pastel hues, to army-themed combat pants with a multitude of different utility pockets for the fashion-savvy traveller.

Unlike her previous work, these new collections took on a distinctly ethical aspect. She especially took over supply chains, desperate to ensure her own success was never at the expense of the environment. Hamnett herself has claimed this obsession with the future of the planet was inspired by the birth of her two sons, in 1976 and 1981. It was not until 1983, however, that this message became overt with the launch of her iconic protest shirts. These pieces were incredibly direct; plain white T-shirts upon which san-serif slogans were printed in black – demanding those who glimpse them to, 'CHOOSE LIFE', 'SAVE THE RAINFOREST' or enact 'WORLDWIDE NUCLEAR BAN NOW'. Brilliant in their simplicity, these shirts became an aesthetic cornerstone of their era. Her clothes were soon stocked in 700 stores in over 40 different countries, yet they still boldly defied the Thatcherite consumerism of 1980s England.

Despite, or perhaps because of, this irreverent attitude, in 1984 Hamnett was named the British Fashion Council's Designer of the Year. Never shy of controversy, she used this platform to amplify her views. She soon took this message all the way to the prime minister herself, Margaret Thatcher, sporting a '58% Don't Want Pershing' shirt to a reception at 10 Downing Street. Confronted by this clear protest against American militarism, Thatcher was photographed looking visibly taken aback.

Given the radically eye-catching simplicity of her work, it is unsurprising that Hamnett also inspired a raft of imitators. When Frankie Goes to Hollywood performed their hit single 'Relax', they did so in Hamnett-inspired 'FRANKIE SAYS RELAX' T-shirts. Her 'CHOOSE LIFE' slogan, made popular by George Michael in the video for 'Wake Me Up Before You Go Go', made an early 1990s return in the opening lines of Danny Boyle's iconic *Trainspotting* movie. Around the same time, Hamnett opened a flagship store on Sloane Street, the interior of which was designed by the then up-and-coming designer Tom Dixon and featured a massive bespoke fish-tank in its window, which seemed appropriate given her longstanding interest in ecology and the natural world.

To this day, Hamnett continues to campaign for a range of causes, with her garments protesting political projects such as the Iraq war and Brexit. Within fashion, she has lobbied against sweatshop labour and the use of pesticides in cotton-growing. In 2005 she relaunched the Katharine E Hamnett collection with manufacturing guidelines focussing strongly on the ethics of international production.

KATHARINE HAMNETT

Opposite: Slogan T-shirts range, 1980.

This page, above: 1986 advertising campaign; left: Satin bomber jacket, 1979; below: Fashion Aid event at the Royal Albert Hall, London, 1985, for which Hammett created a series of slogan T-shirts.

INEKE HANS

CONTEMPORARY · FURNITURE · LIGHTING · PRODUCT

Dutch/British
b. Zelhem, The Netherlands, 1966

Ineke Hans, like many Dutch designers working today, takes an eclectic approach to design and making, and enjoys experimenting with age-old craft skills alongside high-tech manufacturing processes. Her research-based designs often possess a thought-provoking rhetoric, while also having an engaging mutant quality. Through her work, Hans invites us to reflect on the socio-economic issues surrounding globalized contemporary design, while her human-centred approach to design and making shows how resources can and should be used more efficiently. As she notes, 'Many of my designs are rooted in questions on techniques and materials and human habits. Exploring these is often a conscious choice.'[1]

Hans initially studied art and design at what is now AKI ArtEZ Academy for Art and Design in Endshade, graduating in 1991. Two years later she did an MA in furniture design at the Royal College of Art, London. After completing her studies in 1995, she was hired as a furniture designer by Habitat and, while there, branched out into the design of accessories. She stayed at Habitat for three years and around 20 of her designs made it into production, including her Rondo ceramic outdoor stool (1997). Hans created her first Furniture as Pictograms collection, which she exhibited in 1997 at a show in The Tramshed in London's East End. The range included her felt-covered Johanna I and blow-moulded Johanna II stools, which cleverly employed three identical legs to form a single seat. At that show she also showed her Tête à tête table set (1997), which 'started off with a wish to design furniture that would not look over-designed but be an ordinary product. A simple construction based on trial and error, like our ancestors used to do when they needed a table or a chair.'[2] This design was the first of her Ordinary Furniture sets,

which are made from a robust, UV-resistant, recycled, plastic material with a sort of *faux* 'wood grain' that is a result of its production process. Hans realized that this industrial material, which is frequently used along canals in Holland because it is able to withstand wind, water, salt and acid, would also be perfect for making outdoor furniture thanks to its impressive resilience. Having a curious handcrafted aspect, yet utilizing an emphatically man-made material, Hans's Ordinary Furniture sets were nominated for the Rotterdam Design Prize in 1999.

Since then, one of the main themes running through Hans's work has been the idea of re-use, with many of her designs not only utilizing recycled materials but also being devised themselves in a way that they can be efficiently recycled. For instance, her award-winning Ahrend 380 chair (2010) comprises two injection-moulded 100 per cent recyclable elements for easy assembly and disassembly, with its flexible back section moulded from Xenoy, a polymer made from recycled PET bottles. Another theme found in Hans's work is space-saving efficiency. The two elements of her Ahrend 380 chair, for example, were cleverly devised so they would stack together when unassembled for more efficient transportation. Similarly, her practical and playful Plektra stool/table/storage container for littala boasts an impressive multifunctionality within its compact form. As she notes, 'To me there is a practical functionality where things have to work and do their jobs and there is mental functionality where products are poetic or in another way nice for your mind. Functionality can give products a longer life and add to their durability.'[3]

Opposite, from far left:
Ahrend 380 chair for
Royal Ahrend, 2010;
Plektra nesting storage
stools for Iittala, 2015.

This page, above: Johanna
I stool, 1995; left: Tête à
tête set, 1997.

EDITH HEAD

American
b. San Beranadino, USA, 1897
d. Los Angeles, USA, 1979

Arguably one of the most famous costume designers of the twentieth century, Edith Head is best known for the looks she produced for films such as *Roman Holiday* (1953), *The Sting* (1973) and *All About Eve* (1950). And, with her trademark severe fringe and thick-rimmed glasses, she was one of the most recognizable figures of Hollywood's Golden Age. Her father, a gold miner, emigrated to California to escape the anti-Semitic violence plaguing his native Prussia, while her mother was from Missouri. The family operated a small haberdashery shop and struggled financially. Her parents separated and her mother married Frank Spare, a travelling mining engineer, who treated Head as his own child. After living in Nevada, Arizona and Mexico, the family settled in Los Angeles, where Head attended high school.

In 1919 she graduated from the University of California, Berkeley, and the following year earned a master's degree in romance languages from Stanford. She took a job as a French teacher at the Hollywood School for Girls but became dissatisfied with her level of pay. By exaggerating her qualifications, she secured a second, income-boosting post as an art teacher – a role for which she had no formal training. Keen to match her fictionalized credentials, Head took evening classes in drawing. Through a friend she made there, she met Charles Head – a travelling salesman whom she married in 1923.

In need of work during the long summer break, Head noticed a classified ad placed by Paramount Pictures for a costume sketch-artist to work under the famed designer, Howard Greer. She was not confident enough of her own drawing ability, so she borrowed portfolio-filling artwork from her night-school classmates – a hotchpotch of portraits, landscapes and architectural drawings. With this falsified portfolio, she secured the role. On the job, she was quickly taught to draw in the style of Greer so that he could pitch his employee's images as his own. Within a few short years, Head had enough experience to transition from sketcher to designer.

Her first major job was the design of costumes for *The Wanderer* (1925), a silent drama set in Old Testament times. This was followed by a raft of other film-costume commissions. Head became famed for her ability to collaborate with the actresses she dressed, producing garments in which her stars could feel totally comfortable. She became a close confidante to many of the most famous female leads of the day, including Grace Kelly, Marilyn Monroe, Audrey Hepburn and Elizabeth Taylor. Unusually, Paramount allowed her to work with these actresses in films for other studios, understanding that their relationships were more valuable than any one title. Head's style was restrained and she eschewed adornments and details that would date. Every look she created was the result of painstaking story and character research, and placed within the context of the script using pioneering storyboarding techniques. Using this approach, she produced one of her most famous designs in 1936 – the Sarong dress for Dorothy Lamour in *The Jungle Princess*. It was a strapless, figure-hugging affair with a naïve jungle print reminiscent of Henri Matisse's collage studies, and helped launch Lamour's career.

Such was Head's growing reputation, that in 1938 she replaced Travis Banton as chief costume designer at Paramount and retained the role for 29 years. In an industry dominated by men, she was one of the few female outliers. In 1940, with her first marriage in tatters, she married the art director, Wiard Ihnen. She kept her Head surname, however, because it had become so well known within the industry. Her work during this period was so extensive and stylistically diverse that it is almost impossible to categorize, but it was the humble street dress designed for Audrey Hepburn as the princess in *Roman Holiday* that was probably her most famous look, and helped make Hepburn a household name.

In 1967, Head moved from Paramount to Universal Pictures. Alfred Hitchcock had moved his studio there and Head had already styled a number of his films, including *Rear Window* (1954), *Vertigo* (1958) and *The Birds* (1963). During the 1970s, she stepped outside the world of film, producing uniforms for female members of the United States Coast Guard, a commission she claimed was her proudest professional moment. She also designed iconic costumes for Pan Am airline staff and for tour guides working at the United Nations Building in New York. By 1974 Head had worked on over 1,100 motion pictures, winning eight Academy Awards for best costume design, having been nominated a record-breaking 35 times. In recognition of these achievements, she was granted a star on the Hollywood Walk of Fame in 1974 and, to this day, is remembered as the unassailable grande dame of Hollywood costume design.

Clockwise from left: Hedy Lamarr in a costume designed by Head for *Samson and Deliah*, 1949; Ivory lace dress for Audrey Hepburn, which she wore to the 1954 Academy Awards before winning an Oscar for best actress for *Roman Holiday*, 1953; Flame-coloured crepe evening dress with magnolia print for Dorothy Lamour, which she wore in *Tropic Holiday*, 1938.

MARGARET HOWELL

1970S–CONTEMPORARY · FASHION

British
b. Tadworth, UK, 1946

Right: Fashion sketch for Autumn/Summer 1995 collection.

Opposite, clockwise from top left: Spring/Summer 2017 collection; Spring/Summer 2018 collection; Spring/Summer 2017 collection; campaign photograph, 2013.

Margaret Howell was born in a quintessential Home Counties commuter village, set on the Epsom Downs in Surrey. Her father was a managing clerk in a solicitor's office, while her mother worked in a local dress shop. From this quiet, suburban upbringing emerged one of the country's most respected clothing designers. Inspired by British Modernism and English sartorial understatement, she has incorporated traditional Harris tweeds, Irish linens and high-quality corduroys into her own vision of strikingly modern simplicity throughout her career.

Remarkably, the technicolour chaos of late 1960s Swinging London passed her by as she eschewed pyschedelia for structure and clarity. She preferred instead the stripped back beatnik look of the 1950s and early 1960s. Her stylistic affinity was with the understated workman over the contemporary dandy.

Upon graduating in 1969, Howell assisted at her sister's small scarf-printing company. It was there she gained an understanding of design as a route to commerce. Ever the pragmatist, she fell in love with the idea of producing universally desirable objects. Thus, as a sideline, she began creating fine papier-mâché beads, which were soon stocked by Browns, a newly opened fashionable boutique on London's South Molton Street. Before long, she was asked to produce a beaded top for the film-star, Elizabeth Taylor. While the intricate look of the beadwork she produced was quite outside the pared-back style for which she would become known, this was her first taste of commercial success, and it spurred her on to continue creating.

Practical inquiry into the cultural role of craft always informed Howell's output and eventually led her to men's shirtmaking. By carefully recreating, and then modifying, the structure of garments found in second-hand shops, she discovered that she was able to produce garments that were beautifully relaxed in their shape. Initially, she made these shirts herself in her flat in Blackheath, south-east London, and, before long, both Paul Smith and Browns started stocking them. It was, however, her partnership with the fashion entrepreneur Joseph Ettedgui that proved most fruitful, culminating in his funding of her first dedicated, stand-alone menswear shop in 1977.

As the Margaret Howell brand grew over the succeeding decades, Howell broadened her range to include clothing for women that contained within their cut the same utilitarian menswear sensibility. She also wove the importance of quality manufacturing into the very fabric of her expanding organization by establishing her own shirt factory in Edmonton, north London. At the same time, she was influential in championing the cause of Modernist British design by showing in her eponymous stores carefully curated selections of wares – from Robert Welch candlesticks to Ercol furniture – that perfectly complemented the very British ethos of her own beautifully tailored clothes.

As fashion became globalized, in the last decades of the twentieth century, whole new markets opened up to the Margaret Howell brand. The Japanese audience, especially, found an affinity with the reserved, detail-oriented nature of Howell's garments. Perhaps that country, more than any, understood the philosophy that has remained a constant behind the Margaret Howell brand for over half a century – that a quiet and patient attention to detail can satisfy the senses more than trends and gimmicks.

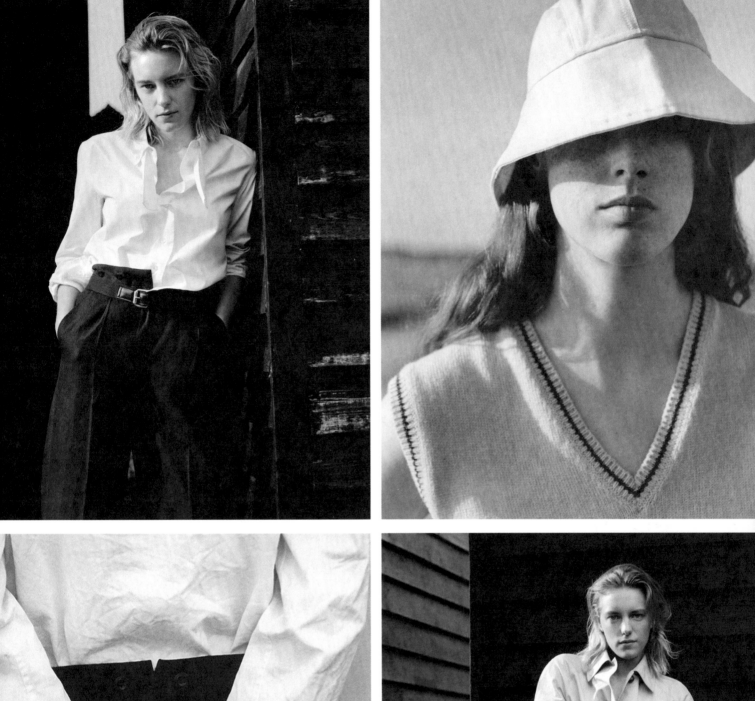
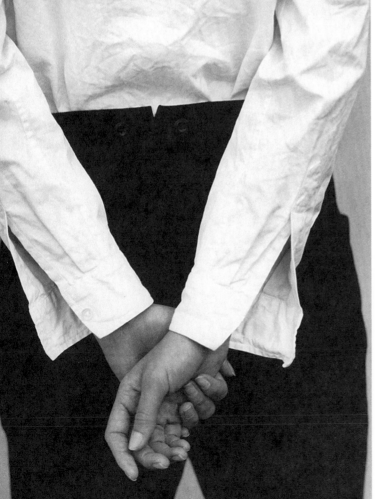

MAIJA ISOLA

This page: Kaivo textile for Marimekko, 1964.

Opposite: Unikko textile for Marimekko, 1964.

1960S–1980S · TEXTILES

Finnish
b. and d. Riihimäki, Finland,
1927-2001

At the vanguard of contemporary Finnish design, Maija Isola produced over 500 textile designs remarkable for their stylistic diversity. From the late 1950s to the 1970s, she created some of the most iconic textiles of the twentieth century, including her Unikko print (1964) with its oversized abstracted poppies, now synonymous with its manufacturer, Marimekko, and an enduring icon of Finnish design.

Isola grew up in southern Finland and studied painting at Helsinki's Taideteollinen Korkeakoulu (University of Art and Design). At 18, she became pregnant with her daughter, Kristina, and married the commercial artist, Georg Leander, in 1945. Three years later, visiting Oslo, she encountered a display of classical amphorae at the Museum of Decorative Arts and Design. This inspired her to create her Amfora print, which, with other designs, attracted the attention of Armi Ratia of the Printex textile company, who hired her as principal designer in 1949. Her marriage to Leander over, she became romantically involved with the painter Jaakko Somersalo, whom she subsequently married. It was he who taught her woodcut-printing techniques and encouraged her to paint.

At Printex, Isola designed many furnishing textiles, some of which were inspired by the African art she had seen on another trip to Norway in 1949. From 1951, she designed bold fashion and interior textiles for Printex's newly founded sister company, Marimekko. As this new venture's first full-time designer, Isola was responsible for its first fashion show, staged at the Kalastajatorppa restaurant on the outskirts of Helsinki in 1951. After the rationing and shortages of World War II and its immediate aftermath, which in terms of textiles had meant either wartime muted cloth or cheap artificial silks, Isola's simple patterns, silkscreen printed onto inexpensive cotton sheeting, must have felt like a gust of fresh Nordic air blowing through the Finnish design community.

During the 1950s, Isola's textiles were inspired by African art and by Slovakian folk motifs. From the early 1960s, however, she began designing bolder textiles that reflected the Finnish love of strong graphic patterns. Many of her textiles were based on her observations of the natural world, for instance, Joonas (1961), which was inspired by the shapes made by sunlight on salt water on a holiday in the Mediterranean. Likewise, her Melooni textile (1963), with its iconic patterning of differently coloured concentric ovals, was inspired by the form of a cut melon. It was, however, her Kaivo textile, introduced in 1964, that heralded a new era of extra-large patterned textiles. This design was part of Marimekko's revolutionary Architects series (of which Unikko was also a part), which had been conceived by Ratia to entice architects and interior designers into using large-scale textile hangings within public and commercial spaces. Boldly abstracted and vibrantly coloured, Kaivo became Isola's most enduring design. It reflected the influence of American Colour Field painting, while also expressing the youthful spirit of Pop design. A cultural nomad, Isola's textiles were also influenced by her travels to the then Yugoslavia, Italy and Greece in the 1960s and, in the 1970s, time spent living in Algeria and the United States. In the 1980s she co-designed a number of textiles with her daughter, but eventually left Marimekko in 1987 and dedicated the rest of her life to painting.

Isola received numerous design accolades, including two International Design Awards in 1965 and 1968. In the early 2000s two retrospectives of her work were staged, in Helsinki and Glasgow. Today, Maija's eye-catching patterns are recognizable throughout the world, their enduring popular appeal springing from an engaging visual freshness that transcends cultural boundaries.

GRETE JALK

1950S–1960S · FURNITURE · TEXTILES

Danish
b. Copenhagen, Denmark, 1920
d. Denmark, 2006

Regarded as 'the Grande Dame of Danish Design',[1] Grete Jalk helped to transform the notion of Modernism in Denmark with her own forward-looking pieces. Despite having been thoroughly grounded in the cabinetmaking tradition, she dared to break free from it by creating furniture that reflected a new and more youthful sculptural direction. Her innovative designs brought her international recognition as a high-profile, yet unconventional, female pioneer of Scandinavian design.

One of the main reasons she was able to succeed in the furniture design field, although it was still very much a male-dominated world, was her undeniable technical abilities and consummate design skills. After finishing high school, she went to Copenhagen University to study philosophy and law, but became disillusioned with this and, after completing

the philosophy element, dropped out. She went on to study drawing for a year at the Tegne- og Kunstindustriskolen for Kvinder (Drawing and Applied Art School for Women) and then served a cabinetmaking apprenticeship with Karen Margrethe Conradsen from 1941 to 1943. During the final year of this apprenticeship she began training as a furniture designer under the exacting tutelage of Kaare Klint at the Furniture School of the Royal Danish Academy of Fine Arts, Copenhagen. As one of Klint's pupils, she was made to measure meticulously and analyze the 'ideal' forms and constructions of antique furniture archetypes. She was also taught anthropometrics and was encouraged to marry rational design principles with well-honed craft skills.

The year she graduated, 1946, she was awarded first prize in the annual cabinetmakers' competition in Copenhagen, a truly remarkable achievement given both her youth and her gender. She subsequently showed her furniture designs at the Milan Triennale in 1951 and, two years later, won first prize in a competition organized by renowned silversmith Georg Jensen. In 1954 she established her own design office and worked for a number of different furniture

manufacturers, including Fritz Hansen, France & Son, Søren Horn, Henning Jensen and P. Jeppensens. Her early designs tended to be contemporary interpretations of traditional furniture models and were typified by the skilful incorporation of hidden joints and subtly curved lines.

In 1963 Jalk won an international furniture design competition sponsored by the *Daily Mirror* newspaper in Britain, with her Bow chair made from two pieces of moulded plywood. Radically different from her earlier furniture pieces, this sculptural design marked a new progressive agenda in her work. Despite its prizewinning success, however, this innovative design was never produced on a large scale – initially only around 300 units were made, perhaps because of the technical challenges posed in bending plywood into the small radii of its curved surfaces. Undeterred, the following year she created a cantilevered chair for Race Furniture that was, if anything, even more radical in terms of its construction, with a continuous looping frame made of laminated pine.

Apart from designing furniture, Jalk also created wallpaper and upholstery textiles for manufacturer Unika Vaev, as well as silverware for Georg Jensen. She was also co-editor of the influential Danish design journal *Mobilia* (1956–62 and 1968–72), with her tenure marking its golden period. Henrik Lange, who owns the licence to produce some of her designs, once noted, 'Grete Jalk's honesty and genuine interest in every aspect of quality has made her the conscience of Danish design.'[2]

As with other female designers working in Scandinavia, Jalk benefitted greatly from the Nordic countries' ethos of social inclusivity and, as a result, was able to rise to prominence within her chosen field entirely on the merit of her work. Furthermore, as she flourished, she helped in no small part to revolutionize Danish furniture design in the process.

Opposite: Lounge chair
for France & Son, 1950s.

This page, clockwise
from top left: Bow
chairs for P. Jeppensens
(later Lange), 1963;
Lounge chairs, 1968;
Teak coffee table for
Glostrup Møbelfabrik,
1960s; Daybed for P.
Jeppensens, c. 1965.

GERTRUDE JEKYLL

ARTS AND CRAFTS · GARDENS

British
b. London, UK, 1843
d. Godalming, UK, 1932

Gertrude Jekyll completely redefined the English country garden. Influenced by the writings of John Ruskin and William Morris, she was closely aligned to the British Arts and Crafts Movement and, in her creation of gardens, took on board its respect for the natural environment. This resulted in landscaping schemes that had a naturalistic aspect. During her career she designed over 400 gardens and penned 15 books, as well as some 2,000 articles on gardening, all of which helped disseminate her design ideas.

Born in Mayfair, London, she was the fifth child of Captain Edward Joseph Hill Jekyll, an officer in the Grenadier Guards. In 1848, when she was five, the family leased Bramley House, set amid the heaths and woodlands of the

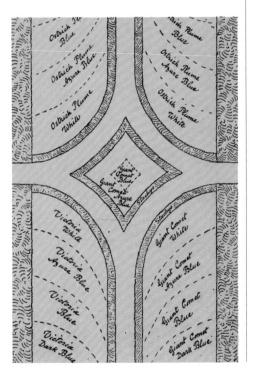

rolling Surrey hills. It was here that Jekyll spent her childhood, playing in its large garden and collecting wild flowers in the surrounding countryside. Her father set up a workshop there, where he made models and conducted experiments, which instilled in her a love of 'working and seeing things grow under my hand'.[1]

At the age of 18, Jekyll enrolled at the South Kensington School of Art (later the Royal College of Art) in London. Here, aside from her fine art studies, she was tutored in the related subjects of botany, anatomy and colour theory, which she keenly embraced. After completing her studies in 1863, Jekyll pursued an active social life that brought her into contact with some of the leading artists of the day, including G.F. Watts and Hercules Brabazon. Even more importantly, she met William Morris and became a devotee of his Arts and Crafts Movement. She also travelled to Greece, Italy and Algeria, and not only painted but also undertook embroidery and other craft work.

Between 1865 and 1870, she exhibited nine paintings of animal subjects but, all the while, her interest in gardens was growing. In 1875 she met the editor of *The Garden* magazine, William Robinson, who had five years earlier published *The Wild Garden*, which urged for less regimented planting and the use of more species of hardy exotic plants that could look after themselves. In 1876 Jekyll moved back to Surrey and began designing the garden of her newly widowed mother's new house on Munstead Heath, near Godalming. She was finally able to consolidate her knowledge of plants and garden design, including Robinson's ideas, into a scheme that received much praise from leading horticulturalists. In 1881 she began contributing articles to *The Garden* and, two years later, acquired 15 acres of heath and woodland opposite her mother's property. From this natural wilderness she created her own garden, Munstead Wood,

which was laid out as a series of themed gardens, each with its own specific scheme of flowers and shrubs.

In accordance with the Arts and Crafts Movement's principles, Jekyll was interested in the idea of *gesamtkunstwerk* (total design unity). In 1889 she met the young architect Edwin Lutyens and they began working together – he designed clients' houses, while she designed their surrounding gardens. One of their earliest collaborations was her house at Munstead Wood, completed in 1897. Two years later, she published her first book *Wood and Garden* (1899). It was, however, her last book *Colour Schemes for the Flower Garden* (1918) that became her most influential. In it, she advised dedicating different areas of a garden to the different seasons, grouping plants according to their colour, texture and shape, and creating coordinated 'cool' and 'hot' beds. It also revealed her remarkable ability to visualize a garden, as well as her impressive knowledge of horticulture.

It is, however, Jekyll's surviving gardens, with their Impressionistic compositions of colour, that remain the most tangible testament of her genius. By introducing a new painterly sensibility to garden design, informal and in harmony with nature, Jekyll fundamentally changed the concept of gardening. To this day, her influence can be detected in contemporary garden design, for, as she once noted, 'The love of gardening is a seed that once sown, never dies but always grows and grows to an enduring and ever-increasing source of happiness.'[2]

Opposite: Planting plan from *Colour in the Flower Garden*, 1908.

This page, clockwise from top: The Aster Garden at Munstead Wood, designed from 1883 onwards; a formal garden at Hestercombe in Taunton, Somerset, designed c. 1903; a signature hot-colour border at Munstead Wood.

BETTY JOEL

Below: Walnut bureau, executed by W.G. Evans at Token Works, 1929.

Opposite, above: Art Deco living room designed by Betty Joel, incorporating her furniture and rugs, 1930; below: pair of mahogany bookcases, executed by J. Emery, 1931.

ART DECO · FURNITURE

British
b. Hong Kong, 1894
d. Andover, UK, 1985

Throughout the 1920s and 1930s, Betty Joel designed luxurious furniture, textiles and interiors that combined elements of the British Arts and Crafts tradition with both Oriental and Modernist influences. Joel did not utilize overtly Modernist industrial materials, such as steel or glass, in her furniture designs, preferring tropical woods imported from across the British Empire, including teak, Indian laurel and greywood, and Queensland silky oak. This meant that, rather than exuding a sense of modish continental utilitarianism, her work had more of a transitional Art Deco quality.

The daughter of Sir James Stewart Lockhart, Joel was born in Hong Kong. Her father, a noted sinologist, had risen through the ranks of the civil service and, a year after her birth, was appointed colonial

secretary. Spending the early part of her childhood in the Far East was hugely formative and, throughout her subsequent career, Joel's designs embodied a stylish and subtle Orientalism. Finishing boarding school in England before World War I broke out, she joined her father in Weihaiwei (now Weihai), then a British-leased territory in north-east China, where he was civil commissioner. Her mother and siblings were stranded in Britain for the duration of the war and so Joel, finding herself pretty much isolated in this Chinese port, began studying Oriental art under the tutelage of her father.

In 1918 she married David Joel, a naval officer. The newlyweds returned to England and set up their first home on Hayling Island, near Portsmouth. As she later noted, 'I personally began to design furniture because I despaired of trying to adapt old furniture to the needs of my own entirely modern house.'[1] Friends admired the furniture and began commissioning pieces. This prompted the couple to establish Betty Joel Ltd in 1919 and to set up Token Works on the island – the workshop's name being a play on the words teak and oak, cleverly reflecting the influence of both Orientalism and Britishness in Joel's work. Initially modest in scale – just a small timber-built workshop employing one or two craftsmen – as orders increased, the firm outgrew its premises and moved to a more modern works in Portsmouth. Many of the craftsmen who worked there had previously been employed as yacht fitters and shipbuilders, which gave Betty Joel's furniture a very distinctive carpentry style.

Initially, they had a small shop in London's Sloane Street but around 1925, Joel opened a larger showroom in fashionable Knightsbridge and eventually moved manufacturing to a large purpose-built factory in Kingston upon Thames. While her early furniture had exhibited a curious neo-Georgian aspect, her

designs became increasingly Modernist in tune with changing fashions and can be seen as a very British answer to the contemporaneous Moderne style in America. In 1935 her work received much acclaim at the 'British Art in Industry' exhibition at the Royal Academy. Two years later, her coronation-related exhibition, at the Betty Joel Galleries, reaped similar praise. According to the *Nottingham Evening Post*, it was 'the first important exhibition of George VI fabrics and furniture',[2] while *The Studio* reported that any visitor to the show would 'not only have been struck by the fine craftsmanship evident in the pieces shown, but also by the tasteful arrangement of the rooms'.[3]

During the 1930s, Joel also undertook private interior design commissions for, among others, the Countess of Iveagh, Lord Mountbatten, the Duchess of York and Winston Churchill, as well as numerous commercial decorating projects, including interiors for the Savoy hotel and various high-profile stores. She brought a thoughtful touch to every interior design project she undertook, while her furniture was always beautiful in its design and execution, as well as being eminently practical.

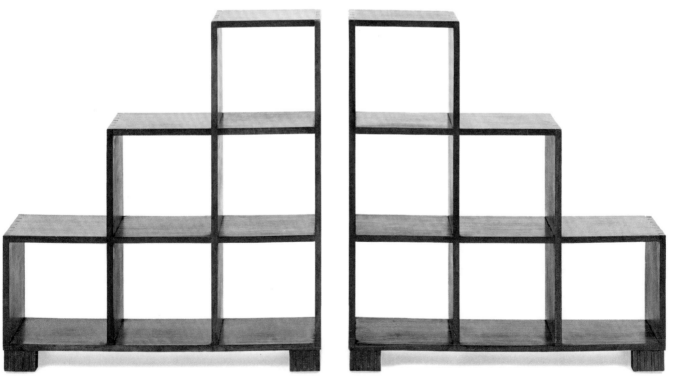

HELLA JONGERIUS

CONTEMPORARY · FURNITURE · TEXTILES · PRODUCT

Dutch
b. De Meeren, The Netherlands, 1963

Since the emergence of the De Stijl artistic group in the early twentieth century, the Netherlands has had a reputation for boundary-pushing architecture and design. In the late 1980s and early 1990s, thanks to a far-sighted government initiative to support innovative design start-ups and a number of world-class schools and institutions intent on pushing the boundaries of design education, a new wave of Dutch avant-garde design emerged that was every bit as revolutionary as De Stijl.

At the centre of this creative resurgence was the renowned Design Academy Eindhoven (DAE), many of whose students went on to become part of what became known as the New Dutch Design movement. Hella Jongerius, who had studied industrial design at the DAE from 1988 to 1993, is a prominent member of this group. For her final degree project, she created her Bath Mat (1993) using an off-

the-shelf cushioning material used in the bronze-working industry onto which large half-droplets of polyurethane were applied. The resultant design, which looked like it had water pooled on it, not only had a Postmodern symbolism but its thought-provoking repurposing of materials also perfectly chimed with the on-trend craft–tech sensibility of the times. It was exhibited in the first Droog design exhibition held at the 1993 Milan Furniture Fair and, as a result, was publicized internationally within the design press. This high-profile exposure helped to establish Jongerius's credentials very early in her career.

On graduating, she established her own studio, JongeriusLab, in Rotterdam in 1993, its title reflecting her research-based approach to problem solving. Like other designers associated with New Dutch Design, Jongerius has always enjoyed exploring the creative potential of traditional craftsmanship using new materials and processes or, conversely, using 'old' materials in 'new' ways. This has imbued her work with a craft-meets-industry quirky aesthetic that is totally at odds with the standardized perfection of so much of today's mass-produced designs. In fact, her work often celebrates imperfection. For instance, her Soft Urn and Soft Vase series (1994) cast in undyed polyurethane rubber or coloured silicone rubber explored how synthetic materials age over time.

It was, however, her Long Neck and Groove Bottles (2000) that really reinforced her reputation as a creative force to be reckoned with. Each bottle was constructed from two moulded elements made of glass and ceramic – materials that cannot physically be joined because of their different melting points – that Jongerius playfully stuck

together with bespoke packing tape labelled 'FRAGILE'. With these design–art pieces, 'the usual hierarchy is reversed because a simple plastic tape has become the constructional device of each vase'.[1] Crucially, this range of bottles also revealed that Jongerius was not only a talented form-giver, but also a gifted colourist and that helped open other creative doors.

In 2002 she began designing eye-catching textiles for Maharam, which also demonstrated her gift for patternmaking. Three years later, she started working for the Swiss manufacturer Vitra, first as a designer and then as an art director, overseeing the colours and materials that the firm uses for its various collections. Her simple, pebble-like Magnet Dots (2016), available in four ranges of harmonious hues, have since gone on to become bestsellers for the company and testify to her remarkable eye for colour. This was also unequivocally demonstrated by her eye-popping installation-based 'Breathing Colour' exhibition held at London's Design Museum in 2017, which explored our perception of colour in design. Above all, throughout her career Jongerius has instilled a sense of individuality and character into her work, which is what helps us to so easily connect with it on an emotional level.

Opposite, far left: Soft Urn vessel for JongeriusLab, 1993; left: Mochi pouf for Vitra, 2013.

This page, clockwise from top left: Long Neck and Groove bottles for JongeriusLab, 2000; cushion for Vitra made using Vases textile manufactured by Maharam, 2012; 'Breathing Colour by Hella Jongerius' installation view at the Design Museum, London, 2017.

ILONKA KARASZ

ART DECO · METALWARE

Hungarian/American
b. Budapest, Austria-Hungary, 1896
d. Warwick, NY, USA, 1981

Modernist pioneer Ilonka Karasz found success across a remarkable range of design disciplines: textiles, wallpapers, furniture, metalware, ceramics, graphics and interiors. Once described as a 'twentieth-century design polymath',[1] she not only challenged the male domination of industrial-design practice in America, but also designed the first Modernist nursery in the United States and was, for a time, 'the country's leading wallpaper artist'.[2] During a career that spanned five prolific decades, she also designed an astonishing number of covers for *The New Yorker* magazine – 186 in total.

Born in Budapest to a silversmith father, as a child Karasz showed a passion for the fine and decorative arts and went on to study at the Hungarian Royal Academy of Arts and Crafts in Budapest, whose

curriculum was heavily influenced by the Viennese Secession movement. Aged 16, she became the first ever female student to be given a solo exhibition there. Her studies were curtailed by her father's early death and in 1913 she emigrated to New York with her sister Mariska (who went on to become a noted fashion and textile designer). Karasz settled in bohemian Greenwich Village and worked as a graphic designer and illustrator for progressive periodicals in the area.

In 1915 she co-founded, with artist and graphic designer Winold Reiss, a collective of European-born creative émigrés known as the Society of Modern Art. Shortly thereafter, she received her first high-profile commission to create advertisements for the Bonwit Teller department store. Her work was also featured in the inaugural issue of the Society's journal, *Modern Art Collector* in 1915 and, the following year, three of her textiles were published in *The American Silk Journal*. Around the same time, she taught textile design alongside the trendsetting artist–designers Marguerite and William Zorach at the progressive Modern Art School. Between 1916 and 1921, Karasz won three textile-design competitions sponsored annually by *Women's Wear Daily*.

Unsurprisingly, given her Austro-Hungarian background, Karasz's early work reflected the stylistic influence of the Wiener Werkstätte, especially her boldly abstracted floral and geometric textiles. Having married in 1920, she and her husband built a house in Brewster, New York State, that was featured in *House Beautiful* magazine, her contemporary interiors being highly commended. She also lived for several years in Europe and Java in the 1920s but on her return to the United States Karasz threw herself back into her design career. By now, her work had become increasingly Modernist with the clean

geometric lines of her metalware and furniture mirroring those found at Bauhaus. One of her most notable designs was a set of silver-plated geometric homewares (c. 1928) for Paye & Baker Manufacturing, with an uncompromisingly clean aesthetic.

In 1928 Karasz produced an installation for the American Designers' Gallery in New York, which is generally regarded to be the country's first Modernist children's nursery design, and the earliest of several she devised. The following year, she designed forward-looking Moderne-style furniture for the Film Guild Cinema, designed by the architect–artist Frederick Kiesler. Karasz's work was certainly respected by her peers during her lifetime and design consultants Donald Deskey and Gilbert Rohde both featured her textiles in their interiors. Likewise, Paul Frankl illustrated her work in his publications on modern design. Karasz was also a founding director of the influential Design Group Inc. agency and a proponent of Jacquard-woven textiles. In the late 1920s she helped the DuPont company improve the feel and texture of rayon, while in the 1950s she experimented with the Alcoa Corporation on the development of aluminium wallcoverings. Although not as well known as some of her European female contemporaries, Karasz undoubtedly deserves more recognition for her contribution to early American Modernism.

Opposite: Cover design
for *The New Yorker*
magazine, 16 July 1966.

This page, above: Electro-
plated nickel silver
sugar bowl and
creamer for Paye &
Baker Manufacturing,
c. 1928; below: Java
Desk, c. 1930.

SUSAN KARE

1980S–CONTEMPORARY · INTERFACE · DIGITAL

American
b. Ithaca, NY, USA, 1954

Hailed by *Wired* magazine as 'the Woman Who Launched a Billion Clicks',[1] Susan Kare is one of the great trailblazers of on-screen digital design. Not only did she develop some of the earliest successful digital fonts, she also designed the first-ever computer icons for Apple – which helped to establish a new visual language for digital-interface design.

Kare studied art at Mount Holyoke College, prior to undertaking a PhD in fine art at New York University. After completing her studies, she worked in a curatorial role at the San Francisco Museum of Modern Art. In 1982, however, at the behest of Andy Hertzfeld – a friend from high school who had recently joined Apple as one of its computer scientists – Kare began working for the California-based firm designing graphics, fonts and icons for its nascent Macintosh operating system. The family of icons she came up with for the Apple Mac represented one of the first graphical user interfaces ever to be used on a commercial computer. The upshot of this was that, instead of having to type in complicated lines of text commands, users could interact with easy-to-understand pictogram images, making the operation of computers infinitely easier. Kare's clever click-to-command icons must be largely credited for the desktop computing revolution that followed the launch of the Apple Macintosh in 1984.

The genius of Kare's icons was that they were based on familiar objects – the trash can, the bomb, the paint can, the ticking watch, the floppy disk, the font suitcase, and so on – and they had a whimsical quality that gave them an endearing emotional appeal. Her smiling Happy Mac symbol perfectly summed up, in just a few pixels, what the Apple Macintosh aspired to have – user-friendliness. When a software icon mimics a real-world object, it is known as a skeuomorphic representation and, without question, Kare's trashcan symbol remains the best-known example to this day.

Kare also designed a number of early bitmap fonts for Apple, intended to optimize on-screen legibility. Among these were some of the original Macintosh 'city' fonts: Chicago, New York, Monaco, San Francisco, Geneva and Cairo. Initially, most of these typefaces were named after Philadelphia suburbs where she and Hertzfeld had grown up, but Apple management insisted that they be upgraded to 'world-class' cities, a sensible move, in hindsight, as they were easier to remember.

In 1986, the year after Steve Jobs was ousted from Apple, Kare joined his start-up company, NeXT, as its tenth employee, taking on the role of creative director. Three years later, she founded Susan Kare Design, a practice specializing in user-interface graphics. Since then, she has developed 'thousands of icons for hundreds of clients',[2] while working on other graphic design projects. As one of Silicon Valley's leading interface designers, she worked as a designer for IBM and also helped to define the look of the Microsoft Windows 3.0 operating system. She also devised hundreds of virtual gift icons for Facebook, including a birthday cake, ice-cream, lucky clover and rubber duck, with such clarity that they could be universally understood.

As she explained in an interview with *Wired* magazine in 2013, 'You aim to create an image that's visual shorthand for a concept. If you do your job well, that image becomes meaningful as a symbol – something easy to recognize and remember.'[3] Since 2015, Kare has worked as a creative director at Pinterest and is a partner of kareprints.com, which sells limited-edition prints of some of her most iconic artworks. Her remarkable ability to reduce real-world objects to a universally understood, pixelated visual symbol is based on her belief that bold simplicity equals functional effectiveness. Kare's icons have an engaging playful charm and her pioneering work quite simply revolutionized the way people interacted with digital technology. And yet, for many years, her game-changing contribution to design was largely overlooked. It was only in the late 2000s that Kare finally received the recognition she so richly deserved as one of the most influential designers of her generation.

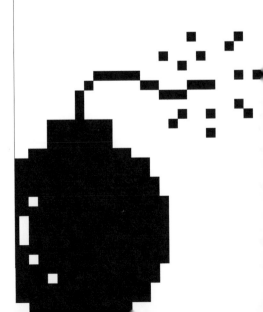

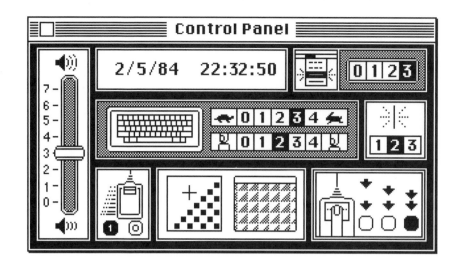

Opposite: Apple
Macintosh computer
icons, 1983.

This page, clockwise from
top left: Queen of Hearts
card from Microsoft
Windows 3.0 Solitare
Game, 1990; Apple Mac
control panel, 1983;
Apple Mac icons, 1983;
Apple MacPaint interface
graphics/japanese wood-
cut image, 1983; Apple
Mac icons, 1983.

REI KAWAKUBO

1970S–CONTEMPORARY · FASHION

Japanese
b. Tokyo, Japan, 1942

As the founder of both fashion label Comme des Garçons and its retail arm, Dover Street Market, Rei Kawakubo has had a profound influence on the design and retail of modern fashion. Born in wartime Japan, her father was an administrator at the liberal, Western-facing Keio University and Kawakubo herself studied art history there. At this institution, she was exposed to the aesthetic canons of both European and Asian culture, as well as early-twentieth-century progressive movements in art and design. After graduating in 1964, she took a job in the advertising department of Asahi Kasei, a large chemical company producing advanced synthetic materials for the clothing industry – her first experience of the fashion business.

Kawakubo left the firm in 1967 to pursue her own sartorial ambitions, beginning as a freelance stylist. She found, however, the looks she wanted to achieve were not possible with the clothes then available in Japan, so she started designing and making her own. At that time, Paris was still the centre of the fashion universe, so she adopted a French name for her label – Comme des Garçons. The company was founded in 1969 and formally incorporated in 1973. Her early womenswear designs proved very popular, allowing her to open a Tokyo boutique in 1975 and then, in 1978, to diversify into menswear. While her work developed in parallel with British punk, it followed a more minimal, structured line – mostly consisting of cleverly layered black garments. The Japanese media was captivated by the look, referring to her black-clad followers as 'The Crows'.

In 1981, this monochromatic fashion look had its international debut in Paris. Western culture was entering a new glitzy, consumer-friendly period but, by contrast, Kawakubo's Destroy collection was a ragged vision of deconstruction. At the time, Western critics insensitively dubbed this style 'Hiroshima chic', and, certainly, it was far removed from the 'party dress' vision of femininity so popular within the fashion establishment. Essentially, Kawakubo's models served merely as frames for sculptural experimentation. The lack of chromatic variation laid bare her visible thread work to great effect and she continued to exploit this signature feature, even after introducing scarlet to her severely restricted colour palette in 1988.

Throughout this period, Kawakubo also designed and produced a line of spartan Postmodern furniture. Fashioned from steel and blonde wood, the chairs and benches she produced were forbidding in their Zen-like austerity. Like her garments, these designs have an ambivalent relationship with the human form – for

instance the Chaise n°24 (1989) offers only a vertical pole for back support.

The refusal to conform ergonomically to the human figure is perhaps Kawakubo's most prominent visual idea. This was pushed to its furthest extent in her Body Meets Dress, Dress Meets Body collection (1997). Each garment was produced simply in gingham check – yet each wearer bore a series of tumour-like padded growths, which their dresses were structured to accommodate. The effect was part Willendorf Venus, part distorted hunchback. Much like the Modernist sculptors and architects Kawakubo had studied in her youth, she develops her ideas through radical formal experimentation over time. Her distortion of the female silhouette has become a kind of leitmotif, which recurs in her recent work, be it the schematic structural exaggeration of her Autumn/Winter 2012 collection, or the expressionist ad-hoc forms of Autumn/Winter 2017, entitled The Future of the Silhouette. This is but one theme amongst many that run through her complex oeuvre – a body of work that intentionally evades easy analysis or reading.

The impact of Kawakubo's garments is often greatly intensified by the drama and mystique surrounding their presentation, which can be seen as a form of theatrical 'saleswomanship'. Certainly, her marketing savviness was a motive for her founding Dover Street Market in 2004, launching an international string of shopping destinations. This commercial presence, alongside a continued spirit of unconventional experimentation, has kept Kawakubo's work in the spotlight for nearly four decades. Her 2017 exhibition at the Metropolitan Museum of Art, New York, entitled 'Comme des Garçons: Art of the In-Between', resulted in the entire Met Gala that year to be staged in homage to her work, testifying to her continuing relevance as one of the great form-givers of fashion design.

Opposite: hand-knotted
jumper with padded
cotton jersey skirt for
Comme des Garçons,
1982.

This page, above: Body
Meets Dress, Dress
Meets Body collection for
Commes des Garçons,
1997; right: structured
dresses for Commes des
Garçons, Autumn/Winter
collection, 2008.

FLORENCE
KNOLL BASSETT

MID-CENTURY · FURNITURE

American
b. Saginaw, MI, USA, 1917
d. Coral Gables, FL, USA, 2019

Florence Knoll Bassett revolutionized the design of workplaces, redefining the concept of modernity in the postwar era, and beyond. A gifted designer, she had a sharp eye for colour, form and space, and a steely determination, which was summed up in her famous adage, 'No compromise, ever'.

The daughter of German-speaking immigrant parents, Knoll was orphaned at the age of 12 and sent by her guardian to Kingswood School for Girls in Bloomfield Hills, Michigan. There, she became a close friend of the future architect–designer, Eero Saarinen, whose father, Eliel, was the first director of the adjacent Cranbrook Academy of Art. This friendship led to Knoll studying at the academy alongside future architect Ralph Rapson and designer Harry Bertoia. Armed with recommendations from both Eliel Saarinen and the architect Alvar Aalto, Florence continued her studies under Marcel Breuer and Bauhaus founder Walter Gropius at Harvard's Graduate School of Design and, later, with Ludwig Mies van der Rohe at the Armour Institute

of Technology in Chicago. These three towering figures of European Modernism could not have given the young 'Shu', as she was known, a better grounding in design and architecture.

Florence moved to New York in 1941 and met Hans Knoll. He was from a German furniture-manufacturing dynasty, his father having produced Modernist furniture by Mies, Breuer and Gropius. Hans had already set up the Hans G. Knoll Furniture Company and begun manufacturing his first range of Modernist furniture. Knoll worked as an interior designer for him, helping to move the company's product line away from the Scandinavian look towards the sophisticated International Style. In 1946, they married and renamed the firm Knoll Associates, in recognition of their partnership. The venture flourished thanks to their perfectly balanced skills: his business acumen and salesmanship and her formidable design talent. The company found early success with furniture designed by Eero Saarinen, Harry Bertoia and Isamu Noguchi that set a new level of aesthetic refinement within the American furniture industry. It also acquired the production rights to Mies's furniture designs in 1948.

During the 1950s, by incorporating these designs into her interiors, Knoll

pioneered a distinctive 'Knoll look'. She oversaw all aspects of Knoll's corporate projections, from the spatial clarity and detailing of its showrooms and interior design projects, to the design of graphics, including the company's famous 'K' logo devised by Herbert Matter.

In 1955 Hans was killed in a car accident but, under Knoll's direction, the company continued to flourish. Unlike most interior designers, she had an in-depth understanding of architecture and could exploit the potential of colour, initially favouring a De Stijl-inspired palette of primaries and later adopting a more muted palette of rich, earthy hues. She also had a gift for finessing designs by others, which she famously did with Charles Pollock's Executive chair – a Knoll manager noting that she 'critiqued the hell out of it, and made the proportions right'.[1]

Her revolutionary Knoll Planning Unit (1943–71) set the standard for modern corporate interiors through its introduction of space planning and total design. Knoll was responsible for a number of iconic furniture pieces, including her thoroughly rational, modern – yet timeless – Lounge Collection (1954) and her perfectly proportioned Credenza (1954). She modestly described these designs as 'fill-in pieces', explaining that if she needed a certain piece of furniture 'for a job' and it was not available, 'I designed it'.[2] Throughout her career, she championed the cause of good design and, as the female president of an internationally respected, design-led company, she was a veritable trailblazer for other women designers.

Opposite: Hairpin stacking table, 1948 (originally sold as the Model 75 stool).

This page, from top to bottom: Office interior, c. 1966, featuring the designer's own table and credenza designs and Charles Pollock's Executive chairs, of which she oversaw the development; interior, c. 1960s, featuring the designer's own sofa, chair and tables designs; Florence Knoll Lounge Collection sofa, 1954.

FLORENCE KOEHLER

ARTS AND CRAFTS · JEWELLERY

American
b. Jackson, MI, USA, 1861
d. Rome, Italy, 1944

After an early career in ceramics, Florence Koehler became one of the leading jewellery designers of the Arts and Crafts Movement, both in America and Britain. Her exquisite gem-encrusted pieces earned her widespread acclaim, with the critic Roger Fry citing her as an influential force in the 'modern revival of craftsmanship' in *The Burlington Magazine* in 1910.

According to her friends, Koehler never spoke about her childhood background, which led them to surmise that she had a 'rather humble origin and grim early environment'.[1] In fact, she had grown up in Missouri, where her father was a grain and coal merchant, but, as for her education or early career, little is known. In correspondence dating from 1881, however, she does mention her 'pictures'.[2] That same year, she moved to Kansas City, where she subsequently married Frederick Koehler. It would appear that she must have branched out into the applied arts at some stage, as, in about 1893, she is known to have been working as the head of ceramics at Kansas City Art School. Around this time, she relocated with her husband to Chicago, which was then an influential centre of the American Arts and Crafts Movement. Here, she exhibited her ceramics at the World's Columbian Exhibition and established a short-lived interior decorating business with a recently widowed friend in the Marshall Field building.

In 1897 Koehler became a founding member of the Chicago Arts and Crafts Society, where she taught jewellery design and metalsmithing. She also taught china painting in 1898 to members of the Atlan Ceramic Art Club, who profited immensely from her 'thorough and exhaustive study of Oriental pottery'[3] and her exacting technical tuition. That same year, she travelled to London in order to study enamelling techniques and jewellery-making with the silversmith Alexander Fisher, who once wrote that enamels 'should be creations ... they are for the representation and embodiment of thoughts, ideas, imaginings'.[4] On her return to the United States, she concentrated on designing jewellery, which was often inspired by historic designs, most notably those from the Renaissance era. She preferred using cabochon gems to faceted stones and her work often featured intricate floral motifs and beautiful enamelling.

Sometime after 1900, Koehler separated from her husband and gave up her studio in Chicago. She became a travelling companion of the wealthy art collector, Emily Chadbourne, and the pair eventually settled in London around 1909, where Florence established a new studio. While living in London, she mixed in artistic circles, becoming friends with, among others, the artist Augustus John and writer Henry James – the latter dubbed her 'The Conversationalist'. She left for Paris in 1912, where she became friendly with Henri Matisse and his family. Eventually, she moved to Rome in the 1930s, where she spent the war years. She died in 1944, just before American troops took the city. A restless creative spirit, Koehler left a remarkable body of work – many of her jewellery pieces are now in the Metropolitan Museum of Art – that testifies both to her immense talent in her chosen design discipline and to her remarkable eye for detail, composition and colour.

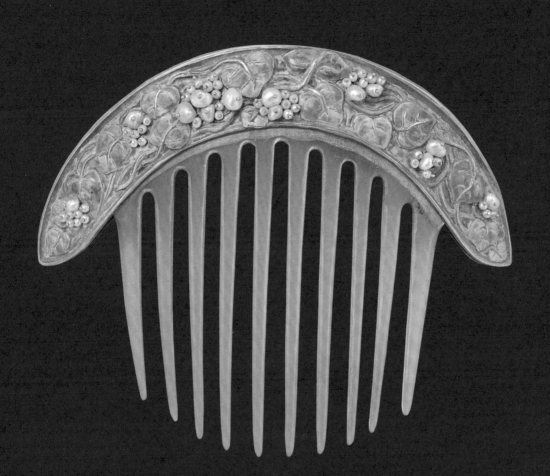

Opposite: Emerald, sapphire and enamelled gold ring, c. 1905; enamelled gold and sapphire Heart ring, c. 1905–35.

This page, clockwise from left: Enamelled gold comb, c. 1905–35; emerald, sapphire and seed pearl enamelled gold brooch, c. 1905; 'antique' medallion pendant, c. 1905–35.

BELLE KOGAN

ART DECO/POSTWAR · CERAMICS · METALWARE · PRODUCT

Russian/American
b. Ilyashëvka, Ukraine, 1902
d. Petach Tikva, Israel, 2000

Belle Kogan is generally credited as having been the very first female professional industrial-design consultant in America. Certainly, she was the first to open her own office and to establish her name in this field. She contributed significantly to the professionalization of design consultancy in America and must be seen as an influential torchbearer for the generations of female industrial designers who have followed in her wake.

Kogan moved with her parents to the USA as a four-year-old. The eldest of eight children, she showed a remarkable aptitude for art even as a young child and, at high school in Bethlehem, Pennsylvania, was encouraged by her art teacher to study mechanical drawing, even though she was the only girl in the class. Throughout her professional design career she would become quite used to this lone-female status.

On graduating from high school, she taught mechanical drawing there and would later observe that it was knowledge of this discipline that enabled her 'to provide my clients with exact working drawings'.[1] She then went to the Pratt Institute in Brooklyn, but was forced to abandon her studies to spend the next decade helping to raise her younger siblings, while also managing her father's jewellery store. She began designing pieces of jewellery and attended classes at the Art Students League in New York, when she could find time. Her big break came in 1929, when she was hired as a freelance designer by the Quaker Silver Company to design silver and pewter homewares.

In 1931 she established her own design studio, specializing in metalware, and, although these were, as she put it, some 'cruelly discouraging years'[2] being a woman designer, she did not give up.

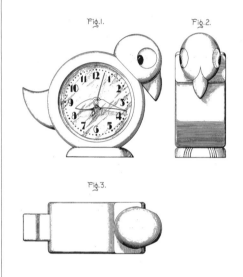

By the late 1930s, Kogan had a string of clients and three female designers working for her.

In the mid 1930s, she became an early adopter of plastics in designs destined for mass production. Her whimsical Quacker Model 7F63 electric alarm clock for Warren Telechron (1934) incorporated a housing of canary yellow, royal blue or black Plaskon and a beak of red plastic. For the Boonton Molding Company, she designed the Boonton Belle range (1954) in durable melamine. Kogan also exhibited a polystyrene container for poker chips at MoMA's landmark packaging exhibition held in 1959. She was the only named women designer.

Kogan famously designed at least four different lighters for Zippo during the late 1930s, emblazoned with fashionable Art Moderne motifs. She is best known, however, for her wares for Red Wing Pottery.

Her first commission from the firm, in 1938, was to design 150 different 'art wares'. Of these, 100 were put into production as the Belle Kogan 100 range, including Art Deco-styled vases and ashtrays that came in an assortment of then-fashionable hues of peach, brown, ivory and aqua. The following year, Kogan created the Terra-Craft line, featuring 14 art wares that were intended to look hand-thrown despite being slip-cast moulded. In 1940 her ivory-glazed Magnolia line of 24 pieces was launched, which was relief-decorated with on-trend magnolia blossoms. She also created other lines for Red Wing, notably Tropicana (1950), Textura (1950), Deluxe (c. 1951) and Prismatique (1962–67). This last eye-catching range with its sharp faceted lines – said to have been inspired by the geometry of tooth root – went on to become her biggest seller.

Throughout her career, Kogan responded confidently to trends in design, while working within the constraints of mass production. In 1994 the Industrial Designers Society of America somewhat belatedly awarded her the Personal Recognition Award – making her the second women ever to receive this accolade. That same year, she became a fellow of the Industrial Designers Institute and moved to Israel, where she died six years later at the age of 98.

Opposite: Patent for the bird-shaped electric alarm clock for Warren Telechron, 1934.

This page, from top to bottom: Boontonware melamine jug and covered sugar bowl for Boonton Moulding, 1958; Prismatique 787 vase for Red Wing Art Pottery, 1962; Model 7F63 Quacker electric alarm clock for Telechron, 1934.

VALENTINA KULAGINA

MODERNISM · GRAPHICS

Russian
b. and d. Moscow, Russia, 1902-1987

During the early Soviet era in Russia, despite the widespread use of propaganda promoting female emancipation and gender equality, in reality little progress was made on women's rights. This was largely due, on the one hand, to the culturally ingrained chauvinism of men and, on the other, to a lack of solidarity between the various women's groups committed to the Soviet cause. It did not help that Stalin had repealed the Bolshevist reforms governing matrimonial laws and sexual ethics that had been introduced in 1917–18. Nevertheless, a definable 'sexual revolution' did take place, especially among those associated with the art and design avant-garde, giving women a greater level of creative autonomy. Even so, most women associated with Russia's artistic community generally took the subservient role of either muse or comrade–

РАБОТНИЦЫ – УДАРНИЦЫ,
КРЕПИТЕ УДАРНЫЕ БРИГАДЫ,
ОВЛАДЕВАЙТЕ ТЕХНИКОЙ,
УВЕЛИЧИВАЙТЕ КАДРЫ ПРОЛЕТАРСКИХ СПЕЦИАЛИСТОВ

wife. That said, there was one woman who, in her own right, became a central figure within Soviet design circles during the post-revolutionary era, and that was Valentina Kulagina.

Born in Moscow, Kulagina studied at the VKhUTEMAS (Higher State Artistic and Technological Workshops) – a progressive design school that can be considered the Soviet equivalent of the Bauhaus. There, she studied under the Abstract artist, Lyubov Popova, and the Constructivist architect–artist, Alexander Vesnin. It was at this college that, in 1920, she met fellow student, photographer Gustav Klutsis. They married the following year and had a son. Throughout the 1920s, the couple lived at the school's headquarters, as did fellow Constructivist husband-and-wife team, Aleksandr Rodchenko and Varvara Stepanova (see pages 212–13).

Ideologically committed to the Soviet concept of production-oriented Constructivism, Kulagina collaborated with her husband on the development of photomontage. They used this new technique, involving cutting and pasting photography into composite artworks, in numerous propaganda posters, to dramatic effect. Certainly, by using this thoroughly modern method and combining it with painting that had a distinctive blocky figurative abstraction, Kulagina was able to produce visually bold work that was immediately attention-grabbing. Indeed, the dynamism of her designs for books, posters and exhibitions powerfully reflected the utopian zeal of the early Soviet period.

In 1928 she participated at the landmark 'Pressa' exhibition held in Cologne and, that same year, joined the radical October Group, a collective of Constructivist artists, of which her husband was also a member. Two years later, Kulagina designed a poster for the 1930 International Women Workers' Day that featured female textile workers wearing red headscarves – a garment strongly

associated with pioneering socialism. This motif was later incorporated into another of her eye-catching posters, captioned 'Women shock-workers! Strengthen shock-brigades, master the machinery, join the proletarian specialists' personnel' (1932).

Kulagina's work portrayed a forward-looking vision of a new, fairer society, in which hero workers could finally take control of their destinies under a benevolent state. The tragic paradox was that her work was actually instrumental in helping to bolster a regime that was increasingly totalitarian and brutally suppressive, as she would find out all too soon: in 1938 her husband was arrested on the trumped-up charge of being involved in a 'fascist plot of Latvian nationalists'[1] and died in custody shortly thereafter, allegedly from a heart attack. Over the next 50 years, Kulagina continued to live in Moscow, never knowing the real circumstances behind her husband's death. It was only in 1989, two years after her own death, that the truth was officially revealed – he had been executed under the orders of Stalin, which is painfully ironic given that he and Kulagina had done so much to glorify the Soviet regime through their innovative work.

Left: 'Women shock-workers! Strengthen shock-brigades, master the machinery, join the proletarian specialists' personnel' lithographic poster, 1932.

Opposite: '1905: the road to October', lithographic poster, 1929.

LORA LAMM

1950S–1960S · GRAPHICS

Swiss
b. Arosa, Switzerland, 1928

From the early 1930s onwards, there was a steady influx of talented Swiss graphic designers into Milan, which rapidly accelerated during the immediate postwar years when the city became Europe's acknowledged epicentre of cool, contemporary design. One of these creative émigrés was Lora Lamm who, in the space of just ten years, designed some of the most iconic Italian advertisements and posters of the 1950s and 1960s for brands such as La Rinascente, Pirelli and Elizabeth Arden. Her playful and poetic work captured the very essence of Italy's design-driven, postwar optimism. Lamm also signalled an original approach to visual communications that successfully mixed Swiss rationalism with Italian exuberance – with the rather dry, direct messaging of the former cleverly counterbalanced with the light-hearted pictorial humour of the latter. But, more than this, Lamm infused her fresh-looking work with a very feminine charm, which was visually engaging and often directly referenced (especially in the case of her work for La Rinascente, Milan's premier department store) the new liberating financial and social freedoms younger women were experiencing, thanks in large part to Italy's postwar *miracolo economico*.

Born in the Swiss Alps close to the Italian border, Lamm studied graphic design at the Kunstgewerbeschule (School of Arts and Crafts) in Zurich from 1946 to 1951, where she was taught by, among others, Johannes Itten, Ernst Keller and Ernest Gubler. The school, along with the Basel School of Design, was one of the two great centres of what became known as The Swiss School of graphic design, which was defined by the use of sans-serif typefaces, bold, pared down layouts, a rigid grid format and universal legibility. Indeed,

Lamm's later professional success is absolutely attributable to her firm academic grounding in the so-called Swiss Style.

Following her graduation, she worked in Switzerland, but moved to Milan in 1953 in search of more interesting work. To this end, she was hired by the highly respected practice, Studio Boggeri,[1] and one of her first assignments was to design packaging for the Milanese panettone manufacturer, Motta. The following year, she joined the advertising graphics team of the high-profile Milanese department store, La Rinascente, led by fellow Swiss expat Max Huber, who had recommended her for the job. In many ways, Lamm could not have found a more perfect place to exercise her skill, for the store was already acclaimed as one of the great champions of avant-garde Italian design thanks to its sponsorship of the Compasso d'Oro industrial design awards. La Rinascente was involved in fashion retailing and greatly needed a design-aware woman's eye to create pitch-perfect campaigns to appeal to young female consumers. As a result, Lamm was given the freedom to experiment and threw herself into designing all sorts of marketing materials, from catalogues and posters to print advertising and packaging, all of which were distinguished by a bold, cheerful illustrative style and playful use of typography. The resulting body of work, with its *faux naïf* portrayals of young women doing fun things, attracted a new female audience to La Rinascente. Given this, it is

not particularly surprising that, when Huber left La Rinascente in 1958, Lamm took over his directorship of the store's advertising team as well as the design and production of its in-store *Cronache* magazine.

That same year, she also started to take on freelance clients and, over the next five years, undertook work for Elizabeth Arden, Latte di Milano, Niggi, Pirelli and department store Upim among others. In 1963, Lamm returned to Zurich, hoping to secure a work visa for the United States, but when it did not materialize she joined a Zurich-based advertising agency founded by Frank Thiessing, whom she later married. Determined not to repeat her earlier work, Lamm abandoned her trademark Swiss–Italian style and embarked on a new stylistic chapter in her career. In 2013 a major retrospective exhibition of her Milanese work was staged at the M.A.X. Museo in Chiasso, Switzerland and, two years later, she was awarded the Swiss Grand Prix for Design – a fitting recognition of her advancement of Swiss design, both nationally and internationally.

la
moda
si diffonde
con
*la*Rinascente

Left: Poster design for La Rinascente, *c.* 1960.

Opposite, clockwise from top left: Poster design for Pirelli, 1960; poster design for Pirelli, *c.* 1960; poster design for La Rinascente, *c.* 1960.

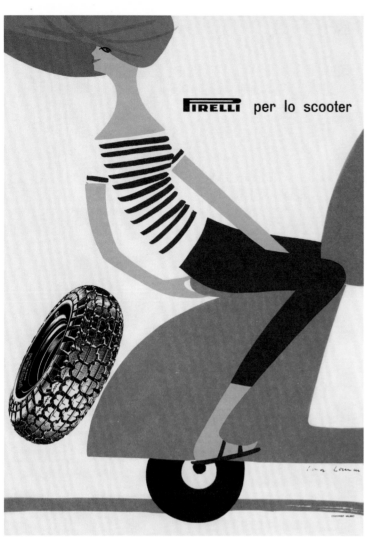

PIRELLI per lo scooter

pneumatici **PIRELLI** per biciclette

estate e mare

JEANNE LANVIN

BELLE ÉPOQUE · FASHION

French
b. Paris, France, 1867
d. Le Vésinet, France, 1946

Jeanne Lanvin was born in 1867 to a middle-class family. The eldest of ten siblings, the young Lanvin learnt to work from an early age. At the age of 13, she glimpsed the trade that would take her to the heights of Parisian society when she took a job as an errand girl with a dressmaker. Sensing that she might have a talent for fashion, she later enrolled as an apprentice milliner at the atelier of Madame Félix. She was soon offered a role as a milliner's assistant at the house of Suzanne Talbot, also in Paris.

The modest income this brought in allowed the young Lanvin to eventually save enough to open her own small millinery workshop, in 1885. This venture became a moderate success and, ten years later, she married an Italian nobleman, Count Emilio di Pietro. It was not until the birth of her daughter in 1897, however, that her work really started paying off. The apple of her mother's eye, baby Marguerite was always dressed immaculately in bespoke dresses. Lanvin's clientele were so besotted with these pieces that they soon asked for them in adult sizes. Poetic allusions to motherhood became a lifelong obsession for Lanvin, who even adopted an illustration of Marguerite and herself embracing as her company logo.

From this small seed grew a great flourishing of creativity, developing into Lanvin's famous *robes de style*. These exquisite, flowing gowns borrowed liberally from Europe's grand history of dressmaking, boasting full skirts supported by fine petticoats and panniers (hoops). These were such a sensation that in 1909 Lanvin was inducted to the Syndicat de la Couture – the hallmark of an establishment dressmaker.

Lanvin resisted the trappings of modernity in her work, even as she refreshed, with a previously unseen

sensuality, the styles that had inspired her. She rejected the sparse, minimal fashions pioneered by Chanel during the 1920s in favour of a more romantic, traditionally feminine mode. As if to underline the historicity of her work, Lanvin adopted the quattrocento blue of an early Renaissance Fra Angelico fresco as her brand's signature hue.

Paradoxically, however, she was also a serial innovator, expanding her range to include sportswear, lingerie, cosmetics and menswear. Through this copious output, she pioneered the four-season fashion year. As if that were not enough, in the early 1920s she collaborated with Art Deco designer Armand-Albert Rateau on a sumptuous range of Lanvin home furnishings. Together, they dressed exclusive private residences with eclectically exotic furniture and textiles – a style that reached its height in their Pavilion d'Elégance at the 1925 International Exhibition of Decorative and Industrial Arts in Paris.

Appropriately, when Jeanne Lanvin died in 1946, the company was passed down from mother to daughter. Today, it remains the oldest Parisian couture house and continues to be highly respected throughout the world for its culture of innovation and elegance.

Opposite: Cyclone evening gown for House of Lanvin, 1939.

This page, clockwise from right: Illustration in *Gazette du Bon Ton* showing Lanvin evening wear, 1920; Fusée evening gown for House of Lanvin, 1938; Roseraie silk dress for House of Lanvin, Spring/Summer, 1923.

ESTELLE LAVERNE

MID-CENTURY · FURNITURE · TEXTILES

American
b. New York, USA, 1915
d. Far Rockaway, NY, USA, 1997

As a high-profile design couple, Estelle and Erwine Laverne helped forge the mid-century modern look in America with their innovative furniture, wallpapers and textiles. Enjoying the freedom that came with running their own company, they produced experimental work that pushed both aesthetic and technological boundaries.

The daughter of a well-to-do Jewish family of jewellery designers and manufacturers, Laverne studied painting at the Art Students League, under Abstract Expressionist Hans Hofmann. In 1932 she met her future soul mate, Erwine Laverne, in the School's cafeteria. He was seven years her senior and had studied at the League in the 1920s. They married in 1934 and established a wallpaper business with Erwine's decorator brother, Louis, but that partnership ended and the husband-and-wife team founded a new business in 1938, Laverne Originals, with a much more contemporary outlook. Four years later, Erwine ventured into Macy's looking for cork placemats but, underwhelmed by the selection available, complained to a salesman. It just so happened he was actually Macy's vice president and he challenged Erwine to design something better, which is exactly what the Lavernes did. Macy's put their designs into production and, after advertisements in *The New York Times*, thousands of orders poured in. On the back of this success, the line was expanded into matching wallpapers and fabrics.

Laverne was undoubtedly more involved in the design side of their eponymous label, while Erwine enjoyed the role of business-impresario and once wryly noted that, with their progressive designs, '... maybe we're designing ourselves out of business'.[1] Their showroom in Manhattan functioned more as a gallery space than a shop, and their designs reflected the influence of contemporary art trends. Laverne's Fun to Run textile (1947–48) paid homage to Henri Matisse's cut-outs. One of the couple's greatest commercial successes was their marbled Marbalia wallpaper range (c. 1944), issued in various fashionable hues. During the late 1940s, they successfully produced textiles by designers Ray Komai and Alvin Lustig. In 1950, they began working with a new design team, Katavolos, Littell & Kelley, who brought a European-style Modernism to their furniture line, most notably with the iconic leather-slung 3LC T-chair (1952).

Four years earlier, the Lavernes had moved into the carriage house of Laurelton Hall – Louis Comfort Tiffany's former mansion, now a foundation for artists. There, they controversially set up a workshop to hand-print wallpapers.

They also developed a series of sculptural seating designs that were breathtakingly innovative in their use of synthetic materials – the first of these, the Lotus chair (1958) featured a single-form seat shell made of lacquered fibreglass. A year later came their revolutionary Invisible Group, including the Lily, Daffodil and Buttercup chairs made of transparent acrylic. Heralding a new aesthetic lightness in design, these revolutionary chairs also presaged the 1960s age of plastic.

Despite international recognition for these inspirational designs, a restraining order filed in 1952 to stop them manufacturing in a residential zone had begun a long and costly legal battle that ultimately led to the Lavernes' financial and professional demise. Mounting litigation costs took their toll, both personally and professionally, and the Lavernes were left penniless. During this time, Laverne had contracted a form of multiple sclerosis leaving her wheelchair-bound and almost blind, although her creative spirit still found an outlet, through poetry. Erwine cared for his beloved muse as best he could, but his health was failing, too. The Lavernes and their work faded almost into obscurity until a new generation of collectors in the late 1980s and early 1990s began rediscovering the extraordinarily forward-looking work of this remarkable design duo.

Opposite: Invisible Group
Lily lounge chair for Laverne
International, 1957.

This page, clockwise from
top left: Fun to Run textile
for Laverne Originals,
1947–48; Printed fibreglass
textile, c. 1953; Figurative
planters for Laverne
International, c. 1953.

147

AMANDA LEVETE

CONTEMPORARY · ARCHITECTURE

British
b. Bridgend, UK, 1955

Amanda Levete is renowned for an interdisciplinary approach to design that is both intuitive and strategic. Her architectural projects adapt advanced materials and constructional technologies from other industries, such as the lightweight composite aerospace material used in her MPavilion (2015) in Melbourne. Levete also enjoys a formidable reputation in product design, creating furniture that pushes the boundaries of technological production. She has created memorable installations, too, that challenge perceptions of form, function and materiality.

Levete is a rebel who enjoys kicking against the status quo. She was expelled from St Paul's Girls' School in London for sunbathing naked on the roof, a story she is happy to relate. After a foundation course at the nearby Hammersmith School of Art, she trained at the Architectural Association. She was taught by architects who, as she recalls, never 'intended to build', so when she graduated she 'didn't know anything about building'.[1] Despite this, it gave her the freedom to explore her creativity, a good basis for her professional

practice. She worked as a trainee for Alsop & Lyall (1980–81), and moved to YRM Architects (1982–84) before working for the Richard Rogers Partnership (1984–89). She also co-founded Powis & Levete in 1983, which, two years later, was nominated for the Royal Institute of British Architects' '40 Under 40' exhibition. In 1989 she became a partner of Future Systems, founded in 1979 by Jan Kaplický and David Nixon, and was part of the pioneering High-Tech movement. Levete married Kaplický in 1991 and they worked together for the next 17 years. Notable early projects in London included the Hauer-King House, Islington (1994), with its all-glass facade, and the Docklands floating bridge (1994).

Levete is known as a 'consummate networker'[2] who helped Future Systems's space-age visions off the drawing board and into construction. The Lord's Cricket Ground Media Centre (1999), a spaceship-like building, sealed Future Systems's reputation as one of the most innovative creative forces on the British architectural scene, winning the coveted Stirling Prize in 1999. Their state-of-the-art Selfridges department store (completed in 2003) in Birmingham's Bull Ring was also highly acclaimed: this landmark building, with its fluid 'blobular' form, is covered in

thousands of shimmering aluminium discs that recall the scaly skin of a gigantic reptile. An otherworldly, space-age building, it demonstrated the transformative power of contemporary architecture on a city. Future Systems began receiving significant commissions from abroad – namely, the Enzo Ferrari Museum (2009) in Modena, Italy, and the unbuilt and controversial octopus-like Czech National Library, in Prague (2007). In 2006 Levete and Kaplický divorced. Having been in the shadow of her older male partner for so long, she founded her own architectural practice in 2009, initially known as Amanda Levete Architects but later rechristened AL_A.

A new and exciting chapter of her career unfolded, witnessing the maturing of her singular architectural vision. Her completed projects include the undulating tile-covered Museum of Art, Architecture and Technology on Lisbon's waterfront (2016), the remarkable Victoria and Albert Museum Exhibition Road Quarter (2017) and a 13-acre media campus and headquarters building for Sky (2016). In 2018 Levete received the Jane Drew Prize, an annual award given by *The Architect's Journal* and *The Architectural Review* to an individual who, 'through their work and commitment to design excellence, has raised the profile of women in architecture'.[3] Other recipients include Denise Scott Brown (see pages 202–203) and Zaha Hadid (see pages 108–109). Levete's exemplary career has been guided by her belief that, 'the point of architecture is to contribute to the culture of the city or the culture of a nation. Architecture changes the way you see yourself, the way others see you.'[4]

SHEILA LEVRANT DE BRETTEVILLE

CONTEMPORARY · GRAPHIC DESIGN

American
b. New York, USA, 1940

During the early 1970s Levrant de Bretteville led a feminist pedagogic revolution in design teaching and is today not only a highly respected professor at Yale University School of Art, but also widely recognised as one of America's most gifted visual communicators.

Levrant de Bretteville initially studied art history at Barnard College, New York, a private women's liberal arts college in the heart of NYC. In 1962 the year she graduated, she also contributed to The Port Huron Statement, an influential student activist manifesto that was the founding document of the Students for a Democratic Society (SDS). Fundamentally an idealistic rallying call to students to become more actively engaged in social reform through participatory democracy, the Statement sought to set out a revolutionary agenda for the younger generation and as such helped to define its aimed-for social goals and values. In its chapter on 'Values', Levrant de Bretteville wrote: 'Independence does not mean egoistic individualism – the object is not to have one's own way so much as to have a way of one's own' – which succinctly sums up her ethos vis-à-vis women in design. She subsequently went on to study graphic design at Yale University, where she obtained an MFA in 1964. After the completion of her studies, she worked as a book designer for the Chanticleer Press and Yale University Press, and for a time also worked as a designer in Olivetti's famed publicity department in Milan. After returning to the United States, she joined the teaching faculty at the California Institute of Arts (CalArts), where she established the Women's Design Program in 1971, which was the first pro-feminist design course of its kind. This year-long program, which only ran for two years, featured alongside its core design studies various other pro-feminist consciousness-raising activities, including performance workshops, group gender-awareness sessions and feminist literature reading circles. Although short-lived, the CalArts Women's Design Program was important in that it highlighted the gendered social implications of visual media, while also introducing feminist concerns and a female perspective on the debate surrounding design and its practice.

In 1973 Levrant de Bretteville co-founded with the artist Judy Chicago and the art historian Arlene Raven the Feminist Studio Workshop in Los Angeles, which was America's first independent feminist art school. It was here that Levrant de Bretteville also established the Women's Graphic Center. In 1975 she organized the 'Women in Design: The Next Decade' conference, held at the Woman's Building at Grandview in Los Angeles. For the event, she designed an eye-catching poster using the process used to make architect's blueprints. As she explains of the poster, 'this choice was informed by the inexpensive aspect of the material to imply that at this conference our visions for the future might guide us in the decade to come. The image of the moon's phases is from a painting by Angelica Kauffman as *The Artist in the Character of Design Listening to the Inspiration of Poetry*. The gridded landscape reflects the influence of utopian images created by Superstudio during the time I was living and working in Milan.'[1] The standout feature of the poster, however, was its field of eyebolts, cleverly referencing the Venus symbol, intended to symbolize women in design. For the conference's attendees, Levrant de Bretteville also made simple eyebolt necklaces, which as she notes 'anyone who wants one can easily make one for under $2.'[2]

In 1981, as one of the foremost design educators in America, Levrant de Bretteville went on to initiate and chair the department of communication design at the Otis College of Art and Design in Los Angeles. A decade later, she joined the Yale School of Art faculty, where she became its first tenured female professor when appointed its director of graduate studies in graphic design. Later, in 2010, she was named the Caroline M. Street Professor of Graphic Design at Yale. Yet, apart from an illustrious career as a design educator, she has also managed to create an impressive body of thought-provoking design work – from posters, books, magazines and newspapers, to various site-specific, graphic-orientated public artworks, including *At the start ... At long last ...* for New York City's Inwood train station and the poignant *Path of Stars* in New Haven that celebrates the lives of ordinary citizens. More than anything Levrant de Bretteville has demonstrated, time and again, that graphic design is about communicating ideas that make people stop and think, and thereby alter their opinions. For Levrant de Bretteville, design is ultimately a powerful communicative tool that can be used to set a more female-centric socio-cultural agenda.

Clockwise from right: 'Pink' poster, 1973; 'Women in Design' conference poster, 1975; *At the start ... At long last ...* graphic installation at 207th Street subway station in Inwood, New York, 1999.

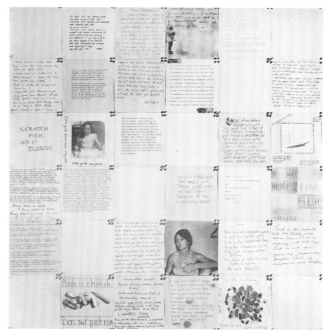

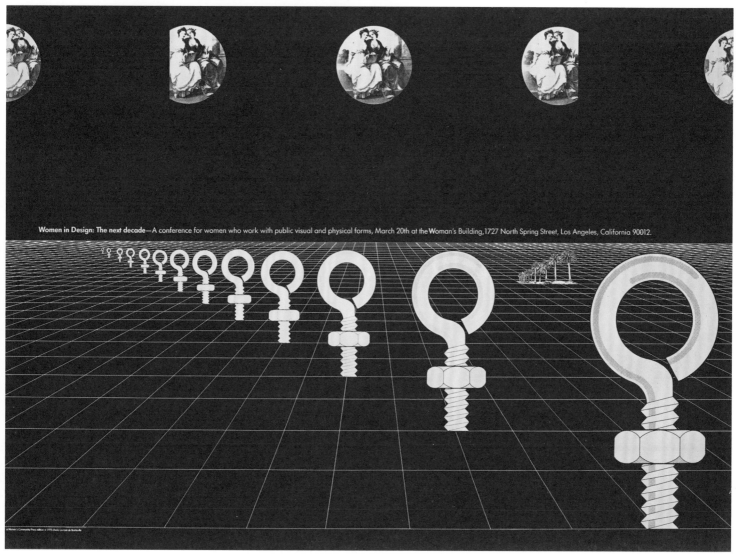

Women in Design: The next decade—A conference for women who work with public visual and physical forms, March 20th at the Woman's Building, 1727 North Spring Street, Los Angeles, California 90012.

151

ELAINE LUSTIG COHEN

American
b. Jersey City, USA, 1927
d. New York, USA, 2016

When she was awarded the AIGA Medal in 2011, Elaine Lustig Cohen was lauded as a 'pioneering graphic designer, artist and archivist' and certainly in each of these roles she made a memorable contribution. It was through her trailblazing graphic design work, however, that she made the greatest waves by pioneering a distinctly American form of Modernism.

As a child Elaine took art classes, which taught her useful drawing skills. At the age of 15, she visited Peggy Guggenheim's Art of This Century gallery and saw an installation of art-furniture by Frederick Kiesler alongside artworks by Wassily Kandinsky. This encounter with contemporary art and design ignited a life-long passion, which prompted her to enroll at Tulane University's Newcomb College – a women-only art school that was famous for its promotion of practical 'industrial' skills that would enable its students to earn a living. One of the many tutors was an inspirational teacher, who taught from a Bauhaus perspective, which gave Lustig Cohen an invaluable grounding in the fundamentals of design and composition. Yet coming from a middle-class Jewish family, she later noted, 'the idea of being an artist never even occurred to me.'[1]

After two years at Newcomb, she continued her art studies at the University of Southern California, and, with a view to becoming a teacher also took an art education course. Upon graduating, she met the graphic designer Alvin Lustig at the opening of Los Angeles's Modern Institute of Art in 1948. Twelve years her senior, the charismatic Lustig had already forged a significant reputation for taking the principles of Abstract Expressionism and Surrealism and applying them to commercial art – or in other words, graphic design. Embarking on a whirlwind romance, they married that December. Elaine was by her own admission his 'blind disciple' and after a year of teaching gave it up to

become his 'office slave'. Although he never taught her the principles of graphic design or how to set type, she learnt them quickly on the job.

When Josef Albers offered Lustig the opportunity to establish the graphic design programme at Yale University in 1950, the couple moved to New York. Around this time, however, Lustig's health began to deteriorate due to diabetes, which he had suffered from since his teens, and as a result Elaine took on an increasing workload in the office, albeit under Lustig's exacting direction. By 1954 Lustig had lost his sight completely and passed away the following year. Yet the seven years they had spent together had equipped Elaine with the creative nous to forge her own graphic design career. Her first commission came from Philip Johnson who tasked her with designing the signage for the Seagram Building. Soon after, the publisher Arthur Cohen asked Elaine to design a series of paperbacks for Meridian Books. In total, she designed more than 100 book jackets for him, most of which were notable for their visual distillation of the subject matter. Employing a combination of abstracted elements, conceptual imagery and expressive typography, her concept-driven book jackets possessed a bold attention-grabbing directness.

In 1956 she married Cohen and on his advice established her own graphic design practice. During her ensuing career she worked on a range of projects – from numerous exhibition catalogues for a host of different museums, to various logos, marketing materials and advertising for the likes of Lightolier, General Dynamics and the Federal Aviation Agency. Having emerged from her first husband's creative shadow, Elaine went on to forge a remarkable career of her own in the ostensibly male-dominated world of graphic design and typography thanks to her remarkable eye for colour, composition and content.

POLITICS: WHO GETS WHAT, WHEN, HOW

HAROLD LASSWELL

elaine lustig

MERIDIAN BOOKS M 58 $1.35 Canada $1.45

A.I.A. File No. 31-F-23

STYLE BOOK SUPPLEMENT

LIGHTOLIER

recent additions to Lightolier's 50th anniversary lighting collection

PICASSO
PICASSO
PICASSO
PICASSO
PICASSO
PICASSO

FIVE MASTER WORKS SEPTEMBER 30 – OCTOBER 18, 1958

KOOTZ GALLERY

MÄRTA MÅÅS-FJETTERSTRÖM

ARTS AND CRAFTS · TEXTILES

Swedish
b. Kimstad, Sweden, 1873
d. Båstad, Sweden, 1941

Any survey of women designers must include the work of Märta Måås-Fjetterström, who revitalized the traditional crafts of Sweden with her Modern rug designs. She was a champion of women designers, who led by example in her highly successful weaving workshop, which is still in operation to this day – a century after its founding.

A vicar's daughter, Märta Fjetterström grew up in a large family and, as a child, enjoyed cultivating flowers in the vicarage garden – an interest that provided fertile inspiration for motifs found in her later textiles. When she was 17, she left home to study art at the University College of Arts, Crafts and Design in Stockholm with a view to becoming an illustrator and drawing teacher. After graduating, she added 'Måås-' to her surname and briefly worked as a teacher. In 1905 she became director of the Malmöhus County Handicraft Association and, four years later, participated in the 'Konstindustriutställningen' ('Industrial Art Exhibition') in Stockholm, organized by the Svenska Slöjdföreningen (Swedish Society of Crafts and Industrial Design). At this exhibition, she showed her large Staffan

Stalledräng tapestry, which, because it bore no relation to the precious, traditional weaves of Scania, in the southern Swedish tradition, meant she was fired from Malmöhus.

She moved to Vittsjö and became director of a new weaving school aligned to an artisanal textile- and rug-making collective founded by textile artist Lilli Zickerman. Here, Måås-Fjetterström found the creative freedom she needed and began designing her own distinctive patterns inspired by the beautiful surroundings of the Scanian countryside. She developed new weaving techniques evolved from Swedish weaving traditions. In 1914 she exhibited at the Baltic Exhibition in Malmö where the nephew of chemist and philanthropist, Alfred Nobel, saw her work. Ludvig Nobel invited her to create textiles for his Skånegården hotel in Båstad and to open her own workshop there. So, in 1919, at the age of 46, she opened her own weaving studio in Båstad, and was able to hire some of her former students.

Eventually, the workshop employed over 20 professional female artist–weavers producing her designs for knotted-pile and rölakan (flat-weave) rugs, wall-hangings and tapestries. These designs earned critical acclaim at various World Fairs as well as at the landmark Stockholm Exhibition (1930) and the Liljevalchs Exhibition (1934). The museum director and curator, Erik Wettergren noted in 1934, 'She is a remarkable storyteller ... who finds her inspiration in legends and meadows, in the Orient and the North, in ancient beliefs and fresh green leaves, in the Bible and buildings.'[1] Moreover Måås-Fjetterström's designs constantly evolved stylistically with contemporary design trends and, as a result, her pictorial Arts and Crafts motifs gave way to more pared-down geometric compositions during the mid 1930s.

Around this time, she stated, 'The connection between technique and form must never be broken',[2] and it was

undoubtedly the mastery of her chosen craft that enabled her to explore her gift for patternmaking with unfettered creativity. During her career, she produced more than 700 textile designs and was regarded by contemporary critics as Sweden's greatest textile designer of all time.

In 1941, at the height of her career, she died through complications from surgery. Her friend and colleague, designer Carl Malmsten, helped save her workshop, with assistance from Wettergren and from King Gustaf V and Crown Prince Gustaf Adolf of Sweden. Over the succeeding decades, this remarkable workshop has not only painstakingly reproduced Måås-Fjetterström's designs, but also textiles by other talented women designers associated with it, including Barbro Nilsson, who, as its new artistic director, helped preserve the rich craft–design legacy that Måås-Fjetterström's left in her creative wake.

Left: Exhibition of Måås-Fjetterström's textiles at the Sundsvalls Museum, 1958.

Opposite, clockwise from top left: Flower Patch woven textile panel, 1939; Rutmattan rug for Märta Måås-Fjetterström AB, 1931; Red Eight carpet for Märta Måås-Fjetterström AB, 1928; Flower Plot textile for Märta Måås-Fjetterström AB, c. 1930.

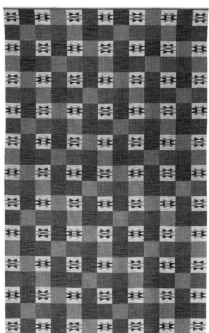

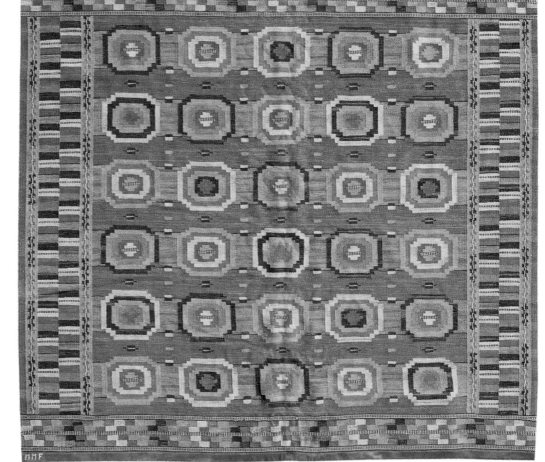

BONNIE MACLEAN

American
b. Philadelphia, USA, 1949

The late 1960s witnessed a shift of social attitudes that saw rock music, sexual liberation, eco-awareness and gender politics become central focuses for a younger generation dissatisfied with the status quo. New, alternative forms of graphic expression were sought to capture the spirit of the time, giving rise to the psychedelic poster. Nothing is more redolent of the Age of Aquarius than the bold, colourful posters and handbills that were created by a small group of artists living and working in San Francisco's Haight-Ashbury district, then the epicentre of the hippie, counter-culture movement. The so-called Big Five psychedelic poster artists – Wes Wilson, Victor Moscoso, Alton Kelley, Stanley Mouse and Rick Griffin – were all men, but there were a number of

female artist–designers working in the genre, too. Of these, Bonnie MacLean was undoubtedly one of the most talented.

Born in Philadelphia, MacLean grew up in Trenton, New Jersey, and later studied at Pennsylvania State University, majoring in French. After graduating in 1961, she moved to New York where she worked at the Pratt Institute, honing her drawing skills at evening classes held there. In 1963, enticed by the more progressive culture of California, she moved to San Francisco, and worked as a secretary at Allis-Chalmers, a manufacturer of specialized machinery. Her boss was Bill Graham, the firm's regional manager, and they fell in love and began living together. When Bill became the business manager of the San Francisco Mime Troupe, MacLean went with him as his assistant. In 1965 members of this radical comedy group were arrested in San Francisco's Lafayette Park for obscenity and Bill arranged three benefit concerts to cover their legal fees – two of which were held at the Fillmore Auditorium. With an obvious talent for event organizing and promotion, Graham and MacLean subsequently put on the Trips Festival in 1966, as well as rock concerts at the Fillmore, which were advertised using psychedelic posters, mainly designed by Wes Wilson. The sale of these posters took off, but Graham and Wilson fell out over money matters.

After Wilson's departure in 1967 MacLean was tasked with designing the posters, as she had already been using a similar graphic style with chalk on two large blackboards announcing current and upcoming bands. Initially, her poster designs paid homage to Wilson's work, but she soon evolved her own signature style. Working as The Fillmore's in-house illustrator from 1967 to 1971, Maclean designed in total 32 'Bill Graham Presents' posters, of which *BG #75* (1967), promoting The Yardbirds and The Doors, is the best known. With its trippy, swirling lettering and

stylized figures, the design reflects the strong influence of Art Nouveau, itself a style associated with drug-induced hedonism. Indeed, this poster has a sort of Aubrey-Beardsley-on-acid quality, while some of her other posters reflect the era's growing interest in Eastern mysticism.

Maclean married Bill in 1967 and their son was born the following year, but his extra-marital affairs led to separation, and eventual divorce, in 1975. During this time, she entered a relationship with the artist Jacques Fabert and moved to Bucks County, Pennsylvania, where she embarked on a new career as a painter. As she recalls, at the time of her posters' creation she viewed them as merely advertisements designed for commercial ends; yet she is happy that this graphic genre has gained status as a quasi-art form over the years. Her designs were included in the 2007 exhibition 'Summer of Love: Art of the Psychedelic Era' at the Whitney Museum of American Art and, in 2015, she was commissioned to design a poster in the style of her 1960s work for the opening of the Fillmore Philadelphia concert hall. The key factor that set MacLean's posters apart from those of her male counterparts was a definable sweetness. Her work was neither overtly sexualized nor shockingly outré, but rather vividly expressed the kaleidoscopic altered perceptions of a 'good' LSD trip.

Left: Fillmore Auditorium poster #84 (Blue Cheer, Vanilla Fudge, The Sunshine Company and Donovan), 1967.

Opposite: Fillmore Auditorium poster #75 (The Yardbirds, The Doors, James Cotton Blues Band and Richie Havens), 1967.

THE YARDBIRDS
TUES. WED. THURS. ONLY

FRI. SAT. SUN. ONLY
THE DOORS

PLUS-ALL WEEK
JAMES COTTON
BLUES BAND
RICHIE HAVENS

JULY 25-30
FILLMORE

B. MacLEAN © BILL GRAHAM 1967 #75   NEAL, STRATFORD & KERR

TICKETS

SAN FRANCISCO: City Lights Bookstore; S.F. State College (Hut T-1); The Town Squire (1318 Polk); Kelley Galleries (3673 Sacramento);
Wild Colors (1418 Haight); Bally Lo (Union Square); BERKELEY: Discount Records; Shakespeare & Co.; SAN MATEO: Town & Country Records;
REDWOOD CITY: Redwood House of Music; PALO ALTO: Dana Morgan Music; SAN RAFAEL: Record King; SAUSALITO: The Tides Bookstore

GRETA MAGNUSSON-GROSSMAN

MID-CENTURY MODERN · FURNITURE

Swedish/American
b. Helsingborg, Sweden, 1906
d. San Diego, USA, 1999

Greta Magnusson-Grossman enjoyed a prolific career spanning four decades and two continents. She effectively brought Swedish Modernism to California, but her contribution was quickly forgotten and it was only when her designs were rediscovered in the 1990s by a new generation of mid-century collectors that her legacy finally began to be reassessed.

Born and raised in Sweden, Magnusson-Grossman benefitted from the socially progressive culture in Scandinavia that enabled female designers to flourish

creatively and to enjoy almost as much opportunity and status as their male counterparts. It could be said that furniture design was in her DNA, coming as she did from a family of Swedish cabinetmakers. After finishing high school, she undertook an apprenticeship at the Kärnan furniture workshop in Helsingborg, then studied industrial design at the Konstfack (University of Arts, Crafts, Art and Design) in Stockholm, graduating in 1933. After completing her studies, mainly focussing on the design of furniture, textiles, ceramics and metalware, with classmate Erik Ullrich she co-founded in 1933 a Stockholm-based store and furniture-upholstery workshop called Studio. That year she married the British-born Jewish jazz musician, Billy Grossman.

With the rise of fascism in Europe and the outbreak of World War II, the couple decided to leave Sweden, despite its supposed neutrality and Magnusson-Grossman having already established a reputation there. On her arrival in California, she declared that she needed 'a car and some shorts' because, as a newly arrived immigrant, these were the most American things she could think of.

Magnusson-Grossman opened a store on Rodeo Drive, Los Angeles, with her business card stating that it specialized in 'Swedish modern furniture, rugs, lamps and other home furnishings'. It was an instant hit, with its progressive, clean aesthetic perfectly chiming with the emerging West Coast Modernism scene in California. Her work attracted a celebrity clientele that included Hollywood actresses Greta Garbo and Ingrid Bergman, both fellow Swedes. Other illustrious patrons included Joan Fontaine, Gracie Allen and Frank Sinatra, and soon she forged a significant reputation within the upper echelons of the architecture and design world, too. She exhibited a wall light manufactured by Ralph O. Smith at the first Good Design exhibition organized by New

York's MoMA in 1950–51, alongside the work of other pioneering women designers, such as Anni Albers, Ray Eames and Marguerite Wildenhain. The following year, she displayed a side chair produced by Glenn of California Furniture at the second Good Design show. During this period, she designed numerous other lighting products for Ralph O. Smith, including her Grasshopper floor light (1947) and hooded Cobra table lamp (1948). She also created many additional items for Glenn of California, notably a desk and related range of tables set at unusual angles and adorned with distinctive ball feet that featured dynamic combinations of walnut and black-laminate elements.

Between 1949 and 1959, Magnusson-Grossman also designed at least 14 Modernist homes in the Los Angeles area, as well as one in San Francisco and another in her native Sweden. Often featuring curtain-wall glazing and open-plan layouts, her houses were light-filled spaces that perfectly suited their environments. Indeed, she worked on several occasions with the landscape architect Garrett Eckbo, ensuring that the interior and exterior spaces seamlessly flowed into each other. Her designs and buildings were featured prominently in *Arts & Architecture* magazine, but, after she retired in the late 1960s, her name and work fell largely into obscurity. However, a major retrospective exhibition held at the Arkitekturmuseet, Stockholm, in 2010, has since led to a major reappraisal of both her life and work.

Opposite: Grasshopper floor light for Ralph O. Smith, 1947.

This page, from top to bottom: Hurley house in Hollywood, 1958; Tiered occasional tables for Glenn of California, c. 1952; Cobra table lamp for Ralph O. Smith, 1948.

CECILIE MANZ

CONTEMPORARY · FURNITURE · LIGHTING · PRODUCT

Danish
b. Zealand, Denmark, 1972

Cecilie Manz is a prominent member of a cohort of designers living and working in Copenhagen who have been responsible for the recent creative resurgence of Danish design. Working for a host of Nordic design-led companies, Manz is probably best known for her designs for furniture and lighting, with her work having been put into production by, among others, Fritz Hansen, Lightyears and Muuto. She has also designed noteworthy glassware for Holmegaard and several elegant portable Bluetooth speakers for the manufacturer Bang & Olufsen, which reveal the multi-faceted breadth of her design talents.

Born on the island of Zealand, Manz trained at the renowned School of Design at the Royal Danish Academy of Fine Arts, graduating in 1997. She also spent time as an exchange student at the University of Art and Design in Helsinki. This, undoubtedly, gave her a broader understanding of Nordic design and its social, economic and aesthetic imperatives. The year after completing her studies, she founded her own studio in Copenhagen, since when she has managed to carve out an international reputation for her aesthetically refined and functionally thoughtful work. Her Caravaggio lamp (2005), for Lightyears, was her first big international success

and spawned a bestselling collection of pendant, table and floor lights.

Like so many Nordic designers working today, Manz mainly produces designs for the home environment but, often, the innate simplicity of her work means it can also be integrated successfully into other kinds of interior spaces. Her Workshop Chair (2016), which playfully reworks a Scandinavian seating archetype, is a case in point, as is her easy-to-assemble Compile shelving system (2016), which can be variously configured against a wall or used as a room divider. These are both produced by Muuto. Her Aitio pocket shelves for Iittala also possess similar home/office crossover potential. As a creative balance to her work within the furnishings and homeware markets, Manz also enjoys working in industrial design, creating products for Denmark's most famous electronics company, Bang & Olufsen. These designs channel the company's august design heritage in a thoroughly contemporary way, by adopting a stripped-down, yet soft-edged, essentialist language of form.

Making experimental prototypes and sculptural one-offs is also an important aspect of the design process for Manz. As she explains, 'I view all my works as fragments of one big, ongoing story where the projects are often linked or related in terms of their idea, materials

and aesthetics, across time and function. Some objects remain experiments or sculpted ideas, others are made more concrete and turn into functional tools. The task or project itself often holds the key to inspiration; ideas don't come from waiting but from leg-work, drafting and trials.'[1] Above all, Manz's work is guided by her in-depth preliminary research into the functional aspect of any project and by her desire for simplicity, which results in a quest for, as she puts it, 'a pure, aesthetic and narrative object'. It is this understanding of design that enables her to create award-winning work that not only has a strong visual simplicity, but an engaging functional simplicity, too.

Left: A1 portable Bluetooth speaker for B&O Play (Bang & Olufsen), 2016; above: Caravaggio lamp for Lightyears, 2005.

Opposite, clockwise from top left: Micado side table for Fredericia Furniture, 2003; Sami knife, 2009; Spectra stacking vases for Holmegaard, 2007; Compile shelving system for Muuto, 2016; TØJTRÆ clothes tree for PP Møbler, 2000 (produced 2008–13).

ENID MARX

MODERNISM · TEXTILES

British
b. and d. London, UK, 1902–1998

Enid Marx is, perhaps, best remembered today for the hardwearing moquette textiles she designed for London Transport in the 1930s. Yet 'Marco', as she was affectionately nicknamed by her friends, also designed around 30 upholstery textiles for the Utility Design Panel during World War II. In addition, she also used her prodigious patternmaking skills to create various eye-catching logos, book covers and book-covering papers during a career that spanned over 70 years.

Marx was initially educated in Hampstead before being sent at the age of twelve to board at Roedean School, a girls' public school near Brighton. It was in the cavernous art room at the school that Marx learnt life drawing at the instigation of the enlightened Head of Art, Dorothy Martin. Indeed, during her final year there, she was allowed to dedicate herself almost entirely to drawing, though she did take carpentry classes, too, which gave her an invaluable 'grounding in the use of tools'. Her father, Robert Marx, an engineering consultant who specialized in papermaking and patented various innovations in this field, also had a formative influence on his daughter and inspired her belief that the machine needed to be harnessed in order to bring good design to the wider public.

Marx went on to study at Central School of Arts and Crafts in 1921 in London, but the following year transferred to the Royal College of Art where she trained under the artist–designer Paul Nash, who encouraged her to work across the disciplines. During her studies at the RCA she began focussing not only on textile design but its manufacture as well, which led to the college's magazine to note of her that 'among all the misses who flirt with Art, she alone woos it seriously.'[1] Despite her obvious talent and commitment, however, she failed her RCA diploma because the assessor thought her work was too abstract – or in other words, too avant-garde.

After leaving the RCA, she apprenticed for a year in the Hampstead-based textile-printing workshop of Phyllis Barron and Dorothy Larcher. Having learnt to mix dyes and carve printing blocks there, Marx subsequently set up her own studio in 1926 and began exhibiting her work to wide acclaim. In 1935 she was commissioned to design seating fabric for London Transport's buses and trains. Incorporating striking geometric patterning in dark multi-coloured hues, the resulting hardwearing wool-based moquette textiles, such as the iconic Shield (c. 1935) and Chevron patterns (c. 1938), demonstrated Marx's ability to find the perfect balance between form and function. The textiles she later developed for the Utility Design Panel during the 1940s were similarly accomplished.

Marx's patternmaking skills were also put to good use at the Curwen Press, where she devised various book-covering papers. She also designed book jackets and produced illustrative engravings for other publishing houses, including Chatto & Windus, Faber & Faber, Hogarth Press and Penguin. Throughout her life, Marx was an avid collector of 'English popular art', as she termed it, which often inspired the motifs found in her textiles and graphic artwork. As she once noted, 'Traditional art – folk art – is, I think, very important.'

Below: Endpaper design for Curwen Press, 1927.

Opposite, clockwise from top left: Spot and Stripe furnishing fabric for Morton Sundour Fabrics Ltd, c. 1945; Chevron furnishing fabric for Morton Sundour Fabrics Ltd, c. 1945; Maidenhare printed velvet for Dunbar Hay Ltd, 1930s; Shield moquette for London Transport, c. 1935.

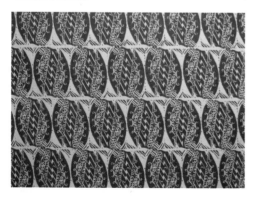

GRETHE MEYER

1960S–1970S · CERAMICS · FURNITURE · GLASSWARE · METALWARE

Danish
b. Svendborg, Denmark, 1918
d. Hørsholm, Denmark, 2008

The Danish architect–designer Grethe Meyer was a pioneering woman in the predominantly male-dominated world of industrial design, who approached design from a scientific standpoint. She specialized in the creation of simple yet practical homewares and her timeless designs won numerous accolades during her career. They are now rightly regarded as true exemplars of Scandinavian design.

Meyer studied at the Det Kongelige Danske Kunstakademi (Royal Danish Academy of Fine Arts in Copenhagen), where she was the only women to graduate as an architect in 1947. From 1944 to 1955, first as a student and then as a recent graduate, she was the assistant editor of an influential guide to the rational planning of homes, entitled *Byggebogen* (Building Manual). The Danish government's institute for research into the building of homes subsequently employed her from 1955 to 1960. In this role, she conducted research into optimized standard measurements for housing, and into consumer products, alongside Paul Kjaergaard, professor of

building art and construction engineering, and architect and design historian, Bent Salicath. During this tenure, she collaborated with the female architect Ibi Trier Mørch on the development of a new line of stacking glassware, called Stub & Stamme (1958) for the Kastrup glassworks in Copenhagen. The design's simplicity and functionality were the direct outcome of her influential research into the standardization of homewares.

Beginning in 1952, Meyer also worked with furniture designer Børge Mogensen on the creation of a revolutionary new storage system that was based on flexibility and adaptability, which was, likewise, informed by her research. They showed an early version of the storage system at the Copenhagen Cabinetmaker Guild exhibition in 1954, and then further refined its design for production. The resultant Boligens Byggeskabe furniture system (1959), which comprised modular shelving, cabinets and desk elements, was constructed from a combination of Oregon pine and a hardwearing laminate. It was produced by furniture manufacturer C.M. Madsens.

In 1960 Meyer founded her own architecture practice and also began

designing tableware for the porcelain company Royal Copenhagen. This fruitful collaboration resulted in three 'classic' ranges: the Blue Line faience dinnerware line (1965), the Whitepot porcelain dinner service (1972) and the Firepot ovenware series (1976). In 1965 the Blue Line range received the Danish industrial design prize, ID, and its aesthetic restraint and utilitarian practicality presaged the neo-Modernist Scandi aesthetic of the 1970s. Meyer's work for Royal Copenhagen not only revealed her in-depth understanding of materials, form and function, but also her knowledge of industrial production techniques. She wanted her designs to be as functional as possible and was only interested in creating 'things people can afford'.[1] For instance, her stackable Firepot range, which won the ID design prize in 1976, came in graduated sizes based on the volumes of various standardized food portions as well as standard oven dimensions; it was also resilient and versatile enough to go from freezer to hot oven and then onto the dining table.

Although Meyer increasingly dedicated her time to architectural projects, she continued to design ceramics and glassware during the 1980s and 1990s. She also designed a simple range of lights with cloche-shaped shades in 1984, the pendant versions of which were eventually put into production by design firm Menu in 2013. Her Copenhagen steel cutlery range, which she designed in 1991 for Georg Jensen, was acclaimed for its elegant ergonomically contoured lines. As she observed in her acceptance speech at the Danish Design Award ceremony in 1997, when working on a project: 'The design must be uncomplicated, and the product easy and comfortable to use, and as simple and anonymous as possible in the expression of its properties. In this way I think that beauty will present itself.'[2] Throughout her career, Meyer practised what she preached and her designs are a lasting testament to this belief.

Opposite, below:
Firepot range for Royal
Copenhagen, 1976; left:
GM 15 pendant lamp for
Menu, 1984.

This page, clockwise
from right: Whitepot
coffee service for
Royal Copenhagen,
1972; stainless steel
candelabra for Georg
Jensen, c. 1990s; Blue
Line teapot for Royal
Copenhagen, 1965.

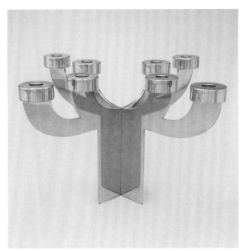

ROSITA MISSONI

1950S–1990S · FASHION · TEXTILES

Italian
b. Golasecca, Italy, 1931

Rosita Missoni was born into a family already knitted into the culture of Italian fashion. They owned a shawl and embroidery factory in Lombardy and it was there, browsing international magazines with her pattern-cutter cousin, that the young Rosita first gained an eye for sartorial form.

In 1948, with her country newly at peace with Britain, she moved to London to study English. It was beneath the statue of the winged lover Anteros in Piccadilly Circus that the teenage Rosita met her husband and lifelong creative partner, Ottavio Missoni. It was the year that London hosted the first postwar Olympic Games and Ottavio was in the British capital as a hurdler for the Italian Olympic team, for whom he had also designed its official sportswear. From this chance meeting a romance ensued, and they married five years later.

They subsequently moved to Gallarate, near her hometown in Lombardy, and put her family expertise to use in their own knitwear workshop. The pair produced their first collection under the Missoni name in 1958. It would not be until the early 1960s, however, that they commenced in earnest the experimentation with materials for which they would become famous, choosing machinery usually reserved for shawls and bedsheets to produce complex, lightweight sweaters and dresses. The resulting garments boasted polychrome stripes of incredible intricacy – a motif that came to define their brand.

The Missonis themselves were voracious collectors of Modernist abstract art, especially Op Art, Vorticism and the Italian Avant Garde. They were also fascinated by the 'primitive' visual cultures of the Aztec and Incan empires, and these influences soon mingled and were synthesized in their increasingly prismatic knitwear, forming their own vibrant world of geometric abstraction. The Missoni name became hypnotically implanted in the minds of the young, fashion-forward Italian elite.

In 1965, Rosita met and began collaborating with famed New Wave Parisian stylist, Emmanuelle Khanh. Together, they embarked on a succession of experimental collections shown to the press through equally boundary-pushing catwalk events. Most famously, in 1967 they were invited to show their designs at the Pitti Palace in Florence. Such was the gossamer delicacy of Missoni's lamé knit, that it was rendered transparent beneath the catwalk lights, revealing that the models were without bras.

Later that year, their Zigzag collection was sported by models floating precariously in the Modernist Solari swimming pool in Milan, atop inflatable furniture created by Khanh's husband, Quasar Khanh, an engineer and architect. Ending with a series of chaotic falls into the pool, this cocktail-soaked extravaganza encapsulated the joyful, future-facing Missoni mood.

By now, the Missonis had every right to be optimistic as their brand was going from strength to strength. It was regularly featured in American *Vogue*, and the Missonis secured a boutique in Bloomingdale's, New York. Bolstered by its international success, in 1968 the company opened a new parkland factory in the beautiful country near Sumirago, Northern Italy. The complex was built on a loan secured on the proviso that it would provide work for the women of the region. Here, Missoni found herself enjoying Alpine views akin to those she had experienced as a child, but with her family now at the helm of an international creative empire. Their daughter, Angela, inherited both the company and her parents' visionary kaleidoscopic experimentation and, as a result, this iconic Italian brand continues to enjoy global success, season after season.

Opposite: Model wearing a Lurex suit in a mosaic print with a flower print shirt, 1972.

This page: Silk knit ensembles for Missoni, 1970s.

MAY MORRIS

ARTS AND CRAFTS · TEXTILES

British
b. London, UK, 1862
d. Kelmscott, UK, 1938

May Morris was a leading female figure of the British Arts and Crafts Movement but, as the younger daughter of William Morris, her contribution to design has often been overshadowed by her father's renown. She was an influential pioneer of art embroidery as well as an accomplished designer of wallpapers, woven textiles and jewellery. She was also active in the emergent Socialist movement in Great Britain, which her father had been so instrumental in founding, and can justly be regarded as an influential proto-feminist.

As the youngest of William and Jane Morris's two daughters, Morris grew up in the midst of politics and art, and many of the Victorian era's most celebrated artists were close friends of the family. Pre-Raphaelite painters Edward Burne-Jones and Dante Gabriel Rossetti designed for Morris & Co. For most of Morris's childhood her family 'lived over the shop' with their Bloomsbury residence also housing 'The Firm'. During her most formative years, she was surrounded by the various craft-based design projects her father threw himself into, as well as the day-to-day running of a thriving design-led business.

Although as a child she was quite a tomboy, Morris displayed an aptitude for fine needlework, which she inherited from her mother and her aunt, Bessie Burden. They taught her stitch-craft to the most exacting standards, including a precise medieval embroidery technique known as opus anglicanum. Since her elder sister, Jenny, suffered from a debilitating form of epilepsy, Morris ostensibly took on the role of 'eldest son'. However, instead of embarking on a formal apprenticeship, as a boy would have done, she undertook an embroidery course at the National Art Training

Below: Garnet and freshwater pearl silver girdle, c. 1906.

Opposite, clockwise from top: Apple Tree embroidered sachet for Morris & Co., c. 1890; design for Honeysuckle wallpaper for Morris & Co., c. 1883; Maids of Honour embroidered panel, 1890s.

Overleaf left: Honeysuckle wallpaper for Morris & Co., c. 1883; right: Arcadia wallpaper for Morris & Co., 1886.

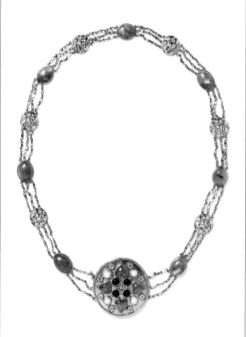

School, which stood her in good stead when she came to take over Morris & Co.'s embroidery department when she was only 23. Working as both a designer and production manager, she produced numerous textile designs that drew inspiration directly from nature and tended to have a more naturalistic aspect than those of her father, or John Henry Dearle who was responsible for most of the Firm's printed textiles. She also designed wallpapers, including one of Morris & Co.'s most iconic patterns, Honeysuckle (c. 1883).

Despite the fact that many women were involved in the Arts and Crafts Movement, its main organization, the Art Worker's Guild, would not accept them as members. In response to this exclusion, Morris co-founded the Women's Guild of Arts with Mary Elizabeth Taylor in 1907. It not only actively promoted the work of women designers, but also provided them with an opportunity to discuss the latest trends in art and design. Its members included the jewellery designer Georgie Gaskin, bookbinder Katherine Adams and artist Evelyn de Morgan. May noted in a letter from 1910, the guild was 'as fine a little knot of women with an all-round, not self-centred, view of the arts as you could meet anywhere ... it is a pleasure to meet women who know their work and are not playing at art'.[1] The guild helped raise the professional status of female designers and, with it, their financial bargaining power. Famously, May also had a 'mystical betrothal' with the married playwright, George Bernard Shaw, who she wrote to many years after their affair had ended, 'I'm a remarkable woman – always was, though none of you seemed to think so.'[2] As a prominent torchbearer for women in design, she was absolutely correct in her assessment of herself, for she uniquely combined her talents as a gifted designer with her activities as an influential women's rights activist.

MARIE NEURATH

MODERNISM · INFOGRAPHICS · BOOKS

German
b. Brunswick, Germany, 1898
d. London, UK, 1986

Marie Neurath was a pioneer of information design who, alongside her husband, Otto Neurath, and their small team of designers, developed a new and influential data-visualization methodology based on an 'international picture language'. Taking pictograms as its look, it was originally known as the Wiener Methode der Bildstatistik (Vienna Method of Pictorial Statistics), but in 1935 she renamed it Isotype (an acronym of International System of Typographic Picture Education). Isotype went on to form the bedrock from which the subsequent teaching of info-graphics would flourish. Such was the importance of their ground-breaking invention, that to this day graphic-design students are taught about the Neuraths's revolutionary system of turning dry statistics into visually engaging info-graphics. But Neurath was also a prolific and hugely gifted author and designer of educational books, which skilfully introduced information and ideas to children visually. They were based on

the Isotype approach and ingeniously distilled information into bold and easily understood graphics.

Unusually for a designer, German-born Neurath came from a maths and science background, obtaining a doctorate in mathematics and physics from the University of Göttingen. In 1924 she went to Vienna on a study trip to learn about the city's programme of school reform. There, on the advice of her mathematician brother, Kurt, who was teaching at the University of Vienna, she visited the economist Otto Neurath. After graduating, she moved to Vienna to join Neurath's team at the Gesellschafts- und Wirtschaftsmuseum (Social and Economic Museum), recently founded to communicate the city's programme of social reform to the general public. Her role was as the team's main 'transformer' – or, in other words, its lead designer. She was responsible for analyzing raw statistical data and putting it into first-draft pictorial form, based on Neurath's 'language-like technique' (as he put it), to be worked up into its final state, ready for production, by the other artists and technicians on the team. One of her key colleagues was Modernist artist, Gerd Arntz, who helped give the linocut pictograms their distinctive graphic quality. The principal rule of Otto's system was that quantity should be represented by a series of repeated pictograms of the same size, rather than by larger pictograms.

In 1934, in the wake of the Austrian civil war, Otto moved to The Hague where he had already set up the International Foundation for Visual Education. Neurath worked with him there and in 1940 they fled to Britain following Germany's invasion of the Netherlands. The following year they married – she was his third wife and sixteen years his junior. They founded the Isotype Institute in Oxford and continued their pioneering work together. In 1944 they proposed a children's book series based on an Isotype vocabulary of consistent

symbolic forms, a restricted colour palette and a strict layout to the publisher Max Parrish, who later published a large number of children's titles by Neurath.

When Otto died in 1945, Neurath remained director of the institute but moved it to London in 1948. From then until she retired in 1971, along with a handful of assistants, she created over 100 children's books, divided into three main series, 'Wonders of the Modern World', 'The Wonder World of Nature' and 'They Lived like This', all of which offered colourful and diagrammatic, easy-to-understand explanations of science, nature and history. This remarkable body of work is a lasting testament to Neurath's extraordinary design genius and stands as a complete rebuttal to the notion that she enjoyed her key position on the Isotype team because she was the wife of her better-known partner. Indeed, it could be argued that, without her remarkable ability to visualize data graphically, the Isotype project might well never have achieved the international success it did.

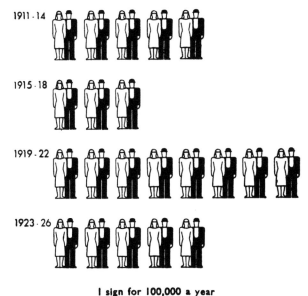

Men Getting Married in Germany in a Year

1911-14

1915-18

1919-22

1923-26

I sign for 100,000 a year

Opposite: *Exploring Under the Sea* for Max Parrish & Co. Ltd, 1959.

This page, clockwise from top: *The First Great Inventions* for Max Parrish & Co. Ltd, 1951; Isotype diagram showing 'Men Getting Married in Germany in a Year', from Otto Neurath's 'International Picture Language', 1936; 'Vote Early at your Polling Station' poster for the Western Regional Government of Nigeria, c. 1955; Tuberculosis poster chart, 1936.

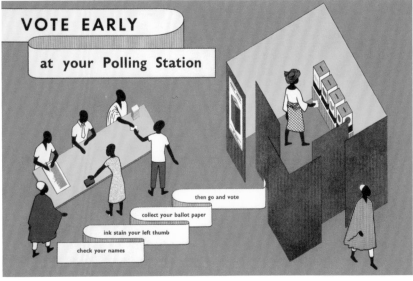

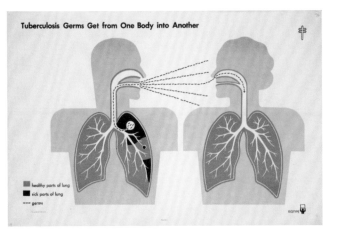

NERI OXMAN

CONTEMPORARY · EXPLORATORY

Israeli/American
b. Haifa, Israel, 1976

The American–Israeli architect–designer, Neri Oxman, is renowned for her thought-provoking experimental designs, which are inspired as much by biology as by advanced computing and state-of-the-art materials engineering. Indeed, she coined the term 'material ecology' to describe her work, which can be seen as design–art explorations into form, function and process.

Oxman was raised in Haifa by her architect parents, Robert and Rivka Oxman, who are known for their research into design theory and practice in the digital age. Given this, it is not surprising that Oxman, who spent much time in her parents' studio while growing up, ultimately chose to study architecture at the Technion – Israel Institute of Technology in Haifa and, later, at the Architectural Association in London, from where she graduated in 2004. The following year, she moved to Boston in order to undertake a PhD in architecture at the Massachusetts Institute of Technology (MIT). Here, her advisor was the Australian-born architect and urban designer, William J. Mitchell, who specialized in relating design practice to advanced computing and other cutting-edge technologies. The subject of her 2010 thesis was material-based design computation, the summary of which described her focus thus: 'Inspired by Nature's strategies where form generation is driven by maximal performance with minimal resources through local material property variation, the research reviews, proposes and develops models and processes for a material-based approach in computationally enabled form-generation.'[1] Put simply, it was all about harnessing the constructional potential of new materials and technologies, and using generative software programmes to explore new formal and/or functional possibilities within the realm of design practice.

In 2010 Oxman became an associate professor at MIT Media Lab, where she leads the mediated-matter research

group that undertakes 'research at the intersection of computational design, digital fabrication, materials science and synthetic biology, and applies that knowledge to design across disciplines, media and scales – from the micro scale to the building scale'.[2] The research-based designs that have resulted have been not only thought-provoking but also visually stunning, from her tongue-inspired Gemini chaise (2014) to her wearable 3D-printed skins, including Mushtari (2014), which was inspired by the structure and workings of the human gastrointestinal tract.

Oxman's prototypical Carpal Skin wrist splint (2009/10) is one of her most interesting design concepts to date, intended to work as a glove for carpal-tunnel syndrome sufferers to wear at night. The idea behind the design is that each example can be specially customized in terms of its hard and soft material distribution, according to the discomfort-profile of each specific wearer. As a groundbreaking cross-disciplinary thinker, Oxman has received numerous awards over the last decade and, in 2016, was named a cultural leader at the World Economic Forum in Davos, Switzerland. More than anything, she functions as a design visionary who is helping to direct design practice towards the greater constructional convergence of the biological, the digital, the material and the technological, while her physical explorations of the process can be seen as tantalizing glimpses into where this convergence might, one day, take design.

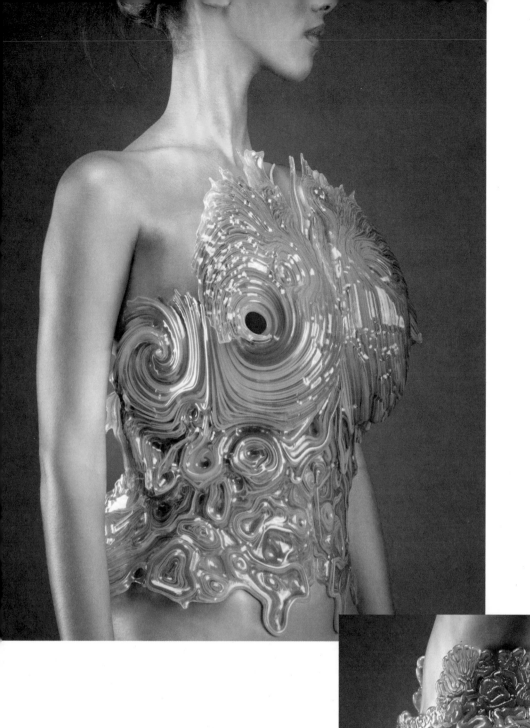

Opposite: Vespers, Series II, mask created for The New Ancient Collection by Stratasys, 2016.

This page: Zuhal (left) and Mushtari (below) from the Saturn's Wanderer series, 2014 (created in collaboration with Christoph Bader, Dominik Kolb and Euromold).

Overleaf: Gemini acoustical twin chaise, 2014 (created in collaboration with W. Craig Carter of MIT's department of materials science and engineering).

MARIA PERGAY

1950S–1970S · FURNITURE

Moldovian/French
b. Bessarabia, Moldova, 1930

Since the 1960s, Maria Pergay has created innovative furniture made of stainless steel that is remarkable for its sculptural boldness. As she notes, 'Stainless steel does not forgive. It has authority, and it helps me not to make errors. But it also shines and glows; it hints at greater things.'[1] It is testament to Pergay's tenacity that she was able to forge a career as a cutting-edge designer in France, despite her work being 'consistently trivialized' by her male contemporaries, who saw it as an aesthetic extravagance not worthy of serious consideration. Her remarkable defiance no doubt stems from experiences she had as a child and is detected in the confident gestural lines she achieves by bending, literally, her material of choice to her creative will.

At the age of seven, Pergay was forced to escape with her family to France to avoid the political turmoil in Eastern Europe, and found solace in drawing as a means of retreating from the tragedies she had witnessed. This love of art eventually led her to study costume and set design in 1947 at Paris's Institut des Hautes Études Cinématographiques (IDHEC; Institute of Higher Cinematographic Studies). She also attended fine art classes at the Académie de la Grande Chaumière in Montparnasse, a neighbourhood known for its artistic bohemianism. There, she studied under the Russian-born sculptor Ossip Zadkine, who instilled in her a love of creative invention. In 1956 she began her design career by making ornate metal elements for the window displays of fashionable Parisian boutiques. This exercise in experimental metalwork led her to design a complete silverware collection, which included silver-plate boxes adorned with ribbons, buckles and tassels. After she exhibited at the Salon Bijorhca (a jewellery tradeshow) in 1957, both Christian Dior and Hermès embraced her objets d'art. Emboldened by this early success, in 1960 Pergay opened

her own shop in the Place des Vosges, Paris, and within the first month had sold her entire stock.

As Pergay's career gained momentum so her work became increasingly experimental, especially when France's foremost steel manufacturer began producing some of her small-scale designs in stainless steel. She instantly recognized the creative possibilities offered by this industrial material and began creating furniture that demonstrated how this shiny alloy could be coaxed into complex sculptural shapes. In 1968, she designed her Flying Carpet daybed that 'challenged the divide between industry, nature and fantasy'[2] and, at a stroke, put stainless steel at the forefront of avant-garde design in France, while sweeping away its previous utilitarian associations. That same year, Pergay's entire steel furniture range was shown at Galerie Maison et Jardin and at the Biennale des Antiquaires, before being purchased in its entirety by Pierre Cardin.

By the 1970s, thanks to Pergay's pioneering designs such as the iconic Ring chair (1968), stainless steel had become a defining theme in contemporary interior design. Despite the male-dominated design community still regarding her work as little more than decoration and having to balance a family life with four children, nevertheless, Pergay managed to win some impressive private commissions from, among others, Hubert de Givenchy, Salvador Dalí, the Shah of Iran and the Saudi royal family. Today, Pergay sees herself as 'a captor of ideas' and 'a servant to her own creative impulses' and, even with her advancing years, she continues to challenge relentlessly the inherent limitations of her chosen material in order to blur the boundaries of art and design.

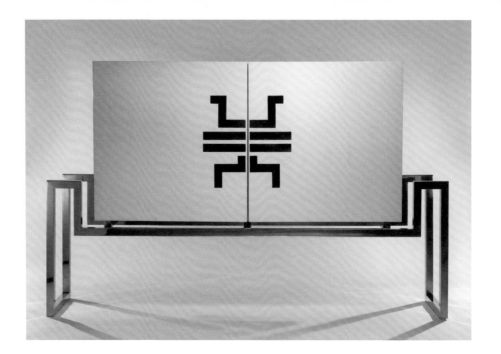

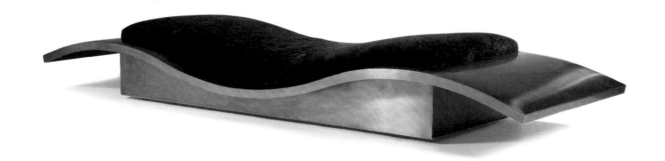

CHARLOTTE PERRIAND

MODERNISM/MID-CENTURY · FURNITURE · INTERIORS

French
b. and d. Paris, France, 1903–1999

Charlotte Perriand helped pioneer a stridently Modernist industrial aesthetic during the late 1920s and 1930s, while working for architect–designer, Le Corbusier. Following her departure from his practice, she worked for the rest of her long career as an independent designer of mainly furniture and interiors that, though still Modernist, had a more humanist bearing. Her post-Corbusier furniture was characterized by the use of natural materials and softer organic forms, while her interiors were notable for their functional flexibility. Inspired by Japanese design, her furniture also had a strong elemental aspect as well as a definable craft aesthetic. Today, original examples of her stylish, yet practical, furnishings command exceptionally high prices at auction thanks largely to the refined aesthetic value that ensures they can be placed in many different types of modern interior setting.

Born into a modest family, Perriand benefitted from being an only child. Her working mother would tell her that 'work is freedom!',[1] inculcating in her a strong work ethic. Having shown an early talent for draftsmanship, Perriand won a scholarship to train as a furniture designer at the École de l'Union Centrale des Arts Décoratifs (UCAD; Central School of Decorative Arts) in Paris. She grew frustrated, however, with the school's traditional approach to cabinetmaking and sought alternative inspiration from the burgeoning industrial modern age, which she witnessed on the bustling Parisian streets with their motorcars and bicycles.

After graduating, in 1926 Perriand married Percy Scholefield 'for a challenge'.[2] Like so many women of her generation, she saw marriage as a rite of passage to adulthood. As she would later explain, 'At the time, marriage was the only way for the chrysalis I was to turn into a butterfly, and a butterfly is a creature that takes flight.'[3] And, indeed, it turned out to be a brief and oppressive marriage that ended in divorce in 1930. It did, however, give rise to her first interior design project – the transformation of the garret apartment she shared with Scholefield from a photographic studio into a chic Modernist design statement. Around this time, Perriand sought work as a furniture designer in Le Corbusier's studio, only to be rudely rebuffed. He showed her the door with a dismissive, 'We don't embroider cushions here'. Some months later, however, Le Corbusier realized his error on discovering her metal and glass Bar in a Garret at the 1927 Autumn Salon in Paris, prompting an apology and an invitation to join his architecture practice, which he ran with his cousin, Pierre Jeanneret.

Two years earlier, Le Corbusier had outlined in his book *Decorative Art of Today* (1925) what he saw as the key requirements for modern furnishings, defining three furniture typologies: type-needs, type-furniture and human-limb objects. During her decade-long tenure in the Le Corbusier–Jeanneret office, Perriand translated these ideas into innovative seating designs using tubular metal. One such design was the B306 chaise longue (1928), on which she posed for a publicity shot, controversially showing her shapely stocking-clad legs. At the 1929 Autumn Salon, as a trio, Perriand, Le Corbusier and Jeanneret exhibited their Interior Equipment apartment installation, which demonstrated unequivocally just how stylishly chic modern living could be. And, by helping Modernism to throw off its utilitarian associations, the work of the three ultimately made Modernism more widely accepted.

In 1937 Perriand left Le Corbusier's studio to work with the artist Fernand Léger. During World War II, she collaborated with Jeanneret and designer Jean Prouvé on the design of aluminium pre-fabricated buildings. In 1940 she became an industrial-design advisor to the Japanese Ministry of Commerce, which involved taking an extensive research trip to Japan. Her guide was the product designer Sori Yanagi, whose father was the founder of the Mingei folk craft movement that sought to preserve traditional craft skills. This two-year long trip was a hugely formative experience, as was Perriand's war-enforced four-year residency in Vietnam, where she met and married her second husband, Jacques Martin, and gave birth to their daughter. While trapped in Vietnam due to a naval blockade, she took the opportunity to study local craft skills. On returning to France, her designs, though still within the Modernist canon, revealed the strong influence of her Asian experience, exhibiting a quasi-Oriental aesthetic refinement. In many ways, these postwar designs were an evolution of her earlier work because, throughout her long career, she never once abandoned the ideals of Modernism. As she explained, 'The most important thing to realize is that what drives the Modern movement is a spirit of enquiry, it's a process of analysis.'[4]

Clockwise from above: B306 (later LC4) chaise longue for Gebrüder Thonet (later Cassina), 1928 (co-designed with Le Corbusier and Pierre Jeanneret); Interior installation at the Salon d'Automne, Paris, 1929 (co-designed with Le Corbusier and Pierre Jeanneret); Shepherd's Stool, for Galerie Steph Simon (later Cassina), 1953; Bloc Bahut sideboard executed by Négroni and Métal Meuble for Galerie Steph Simon, 1958.

MIUCCIA PRADA

1980S–CONTEMPORARY • FASHION

**Italian
b. Milan, Italy, 1949**

Miuccia Prada is a veritable doyenne of Italian fashion as well as a formidable businesswoman. As the heiress to the Prada name, she has guided her family company from leather goods house to multi-billion-dollar international fashion giant. She is also the founder of Miu Miu – a provocative yet sophisticate brand, with a nonchalant attitude, which has been described as Prada's 'other soul'.

As a teenager in the 1960s, Prada became interested in politics – specifically feminism among other left-wing causes – and in 1973 earned a PhD in Political Science from the University of Milan. Soon after this she attended the Piccolo Teatro, where she studied mime for five years. It was during this period that she also became increasingly involved in her family's company, which had been originally established by her grandfather in 1913, when he had opened the first Prada store in the prestigious Galleria Vittorio Emanuele II in Milan.

It was through her involvement with the family business that she met her future husband, Patrizio Bertelli in 1977. Soon after they begun working together, laying the foundations for the future international expansion of Prada. While he pioneered a new business model within the luxury goods sector, which was based on the implementation of rigorous quality controls throughout all stages of production, Prada, with her maverick creative spirit, began commanding international attention for her innovative approach to design, which has always been inspired by her curiosity and unconventional observation of society. Indeed, it is her ability to interpret everyday reality through unusual perspectives that has enabled her to repeatedly anticipate and also influence fashion trends. One of Prada's first designs of note was a waterproof bag, produced in nylon –

a material then usually reserved for coverings and military tents. The breakout success of this model as well as her other early bag designs in the late 1970s and early 1980s, enabled the company to once again expand across the country and into international territory. The subsequent interest in the Prada name also allowed her to launch the company's first shoe line in 1979.

In 1987, she married Bertelli and thanks to his business acumen, the company expanded even further. The launch of her first ready-to-wear collection in Milan the following year once again saw Prada's designs bucking the prevailing fashion trends by displaying tasteful clean lines and careful craftsmanship in a pared-back palette of black, red and tan. These she described as 'uniforms for the slightly disenfranchised'. It could be argued that this sober approach was informed by her feminist, anti-bourgeois political tendencies. Yet her left-wing sentiments certainly did not impinge on her ability to build an enormously successful company.

The year 1992 was an especially important one for the company, for it witnessed the launch of Miu Miu. The following year saw the launch of Prada's first menswear pieces. That same year, 1993, Prada turned her attention to creativity outside of the fashion world, when she and her husband opened the Fondazione Prada, a nonprofit organization that supports up-and-coming designers, artists and architects. She later relocated this foundation to a Milanese complex designed by avant-garde architect and theorist, Rem Koolhaas.

Across myriad collections over the years, Prada has always managed to keep her goal of material creativity to the fore, while maintaining an enviably prestigious position within the fashion mainstream. In 2014 she was named International Designer of the Year by the British Fashion Council and the same year – alongside

Elsa Schiaparelli (see pages 198–99) – was the subject of a major exhibition at the Metropolitan Museum of Art, New York. Following on from this, she was honoured by the British Fashion Council with its Outstanding Achievement Award in 2018. As Nadja Swarovski commented at this time, 'Miuccia Prada is unquestionably one of the most influential designers in fashion history. A true visionary, her dedication to fashion as an art form is endlessly inspirational.'[1] Although not particularly interested in fashion per se, Prada has throughout her career espoused an aesthetic purity in her pursuit of beauty, and this is ultimately the reason for her enduring success.

Opposite: Prada nylon
backpack, 1980s.

This page, clockwise from
below: Prada's flagship
store in Milan; Spring/
Summer 2019 collection;
First ready-to-wear
Autumn/Winter 1988
collection; Autumn/Winter
2003 collection.

MARY QUANT

British
b. London, UK, 1934

Few names are as synonymous with the spirit of 1960s fashion as Mary Quant. She has become a by-word for the sexual and sartorial freedom of her time.

Quant's first shop, Bazaar, opened on the Kings Road in Chelsea in 1955. Although a recent graduate of Goldsmiths College, Quant was able to establish a high-profile presence in the stomping grounds of the infamous 'Chelsea Set' thanks to a healthy investment from her aristocratic future husband, Alexander Plunket Green. Open to the street, open minded and open late, the shop quickly became a social hub for a bubbling London scene, which was just beginning to 'swing'.

Inspired by the strikingly modern approach to life being explored around her, Quant's early designs were a revolution in clean lines, bright colours and youthfully simple forms. These 'beatnik' inspired pieces were light-years ahead of those stocked by more traditional sellers. In fact, most of the garments sold in Bazaar by day were produced by Quant herself in the back room over night. This round-the-clock process allowed for jazz-like formal experimentation. The looks that graced Quant's famous window displays were always a fresh expression of 'the moment' as she saw it.

In 1962 Quant went mainstream with a collection for American retail giant JC Penny and a more affordable diffusion line named Ginger Group for the UK. Seen in retrospect, these high necked, trapeze-line dresses still appear futuristic. According to Quant, however, the look drew equally from her nostalgia for the playful freedom of childhood. As she once explained, she saw no reason 'why childhood shouldn't last forever. I wanted everyone to retain the grace of a child and not to have to become stilted, confined, ugly beings. So I created clothes that

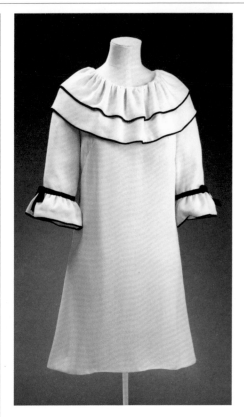

This page, top: Plastic and cotton ankle boots, 1967; above: mini dress, 1964.

Opposite: Models wearing Skindles (bat-wing blouse with striped skirt) and Hammersmith Palais (striped waistcoat and matching trousers, with crêpe shirt), 1975.

worked and moved and allowed people to run, to jump, to leap, to retain their precious freedom'.[1] This toy box innocence is visible in everything Quant designed from the mid 1960s onwards. It contrasts strongly with the more adult connotations of the miniskirt she is often credited with inventing. Though it cannot be said for sure that it was Quant who first sent hems so high up the thigh, she can certainly be credited for another controversial 1966 phenomena – the 'hot pant'.

Quant's mainstream success never deterred her from 'far-out' material experimentation – for example she helped to pioneer the use of PVC in fashion, and produced daring plastic footwear through her Quant Afoot line. This experimentation continued into the 1970s as she diversified beyond garments, licensing the Mary Quant brand to manufacturers in a range of fields. A sea of modish Quant daisies popped up on children's dolls, soft furnishings and make up. Through these licenses she was able to design a whole lifestyle for young women across the world. Eventually, Quant resigned from her cosmetics brand in 2000, but there are still more than 200 stores bearing her name across Japan. And as a result, a new generation of international anglophiles continues to discover the quintessential Quant look.

INGEGERD RÅMAN

CONTEMPORARY · GLASSWARE

Swedish
b. Stockholm, Sweden, 1943

A doyenne of Swedish design, Ingegerd Råman is one of the world's leading designers of glassware and ceramics. In fact, in her own country she is regarded as something of a national treasure thanks to her thoughtfully conceived homewares, which embody the core attributes of Nordic design – utility, timeless simplicity and understated beauty.

Råman trained under Carl Malmsten at his school in Öland (Capellagården in Öland), before studying at the Konstfack (University College of Arts, Crafts and Design) in Stockholm. She then spent a year studying ceramic chemistry at the State Institute for Ceramics in Faenza, Italy. She later established her own pottery in 1967 in the Skåne province in southern Sweden and, over the succeeding years has become not only Sweden's most renowned ceramicist, but also one of its leading 'form-givers'. As she notes, 'I love throwing clay, it is so tactile and direct. It's amazing to really be good at something. I can always fall back on that knowledge, throwing, glazing, firing ... Because I am a master of all those various stages, I personally can be responsible for both the quality and the expression.'[1]

But apart from being a celebrated ceramicist, she has also worked very successfully as a glass designer. Indeed, she seems to straddle the different realms of craft and industrial production effortlessly. She was employed by the Johansfors industrial glassworks from 1968 to 1972, and became a designer for the Skruf glassworks in 1981, where she designed her successful Bellman range, which helped revive the use of tiny schnapps glasses and has been in continuous production since its introduction in 1992. This testifies to Råman's observation, 'Right from the start my vision has been to work traditionally and timelessly with pieces that still feel modern and can be in production a long time.'[2] For Skruf, she also created her Mamsell carafe (1990), the remarkable functional simplicity of which lifted what is ostensibly an ordinary household object into the realms of the extraordinary. Indeed, Råman's designs exude a feeling of inherent 'rightness' that comes from her ability to channel into her designs the intrinsic qualities of whichever material she is working with.

In 1999 she began working with the Orrefors glassworks designing wares that were quite different from the earlier utilitarian pieces, but every bit as accomplished. One of her earliest successes at Orrefors was her delicate Drop of Water bedside decanter (2000), the inspiration for which is self-evident. In 2000 her well-publicized series of vessels for Orrefors – including her Skyline and Slowfox vases as well as the Tanterella decanter – marked a new level of artistic mastery, with their etched motifs enhancing the inherent properties of glass.

Her later Pond series (2006) had an even stronger visual dynamism with its tangled and grass-like etched motifs, while her Bonbon range of vases (2009) explored decorating techniques – cutting, blasting and etching – to dramatic effect. Both these collections were distinguished by a playful artistry and yet retained the formal purity that is so characteristic of Råman's work.

In 2016 IKEA launched Råman's extensive Viktigt collection, comprising handmade glassware and ceramics as well as furniture, lighting and accessories woven from natural fibres. This limited-edition range was inspired as much by her desire for simplicity as her love of craftsmanship. As IKEA's then head of design, Marcus Engman, noted, 'Ingegerd Råman is extremely good at raising the everyday to an exceptional level. At making the ordinary spectacular. She makes us rediscover the everyday.'[3] Råman knows that, when it comes to design, it is the smallest of details that count, even in the most quotidian of things.

Opposite, far left; Bonbon limited-edition vase for Orrefors, 2009; left: Bamboo basket from the Viktigt Collection for IKEA, 2016.

This page, clockwise from above left: Bonbon limited-edition vase for Orrefors, 2006; Råman at her potter's wheel in her studio, c. 2016; Pond bowl for Orrefors, 2006; Drop of Water bedside decanter for Orrefors, 2000.

RUTH REEVES

ART DECO · TEXTILES

American
b. Redlands, CA, USA, 1893
d. New Delhi, India, 1966

Californian-born Ruth Reeves began her artistic education at the Pratt Institute, New York, in 1911. She trained, for the most part, as a painter and, as would be the case throughout her long career, fine art served as a fountainhead of inspiration for her print and textile designs. Following in the footsteps of many of her contemporaries, Reeves moved to Paris in 1920, where she trained at the Académie Moderne until 1927. At this institution she was greatly influenced by her tutor, the noted Cubist painter Fernand Léger. During this period, Reeves also derived great creative succour from the dynamic Parisian Jazz Age arts scene, drawing on the influence of the Fauvist, Raoul Dufy, and Sonia Delaunay's Orphist abstraction (see pages 62–63).

She shared the Cubists' rejection of illusory perspectival space in favour of fragmented mosaic-like surfaces. Into these geometric compositions she wove charmingly simplified flashes of figuration. Jazz bands, animals and petticoated ladies all appear, executed impeccably with pioneering vat dye and screen-print processes. As a fanatical champion of craftsmanship, Reeves sought to channel her lofty abstract influences into practical works for industry.

Well aware of the burgeoning market for mass-produced homewares in America, she returned to the United States in 1927. The artistic vigour of interwar Europe travelled with her, marrying perfectly with the American Moderne mood of brash informality that was sweeping her homeland. The zeitgeist of this period is perhaps best captured in her print Manhattan (1930), in which crosshatched steamships, skyscrapers, workmen and biplanes jostle for visual attention amidst the organized chaos of New York's soaring skyline. Reeves became almost

synonymous with New York City, when she was commissioned to design carpets and wall-hangings, which featured a complex cavalcade of guitar players, dancers and circus performers, for the newly constructed Radio City Music Hall (1931).

Reeves's influence was, however, not confined to the metropolis. In 1934, funded by the Carnegie Institute, she travelled to Guatemala. There, she carried out an in-depth ethnographic study of traditional South American textile and clothing production. She soon found a deep affinity for the subject, especially in its flat, graphic simplification of natural forms. In her opinion, the American continent had developed an advanced and abstract visual sensibility centuries before the European Avant-Garde. In 1935, she produced a series of patterned homages to the craftsmen of Guatemala, which she displayed alongside her personal collection of their work. The critic Lewis Mumford praised her Guatemalan-inspired wall-hangings and

garments, stating that they were 'probably the most interesting work any designer has offered for commercial production today'.[1]

As a continuation of this project, Reeves headed an ambitious initiative to document the entire American continent's traditional visual folk culture. This culminated in The Index of American Design, which comprised nearly 18,000 watercolour illustrations. It was a New Deal Federal Art Project, an initiative devised to support artists during the Great Depression. It was also intended as a central reference for artists and craftspeople wishing to learn more about the rich creative culture of historic Pan-American folk arts and crafts.

Reeves continued her own artistic practice in the United States until 1956 when, fascinated by the task of preserving indigenous folk art against the homogenizing effects of European colonial power, she moved to India on a Fulbright scholarship. There, she served on the All India Handicraft Board and wrote a seminal book on the lost-wax casting technique used in Indian craft production. She died in New Delhi in 1966, leaving a remarkable legacy, both in terms of her own designs and her insightful management of The Index of America Design, which must be considered the most ambitious craft and design documentation project ever undertaken.

This page: 'Petit Dejeuner' tablecloth, c. 1928.

Opposite: Manhattan textile for W. & J. Sloane, 1930.

LILLY REICH

MODERNISM · FURNITURE · EXHIBITION

German
b. and d. Berlin, Germany, 1885-1947

Lilly Reich was a pioneering Modernist, who was respected by her peers for her innovative exhibition and interior design. From a well-to-do family, as a young women Reich learnt how to use a sewing machine to stitch Kurbel embroidery – a technique widely employed for Jugendstil textiles – which led to a life-long love of design. In 1908 Reich was hired by Josef Hoffmann to work as a designer for the Wiener Werkstätte in Vienna. As she later recalled, Hoffmann's office was 'all about design, furniture, interiors and thinking about design in a new way.'[1] A few years later, she returned to Berlin to study at the Höhere Fachschule für Dekorative Kunst (Higher Technical School for Decorative Art) under Else Oppler-Legband, who inspired Reich to pursue her own design career. In 1911 Reich created clothing displays for the Wertheim department store in Berlin, presumably at the instigation of her mentor. That same

year she devised interiors and furnishings for a youth centre in Charlottenburg, while the following year she designed a 'worker's apartment' for the 'Frau in Haus und Beruf' ('The German Woman at Home and at Work') exhibition held in Berlin, which the critic Paul Westhein decried as displaying all the 'failings of the architecturally inept woman'. This rebuke reflected the then widespread perception that it was fine for women to dabble in the decorative arts but not professional design practice.

Yet despite such prevailing beliefs the Deutscher Werkbund invited Reich to become a member in 1912. Two years later, she opened her own studio and devised a living room installation, as well as other displays, for Margarete Knüppelholz-Roeser's controversial 'Haus der Frau' ('House of Woman') pavilion at the first Deutscher Werkbund exhibition held in Cologne. By 1920, such was Reich's professional standing that she became the first woman to be elected onto the Deutscher Werkbund's board of directors.

In 1924 she met Ludwig Mies van der Rohe and soon after became his mistress, soul mate and design collaborator – an association that spanned some 13 years. Together they co-designed the exhibition halls of the Deutscher Werkbund's 'Die Wohnung' ('The Dwelling') exhibition of 1927, and later co-created various exhibits for the 1929 'International Exposition' in Barcelona.

During this period Reich shifted her focus towards interior and furniture design, in all likelihood because they were areas where it was easier for a woman to succeed. In 1931 a range of her tubular steel furniture was launched by Bamberg Metalwerkstätten, which also produced designs credited solely to Mies van der Rohe, although in all probability, it was Reich who assisted in their realization. Certainly, it is thought that Reich helped Mies design furniture for the Tugendhat House (1930) in Brno. In 1930 Mies was appointed director of the Dessau Bauhaus, and Reich subsequently headed the school's weaving studio and interiors workshop, moving with the school to Berlin in 1932. After the Bauhaus's closure in 1933, she continued working as a designer, however, commissions were sporadic. In 1938 Mies emigrated to the United States and although Reich visited him there the following year, she returned to Germany and spent the ensuing war years working in the office of Ernst Neufert. As she later noted when asked about her collaboration with Mies, 'I loved Mies and reflected in his success. Times changed and it's easy not to understand the way things were.'[2] Indeed, it was only when a retrospective of Reich's work was held in 1996 at the Museum of Modern Art in New York that she got the recognition she so richly deserved.

Opposite: View of the German Linoleum Works exhibit at the Deutscher Werkbund's 'Die Wohnung' exhibition at the Weissenhofsiedlung, Stuttgart, 1927.

This page, above: View of the 'lady's bedroom' in the Ground-Floor House at 'Die Wohnung unserer Zeit' exhibition in Berlin, Germany; left: MR 10 cantilevered side chair for Berliner Metallgewerbe Joseph Müller, 1927 (co-created with Ludwig Mies van der Rohe).

LUCIE RIE

POSTWAR–1970S · CERAMICS

Austrian/British
b. Vienna, Austria, 1902
d. London, UK, 1995

Dame Lucie Rie was one of the great pioneers of postwar British studio pottery, whose work introduced a new level of aesthetic refinement that blurred the boundaries of art, craft and design. During her lifetime, her work was internationally acclaimed and brought her financial success as well as various public accolades, including her damehood in 1991.

Born in Vienna, Rie came from a bourgeois Jewish family – her father was a prosperous specialist ENT doctor with progressive tastes and friends.[1] As a child, she enjoyed plenty of outdoor leisure, including skiing, which instilled in her a love of nature. Between 1922 and 1926, she studied ceramics at the Kunstgewerbeschule (University of Applied Arts) in Vienna under the Secessionist ceramicist–sculptor, Michael Powolny. There, she learnt ceramic chemistry, which later enabled her to create her signature volcanic and textural glazes.

The year she graduated, she married Hans Rie, whose family was friendly with hers, and established her own pottery studio. The couple lived in an apartment, given to them by her uncle, that was furnished with Modernist pieces by the

architect–designer, Ernst Plischke. In 1930 some of Rie's designs were illustrated in a book entitled *Austrian Applied Art* (1930), which had a foreword by Josef Hoffmann. Around this time, her work was also exhibited in the Wiener Werkstätte's galleries and she became an active member of the Österreichischer Werkbund.

The political climate in Vienna became increasingly hostile for Jews, culminating in the Kristallnacht pogrom of 1938. Rie and her husband managed to obtain the necessary papers to move to Britain. Hans's plan was to use London as a temporary stop-off before emigrating to the United States, where he had job prospects. Rie, however, had other ideas and the couple parted company: he moved to Boston, while she remained in London. In 1939 she set up a new home-studio in a converted stable block in Paddington, London. During the war she ran a button-making operation from there, using press-moulded clay that she glazed.

After the war, she received commissions for other ceramic items, including tea and coffee sets for the upmarket chocolatier, Bendicks, and pots for Henry Rothschild's fashionable Primavera gallery in Sloane Street. In 1946 Rie met the German-émigré potter Hans Coper, who soon began working as her assistant at her Albion Mews pottery. This was the start of a collaboration that spanned a dozen years. Rie always

modestly insisted that she was actually his student and, while that was not true, he certainly helped her gain the necessary creative confidence to produce truly great pots. Working alongside each other, these technical equals endlessly spurred each other on creatively. They both made ceramics that had a sculptural sensibility, but Coper's had a bolder vocabulary of form whereas Rie's designs had a finer and more precise aesthetic.

During the 1950s, Rie became well known for her tea and coffee sets, but it was her more sculptural bowls, dishes and vases, which came in a myriad of Oriental-inspired forms and glazes, that ultimately made her name. One of her favourite techniques was the raw glazing of stoneware, whereby the clay is not bisque-fired but allowed to interact with the oxides in the glaze. Many of her vessels were also decorated using sgraffito, a technique that involves scoring layers of coloured slip or glaze to reveal the underlying colour. For Rie, each design was an exploration of form, material and technique. As she once noted, 'To make pottery is an adventure to me, every new work is a new beginning',[2] and the attainment of beauty was her ultimate goal. During her long and illustrious career, she took part in numerous exhibitions in Britain, Europe, America and Japan. In the 1960s, her ceramics became chunkier and more textural, in tune with contemporary taste, while in the 1970s, her wares reached their high point of technical and formal perfection. One of the greatest ceramicists of all time, Rie left an extraordinary body of work that, though rooted in craft, was also an exquisitely refined expression of Modernism.

Opposite, left: Stoneware coffee service with manganese glaze, 1958; above: porcelain vase, 1976.

This page, from top: Pots, bowls and vases featuring volcanic glazes on display at Rie's studio, *c.* 1960s; bowl, *c.* 1980; vase, *c.* 1960s.

ASTRID SAMPE

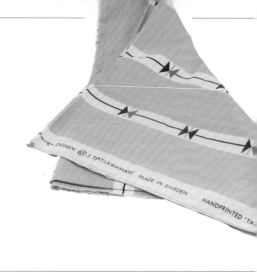

MID-CENTURY · TEXTILES

Swedish
b. and d. Stockholm, Sweden,
1909-2002

Astrid Sampe brought a youthful vitality to textile design during the postwar period and a new sense of professionalism. Fellow textile designer Jack Lenor Larsen later described her as the design world's 'ambassadress without portfolio',[1] while the Cooper Hewitt Museum's then curator of decorative arts, David Revere McFadden, once observed that she 'helped to prove that arbitrary boundaries between art, craft and production need not interfere with creativity, vision and dedication'.[2] Certainly, over her long and distinguished career, Sampe truly earned the sobriquet 'Sweden's doyenne of design'.[3]

Sampe inherited a love of industrial production, and more broadly the arts, from her father Otto, who owned a textile factory in Borås, western Sweden – a city well known for its textile industry. Even as a child, having completed her homework, she would help in the factory. She trained as a textile designer at the Konstfack (University College of Arts, Crafts and Design) in Stockholm, from 1928 to 1932. Completing her studies at the Royal College of Art, London, helped her forge links with the British design community and gain an international outlook.

In 1937 as a designer for the Stockholm department store Nordiska Kompaniet (NK), she created, with architect Elias Svedberg, the NK interior for the Swedish Pavilion at the 'Exposition Internationale des Arts et Techniques dans le vie Moderne' ('International Exhibition of Arts and Techniques in Modern Life'), in Paris. The following year, she was appointed manager of NK's newly established Textilkammare (Textile Chamber), remaining at its helm until 1972, when the studio closed. During her tenure, she

designed numerous textiles that testified to her talents as both a patternmaker and a colourist.

In 1939 Sampe collaborated with the Swedish Modernist architect, Sven Markelius – who had created textiles for NK – on the Swedish Pavilion at the 1939 New York World's Fair. Throughout the 1940s and 1950s, she revitalized the Scandinavian tradition of textile weaving by creating patterns with a definable mid-century Modernist appeal, while also commissioning work from leading Scandinavian designers, including Carl-Axel Acking, Ulla Ericksson, Stig Lindberg and Bjørn Wiinblad. She was the first Swedish designer to experiment with fibreglass cloth, in 1946, and was highly influential in creating textiles for specific architectural settings. Having pioneered the development of textiles based on photographic techniques during the mid 1950s, later in her career she was at the vanguard of computer-assisted data-based patternmaking. Recognized both at home and abroad, she was elected an honorary member of The Royal Society's Faculty of Royal Designers for Industry in 1949 and won a Grand Prix at the Milan Triennale in 1954, as well as the Gregor Paulsson trophy in 1956.

Crucially, Sampe enjoyed a long and fruitful association with Almedahls, the company subcontracted to produce her Linen Line for NK in 1955. Launched at the 'H55' exhibition in Helsingborg, this revolutionary range, which included napkins, runners and tea towels, introduced new sizes, fashionable colours and modern abstracted, Mondrian-inspired patterns to the Swedish textile repertoire. That same year, Sampe designed a printed tea towel emblazoned with her Persson's Spice Rack pattern, a tribute to the ceramicist Signe Persson-Melin, who had attracted huge press attention at H55 with her cork-stoppered spice jars. Today, this pattern, which epitomizes Sampe's fresh, youthfully casual approach to textile design, is still produced by Almedahls. During her long career, she also designed for the Wohlbeck and Kasthall carpet factories in Sweden, for Knoll International in New York and Donald Brothers in Dundee. After the closure of NK's Textile Chamber, she established her own Stockholm-based studio in 1972. Apart from her own remarkable legacy as both a designer and design manager, Astrid was also the mother of the glassware designer, Monica Backström, who is similarly blessed with a rare gift for colour and patternmaking.

Above: Tattoo textile for NK, 1956; left: Kitchen Job Satisfaction teatowels for Klässbols, 1955; opposite: Persson's Spice Rack textile for Almedahls, 1955.

PAULA SCHER

**American
b. Washington, DC, USA, 1948**

Pentagram is the world's largest independently owned design studio and its remarkable success, which spans some five decades, is attributable to its unique structure, whereby its shareholding partners are all practising designers. In 1991, graphic designer and typographer Paula Scher became Pentagram's first female principal, a remarkable achievement in such a male-dominated field. Scher's reputation at the agency's New York office has grown thanks to an impressive portfolio of work undertaken for a roster of high-profile clients, ranging from the not-for-profit cultural to the deep-pocketed commercial. Indeed, she is regarded in

New York as something of a design legend thanks to her Public Theater campaign and identity work for the city's High Line.

Scher trained at the Tyler School of Art in Pennsylvania, majoring in illustration in 1970. She was then employed by Random House, working on book layouts for its children's division. Around the same time, she met the designer Seymour Chwast marrying him when she was 22 years old and, although they later divorced, they eventually remarried. Chwast's ability to mix Pop-inspired illustration with interesting typography was immensely influential to Scher's own development as a skilful visual communicator.

In 1972 she took up a position in the advertising and promotion department of CBS Records creating print ads. A year later she moved to the competing music label, Atlantic Records, and began designing album covers. She returned to CBS in 1974 and collaborated with illustrators and photographers to create hundreds of record sleeves, including rock band Boston's debut *Boston* album (1976), which cleverly featured an illustration of guitar-shaped UFOs by Roger Huyssen, and Eric Gale's *Ginseng Woman* (1976), which combined innovative Japanese-inspired typography with an illustration by David Wilcox. During her decade-long stint in the music industry, Scher won four Grammy awards for her album covers, which perfectly interpreted musical content in a highly poetic visual way. At CBS, she oversaw the production of more than 125 record sleeves per year, and innumerable posters and ads.

In 1982, she went freelance and, two years later, co-founded Koppel & Scher with a fellow Tyler graduate, Terry Koppel. During their six-year partnership, they designed book covers, a Mondrian-inspired identity for Manhattan Records and watch faces for Swatch. Scher also created posters for Swatch including one that controversially paid homage to an earlier artwork by Herbert Matter, which was

regarded as a veritable Modernist icon of Swiss School graphic design. By now she had developed a distinctive graphic style, referencing Art Deco and Russian Constructivism. Hit by the early 1990s recession, Koppel took a position at *Esquire* magazine and, in 1991, Scher joined Pentagram as a partner, to become, as she put it, 'the only girl on the football team'.[1]

The move to Pentagram was momentous in terms of her career trajectory as, being part of a world-class agency, she now had far more ambitious and diverse projects to work on. In 1994 she began a long-running Deco-meets-Rodchenko campaign for New York City's Public Theater, the posters of which perfectly transmitted the organization's creative vitality and diversity. Scher also worked as a logo designer for, among others, Tiffany & Co., CitiBank and Microsoft's Windows 8.

She was inducted into the Art Directors Club's Hall of Fame in 1998 and has since worked on innumerable projects that continue to feature her trademark neo-Pop aesthetic. Her success lies in her ability to translate popular culture into sophisticated high-culture communication, for, as she notes, 'I've always been what you would call a "pop" designer. I wanted to make things that the public could relate to and understand, while raising expectations about what the "mainstream" can be.'[2]

Left: Identity design for the High Line in New York City, 2009.

Opposite: 95/96 Season Poster for the Public Theater in New York, 1995.

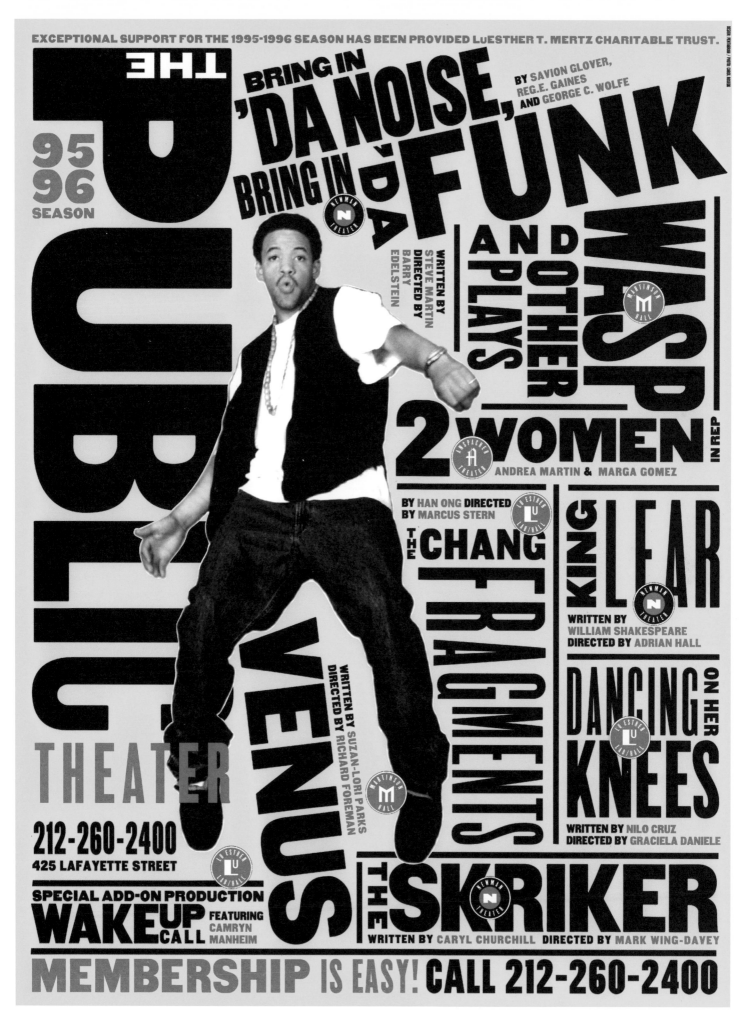

THE PUBLIC THEATER

95 96 SEASON

BRING IN 'DA NOISE, BRING IN 'DA FUNK

BY SAVION GLOVER, REG.E. GAINES, AND GEORGE C. WOLFE

AND OTHER PLAYS

WASP

WRITTEN BY STEVE MARTIN
DIRECTED BY BARRY EDELSTEIN

2 WOMEN IN REP

ANDREA MARTIN & MARGA GOMEZ

BY HAN ONG DIRECTED BY MARCUS STERN

THE CHANG FRAGMENTS

KING LEAR

WRITTEN BY WILLIAM SHAKESPEARE
DIRECTED BY ADRIAN HALL

VENUS

WRITTEN BY SUZAN-LORI PARKS
DIRECTED BY RICHARD FOREMAN

DANCING ON HER KNEES

WRITTEN BY NILO CRUZ
DIRECTED BY GRACIELA DANIELE

THE SKRIKER

WRITTEN BY CARYL CHURCHILL   DIRECTED BY MARK WING-DAVEY

212-260-2400

425 LAFAYETTE STREET

SPECIAL ADD-ON PRODUCTION
WAKE UP CALL   FEATURING CAMRYN MANHEIM

MEMBERSHIP IS EASY! CALL 212-260-2400

197

ELSA SCHIAPARELLI

Italian
b. Rome, Italy, 1890
d. Paris, France, 1973

The Italian fashion designer Elsa Schiaparelli was born in Rome and, owing to her father's expertise in medieval history, she grew up obsessed with ancient cultures and historical archetypal forms and motifs. She studied philosophy at the University of Rome and published an anthology of poetry based on the Greek myth of Arethusa. So explicit was her verse that her parents sent her to a convent as a corrective measure; she escaped, however, by going on hunger strike.

At the age of 22, she fled to London and took a job as a nanny. She also attended lectures in history, literature and art, and fell in love with her teacher, the theosophist Count William de Wendt de Kerlor. They became engaged within 24 hours of meeting. With the outbreak of World War I, the couple left Europe for New York, where their daughter Gogo was

born. In New York, Schiaparelli worked in a boutique owned by the ex-wife of Dadaist artist, Francis Picabia, and soon befriended the artist himself. Her easy social grace and understanding of artistic theory soon led her into a constellation of star artists, such as Marcel Duchamp, Man Ray and Edward Steichen.

Schiaparelli's marriage ended as swiftly as it had begun and she was left divorced and almost penniless. Aided by wealthy friends, she returned to Paris where she was able to make money selling fashion drawings to couture houses, including Maggy Rouff. A shrewd networker, she made her presence felt amongst the artists at the cabaret bar, Le Boeuf sur le Toit. In 1927 a chance encounter with the couturier Paul Poiret encouraged her to produce her own clothing for sale. Inspired by the surrealistic milieu of the time, her early scarf sweater was the first sign of the whimsical visual play that persisted throughout her career. George Hoyningen-Huene photographed this hand-knitted jumper, with its illusory bow, for *Vogue* and, as a result, there was so much demand for her designs that she opened her own ready-to-wear shop, the House of Schiaparelli.

In 1930, in synchrony with Coco Chanel (see pages 40–41), Schiaparelli developed a range of sleek sportswear, under the name Pour le Sport. Highlights included the first split skirt – a functional revolution in women's tennis wear. Further structural innovation came that year when she introduced, for the first time ever, garments with unconcealed zippers – a strikingly modern look. Her relationship with fastenings developed throughout the 1930s, with sculptural elements introduced on buttons. Her lines also boasted brooches and ornamentation by Surrealist luminaries such as Méret Oppenheim and Elsa Triolet, but her experimentation went beyond the superficial and she collaborated with manufacturer, Charles Colcombet to push new synthetic fibres, such as rayon and stretch jersey,

to their limit. A typical experiment of this era was the Glass cape (1934), made of transparent Rhodophane plastic.

In 1937 Schiaparelli moved yet closer to the art world, when she embroidered a line portrait by Jean Cocteau in lavish gold on a linen evening coat. It was, however, the Lobster print dress that launched her collaboration with the most famous Surrealist of them all – Salvador Dalí. The pair followed this with the iconic Shoe Hat (1937), a classic Dalí sculptural inversion. As though to offset the frivolity of this piece, the following year Schiaparelli created the Skeleton Dress (1938), on which black trapunto quilting produced the effect of protruding bones. The year 1938 also saw the appearance of the Tears Dress, a light blue evening gown interrupted by a pattern of Dalí-drawn *trompe-l'oeil* rips. Strangely prescient of punk, it was worn with a veil on which wound-like cuts revealed fleshy magenta rayon. It was shown to the press as part of a cavalcade of acrobats, music and whimsical garments: Schiaparelli's Circus helped establish the form that most modern fashion shows now follow.

A natural-born self-publicist and sensing opportunity in Hollywood, Schiaparelli took commissions in the United States, including dressing the actress Mae West for the film *Every Day's a Holiday* (1937). She then shrewdly used the proportions of West's mannequin for the bottle of her new Shocking fragrance – a curvaceous form packaged in her signature Schiap pink. She also produced a dress to accompany the perfume, which came complete with an inflatable West bust.

She resided in America during World War II, then made a post-war return to France, where she witnessed the rise of Christian Dior's 'New Look'. Struggling to recapture the attention of the fashion press in the postwar years, she closed her fashion house in 1954. Her legacy to fashion remains as bold and daringly original as their creator.

Opposite: Shoe Hat, 1937–38.

This page, clockwise from top left: Hand-knitted woman's sweater, 1928; Lobster printed silk organza dinner dress, 1937 (co-designed with Salvador Dalí); the Skeleton Dress, 1938.

MARGARETE SCHÜTTE-LIHOTZKY

MODERNISM · INTERIOR PLANNING

Austrian
b. and d. Vienna, Austria, 1897–2000

Margarete Schütte-Lihotzky was not only Austria's first female architect, but also a communist activist who fought against Nazism. Today, she is best remembered for designing the Frankfurt Kitchen in the 1920s. This state-of-the-art model kitchen had a rational layout and was innovative because it was based on time-and-motion efficiency studies. It was produced on a large scale and was hugely influential in the development of modern built-in kitchens.

Schütte-Lihotzky was born into a freethinking and well-connected middle-class family, which inculcated in her deep-seated moral values that gave her a lifelong sense of social responsibility. She was the first woman to study at the Kunstgewerbeschule (University of Applied Art) in Vienna, having secured a place with help from a close friend of her mother, the Secessionist artist Gustav Klimt, who had written a letter of recommendation. There, she caught the attention of two of the more progressive tutors, Oskar Strnad and Heinrich Tessenow. She also trained under architect and designer Josef Hoffmann, who was dismissive of female students, observing that 'in any case, women get married'.[1] At this stage, even Schütte-Lihotzky herself never thought her training would lead to professional practice. As she later observed, 'In 1916, no one would have conceived of a woman being commissioned to build a house – not even myself.'[2] Luckily, however, Strnad was a pioneer of social housing and open-plan living spaces, and it was through him that she realized how important it was to design buildings from a user-centric perspective.

After graduating, Schütte-Lihotzky assisted architect and theorist Adolf Loos on housing projects for postwar refugees. The German architect and city planner Ernst May was so impressed by her social-housing work that, in 1926, he asked her to join his team of highly talented architects designing the ambitious New Frankfurt social housing project (1925–31). Working alongside Walter Gropius, Adolf Meyer, Bruno Taut and Mart Stam as part of May's 'brigade',[3] she was tasked with designing a standardized kitchen that could be incorporated into the project's 10,000 new and affordable apartments intended to redress Frankfurt's dire housing shortage. Her remarkably efficient model kitchen boasted numerous space-efficient and labour-saving features, including a fold-down ironing board, a swivelling stool and integrated aluminium storage containers with handles that enabled their contents to be poured easily. The so-called Frankfurt Kitchen was so ingeniously designed it was able to consolidate everything a housewife needed to complete her household chores, from cooking to ironing, into a compact space measuring just 1.9m (6ft 3in) by 3.4m (11ft 2in).

The rational layout of Schütte-Lihotzky's kitchen was informed by two books based on time-and-motion studies: Frederick Winslow Taylor's *The Principles of Scientific Management* (1911) and Christine Frederick's *New Housekeeping: Efficiency Studies in Home Management* (1913). Over and above this, she adapted a railway dining car in which to conduct her own empirical research. This prototype was the blueprint for her prefabricated 'housewife's laboratory', which was manufactured in its many thousands.

In 1930 Schütte-Lihotzky joined another architectural team headed by May, working on large-scale housing and town-planning projects in the Soviet Union. When Stalin's purges began, fearing for her safety, she decamped to London, then Paris and Istanbul. As a committed communist, she returned to Austria in 1940 to join the anti-Nazi resistance movement but was arrested by the Gestapo and sentenced to 15 years in a labour camp. She was liberated in 1945 and resumed work as an architect and planning consultant. It was the Frankfurt Kitchen that proved to be the most notable design of her long career.

But, when interviewed as a centenarian, she obviously felt ambivalent about it, quipping, 'If I had known that everyone would keep talking about nothing else, I would never have built that damned kitchen!'[4]

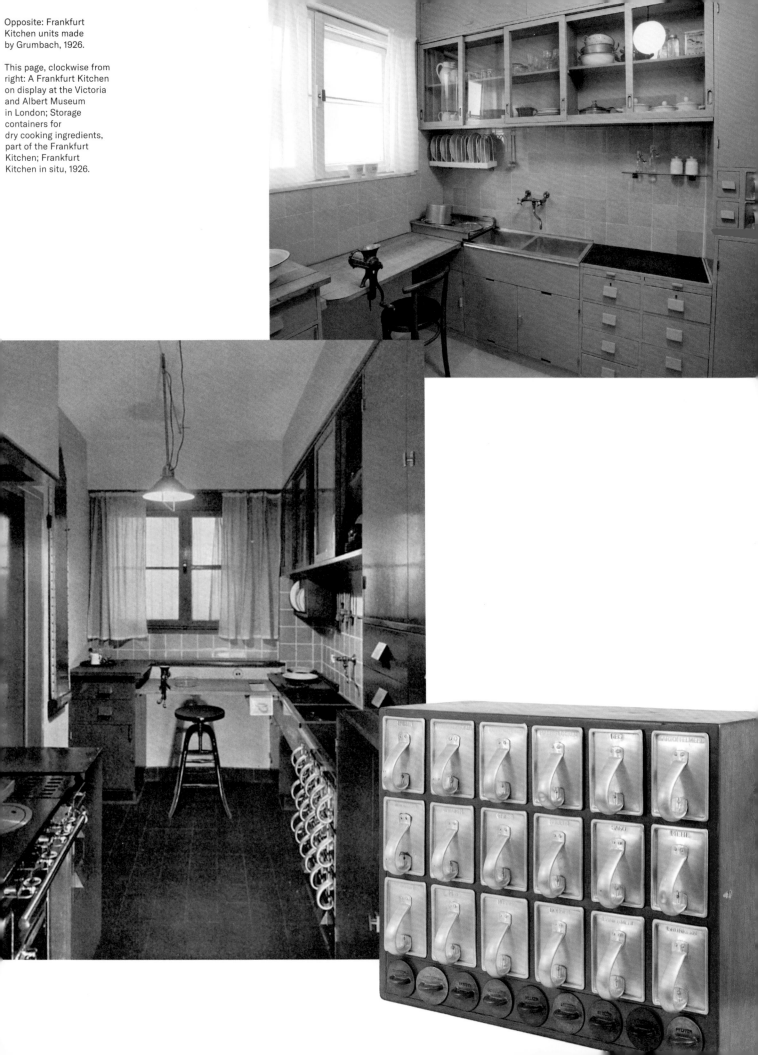

Opposite: Frankfurt
Kitchen units made
by Grumbach, 1926.

This page, clockwise from
right: A Frankfurt Kitchen
on display at the Victoria
and Albert Museum
in London; Storage
containers for
dry cooking ingredients,
part of the Frankfurt
Kitchen; Frankfurt
Kitchen in situ, 1926.

DENISE SCOTT BROWN

1960S–1990S · ARCHITECTURE

**American
b. Nkana, Northern Rhodesia
(now Zambia), 1931**

A great trailblazer of Postmodernism, Denise Scott Brown is arguably the most important female architect and urban planner of her generation, as well as being a prominent theorist, educator and writer. Her projects and ideas have profoundly influenced architectural discourse and practice the world over.

Scott Brown studied at the University of the Witwatersrand in Johannesburg, South Africa, from 1948 to 1952. Having further trained at the Architectural Association in London, she moved to the United States with her architect husband, Robert Scott Brown, to study under Louis Kahn at the University of Pennsylvania. Despite Robert's death in a car crash in 1959, Scott Brown continued her studies, receiving a postgraduate degree in urban planning the following year. She became a faculty member and began teaching, while also embarking on a Master of Architecture, and met fellow teacher, Robert Venturi. Soon afterwards they became partners – both personally and professionally. In 1965, the year she received her professional degree, she wrote 'The Meaningful City', an essay published by the *Journal of the American Institute of Architects* – the first of many influential

texts she produced. In her view, most planners were ignoring the importance of symbolism within urban environments and failing to understand how their inhabitants decipher symbols. As she noted: 'We do not lack for symbols, but our efforts to use them are unsubtle and heavy-handed.' This emphasis on symbolic communication within an urban context was Scott Brown's most important contribution to architectural discourse.

In 1967 Scott Brown and Venturi married, and worked collaboratively thereafter. It was a meeting of intellects, with her focus on symbolism in the urban environment perfectly syncing with his interest in populism. In 1968, with the assistance of Steven Izenour, they co-taught a course at Yale School of Architecture entitled 'Learning from Las Vegas, or Form Analysis as Design Research'. The course analyzed The Strip in Las Vegas, which was 'the archetype of the commercial strip, the phenomenon at its purest and most intense'.[1] A seminal class, it gave rise to the couple's best-selling book of the same name, published in 1972. It became the most influential architectural text of its era, providing the philosophical bedrock from which a new, symbolically laden, international style in architecture and design emerged – Postmodernism.

An earlier book, entitled *Learning from Levittown* (1970), investigated 'the emerging automobile city, the relation of social and physical in architecture and urbanism, and the role of symbolism and communication in architecture'.[2] These two books, along with other writings and Scott Brown's teaching at the Universities of Pennsylvania, Harvard, UCLA, UC Berkeley and Yale, established techniques governing architectural research lasting more than four decades. She also guided their architectural firm, Venturi, Scott Brown and Associates, as principal-in-charge of urban planning, urban design and campus planning. Her urban-planning schemes

include ones for South Street and Old City in Philadelphia, and Miami Beach in Florida. She has produced master-planning studies for universities across America and in China, and contributed to major projects undertaken by the firm: the Sainsbury Wing of the National Gallery in London; the Mielparque resort in Japan's Kirifuri National Park; and the provincial capitol building in Toulouse, France.

Scott Brown has received an impressive number of awards, including the American Institute of Architects Gold Medal, jointly awarded to her and Venturi, in 2016 – the first time the prize had been awarded to more than one architect, acknowledging Scott Brown's exceptional contribution to architectural practice and theory. Today, despite Venturi's passing, Scott Brown continues to publish and present her work. Her contribution to their partnership did not always receive the proper recognition, but together, as intellectual equals, they quite literally changed the face of contemporary architecture.

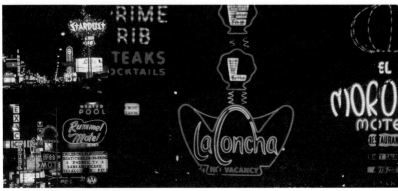

Opposite: Hôtel du Départment de la Haute-Garônne in Toulouse, France, 1990–99.

This page, clockwise from top left: Las Vegas Strip photograph from the Learning from Las Vegas group, 1968; Neon at Night photograph from the Learning from Las Vegas group, 1968; Santa Monica photograph from the Learning from Los Angeles group, 1965; Las Vegas Strip photograph from the Learning from Las Vegas group, 1968; Denise Scott Brown, The Strip, Las Vegas, November 1966.

INGA SEMPÉ

CONTEMPORARY · FURNITURE · LIGHTING · PRODUCT

French
b. Paris, France, 1968

One of the leading French designers practising today, Inga Sempé lives and works in Paris where her small, home-based studio, comprising just her and two assistants, specializes in the design of furniture and homewares for an impressive array of international manufacturers.

Sempé comes from a highly creative family, with both her Danish mother, Metter Ivers, and her French father, Jean-Jacques Sempé, being accomplished painters and illustrators. Unsurprisingly, she inherited their formidable drafting skills, but decided to pursue a career in design rather than in fine art. This led her to study at the ENSCI–Les Ateliers (École Nationale Supérieure de Création Industrielle) in Paris. After graduating in 1993, she worked in various design practices, including a formative internship in the studio of Australian industrial-designer Marc Newson, as well as a two-year stint working for the *grand dame* of French interior design, Andrée Putman, whom she admired greatly, even though the experience made her realize that she did not want to pursue a career in interior architecture.

Sempé established her own studio in 2000. That same year, her first product prototypes were realized under the supportive auspices of the VIA, an organization that promotes innovation within the furniture industry, and she received a residency scholarship at the French Academy in Rome, based in the historic Villa Medici. While there, she took the opportunity to develop her first designs

that made it into production – her Moustache storage shelves with their curious content-hiding fringes made of industrial brush fibres and a range of lights made from a pleated polyamide material held in place with a light and invisible metal structure. These were put into production in 2003 by Edra and Cappellini respectively. The fact that these two Italian companies, well known for their incubation of youthful design talent, were prepared to put such experimental designs into production led to other manufacturers wanting to work with Sempé on projects. She was awarded the Paris Grand Prix de Création in 2003 and the same year, her first solo exhibition was held at the Musée des Arts Décoratifs, Paris. Given that she was then only 35 years old, this was a reflection of the high esteem in which she was already held by the French design community.

Juggling motherhood with a burgeoning design career, Sempé still established an international reputation for skilfully balancing the chic form of French design with an understated Scandinavian practicality. And, while her work might not be as instantly recognizable as that of her long-term partner, Ronan Bouroullec, Sempé has worked with a host of Scandinavian, Italian and French design-led companies, including Alessi, Gärnäs, HAY, Ligne Roset, Luceplan, Moustache, Røros, Samsung, Svenskt Tenn and Wästberg – an impressive client roll call that most designers can only dream of.

Opposite, from left:
Sempé w103 desk light
for Wästberg, 2012; Ruché
sofa for Ligne Roset, 2010;
Collo-alto serving fork and
spoon for Alessi, 2015.

This page: Österlen chairs
for Gärsnäs, 2011.

ALMA SIEDHOFF-BUSCHER

MODERNISM · TOYS · CHILDREN'S FURNITURE

German
b. Kreuztal, Germany, 1899
d. Frankfurt, Germany, 1944

Although her career was short-lived, the Bauhaus-trained designer Alma Siedhoff-Buscher left her mark on design history with a simple but ingenious building-block game that remains in production today, nearly a century after it was first created.

After attending a private boarding school just outside Berlin, Siedhoff-Buscher studied at the Reimann School in Berlin from 1917 to 1920. This was a private and highly regarded college of arts and crafts, which had been founded by the Jugendstil designer and sculptor, Albert Reimann in 1902. It offered vocational training in the applied arts, including textiles, wood-carving, metalwork, poster design and fashion drawing. After this, she studied at the training institute aligned to the Kunstgewerbemuseum (Museum of Applied Art) in Berlin, where she remained until the spring of 1922. Having clocked up five years in art and design education, she enrolled at the Bauhaus in Weimar. She took the school's famous preliminary course taught by the charismatic Expressionist artist Johannes Itten, and also attended classes given by Paul Klee and Wassily Kandinsky. In 1922, she was offered a place in the school's weaving workshop – where the vast majority of female students at the Bauhaus ended up – and was taught loom skills by both Georg Muche and Helene Börner. The following year, however, she managed to switch workshops, swapping weaving for woodcarving, a much more male-oriented discipline. The woodcarving workshop was also under the direction of Muche, but one of her teachers was the sculptor Josef Hartwig, who designed the well-known Bauhaus chess set (1924), its individual pieces reduced to elemental geometric forms. In a similar vein, Siedhoff-Buscher tried her hand at designing wooden toys that would also suit mass production.

For the landmark 1923 'Bauhaus Ausstellung' ('Bauhaus exhibition'), she was asked to design furnishings for the children's room of the Haus am Horn – a showpiece Modernist model dwelling designed by Muche in collaboration with Adolf Meyer and Walter Gropius. For this project, Siedhoff-Buscher created a toy cupboard based on Modernist principles, which was produced in the school's woodcarving workshop. This remarkable nine-piece storage closet was designed specifically with children in mind and comprised storage boxes painted in bright primary colours that could be configured in various ways – as stools and desks or as a stage for imaginative play. It also came with a large trundling container complete with wheels and cut-out handholds, while one of the cupboard's doors was thoughtfully given a cut-out section so it could be put to alternative use as a puppet theatre. This revolutionary children's furniture design was put into production, and it is known that the celebrated architecture critic Nikolaus Pevsner bought one of the sets in 1924, bringing it to London in 1933. Siedhoff-Buscher also designed a handy, wheeled, ladder-like step-chair for the nursery in the Haus am Horn so that children could reach the cupboard's highest shelves. Photographs reveal that, around this time, she also designed other nursery furniture, including a cot and a baby's changing table (c. 1924) that featured various drawers and drop-down elements, as well as an integrated stool/table.

In 1923 she assisted artist Ludwig Hirschfeld-Mack with his colour-light play experiments and designed various games of her own, including the Small Ship-Building Game (1923). Later, in 1924, the Zeiss Kindergarten in Jena, Thuringia, was fitted out with Siedhoff-Buscher's pioneering child-centric equipment, which had been inspired by educational pedagogue Friedrich Froebel's influential 'hands-on learning' approach. Her designs for both children's furniture and toys were subsequently presented at a conference-related exhibition during a Froebel Days event in Jena and included in the 'Youth Welfare in Thuringia' exhibition held in Weimar.

She moved to Dessau in 1925, when the Bauhaus was relocated there and, the following year, while still a student, showed some of her designs at the international Toy Fair in Nuremberg. In 1926 she married Werner Siedhoff, an actor and dancer who took part in Oskar Schlemmer's avant-garde stage productions held at the Bauhaus. When she finally completed her studies at the school in 1927 – having by now spent a decade studying design – she stayed on as a teacher for a while, but her husband's career led to numerous moves for the family over the succeeding years. Siedhoff-Buscher was killed in an Allied bombing raid on Frankfurt in 1944 but, in the late 1970s, some of her wooden toys were put back into production by the Swiss toy-maker Naef, which continues to manufacture her iconic Bauhaus Ship-Building game.

KRAHN

MAIERS BUNTE BAUHEFTE 5

VERLAG OTTO MAIER RAVENSBURG

ALMA SIEDHOFF-BUSCHER

Opposite: *Krahn* (*Crane*) book published by Otto Maier, 1927.

This page, left: Small Ship-Building game (reissued by Naef), 1923; below: Bauhaus catalogue page showing the TI24 children's toy cupboard, designed for the 'Haus am Horn' exhibition, Weimar, Germany, 1923.

ALISON SMITHSON

BRUTALISM · ARCHITECTURE · FURNITURE

British
b. Sheffield, UK, 1928
d. London, UK, 1993

Alison Smithson was one of the leading pioneers of New Brutalism, which was first defined by the architecture critic, Reyner Banham, in 1955. As one half of the most influential Brutalist architectural partnership in the UK, Smithson had a bold and forthright utopian vision for contemporary architecture and urban planning. But, more than this, she was one of the very few female architect–designers of her generation who truly enjoyed professional parity within a husband-and-wife working partnership. As a consequence, she had a higher-than-average profile within her field of expertise, which led her to become an important role model for later generations of women designers.

Born in the north east of England, Smithson studied at the Architecture School of the University of Durham in Newcastle-upon-Tyne. There, she met fellow student Peter Smithson, who she subsequently married in 1949. On graduating, the pair briefly worked as architects at the London County Council

School Division. Having won a competition for the design of the Hunstanton Secondary Modern School (1949–54) in Norfolk, which they had designed at home outside office hours, they established their own architecture practice in 1950.

Together, the couple were also founders of the influential Independent Group, established at the Institute of Contemporary Arts, London, in 1952 and generally credited with having laid the philosophical foundations of the Pop movement in both art and design. They also took part in the group's seminal 'This is Tomorrow' exhibition, held at the Whitechapel Art Gallery in 1956. It was, however, their space-age House of the Future, designed for the *Daily Mail* 'Ideal Home Exhibition' in London the same year, that sealed their public reputation as architectural provocateurs. It was intended as a projection of how a one-bedroom townhouse, with a central courtyard garden, might look twenty-five years into 'the brave new world of tomorrow.[1] Made from plastic-impregnated plaster and with a roof covered in light-reflecting aluminium, the house featured all sorts of futuristic ideas, including a thermostatically controlled bath and an accompanying air-jet shower for drying, as well as a blanketless bed that had a single heated nylon sheet and which retracted into the floor when not in use. While this installation was definitely an exercise in blue-sky design thinking, the Smithsons did go on to design a number of real 'houses of today', of which only a handful were built. They also undertook several conversions of existing dwellings. Such was their

early architectural notoriety, they were invited to join the Congrès Internationaux d'architecture Moderne (CIAM) in 1953. Six years later, however, they formed part of the breakaway Team 10 group, which challenged CIAM's doctrinal functionalist approach towards urbanism and which ultimately led to its dissolution in 1959.

That same year, the Smithsons began the design of *The Economist* complex in St James's, Westminster (1959–64). This, and their later controversial Robin Hood Gardens housing estate in Poplar (1966–72), demonstrated unequivocally their uncompromising architectural vision. Juggling motherhood with her burgeoning career, Smithson was also responsible for writing the Team 10 primer as well as a number of other publications including one (co-authored with Peter) entitled *The Heroic Period of Modern Architecture* (1981), which lauded the work of Le Corbusier and Ludwig Mies van der Rohe, above all others.

The Smithsons also designed a few notable pieces of furniture, including their most famous D38 Trundling Turk 1 (1953), which was an homage to the De Stijl movement. In many ways, this lounge chair encapsulated their shared vision for design: a forward-looking, contemporary modernity that was ideologically inspired by the Modernist movement.

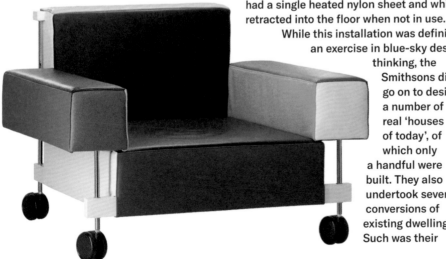

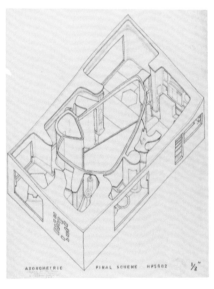

Opposite: D38 Trundling Turk I chair for Tecta, 1953.

This page, clockwise from above: House of the Future created for the *Daily Mail* 'Ideal Home Exhibition' in London, 1956; Robin Hood Gardens Housing Estate in London, completed 1972; axonometric drawing of the House of the Future, 1956.

SYLVIA STAVE

MODERNISM · METALWARE

Swedish
b. Växjö, Sweden, 1908
d. Paris, France, 1994

A prodigiously talented metalware designer, Sylvia Stave is an enigmatic figure whose career trajectory should have been stellar, given her talent, but which was stifled by matrimony. Her story is – at least among women designers – one that has been all too commonly repeated, although perhaps not as starkly as in Stave's case. As Micael Ernstell and Magnus Olausson of the Nationalmuseum, Stockholm, noted, 'Sylvia Stave is one of the great mysteries of twentieth-century design history.'[1]

Born in southern Sweden, Stave lived with her father and stepmother in Kristianstad but, when she was 21 years old, she ran away to Stockholm to escape

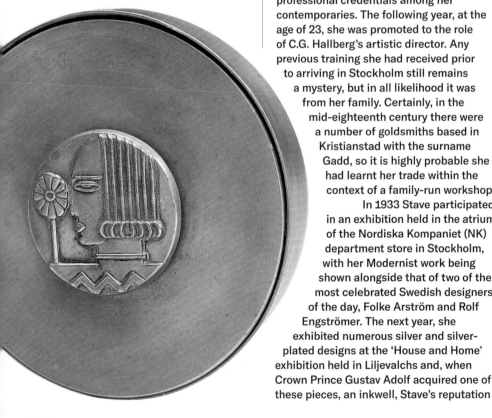

them. Another motivation behind her decampment was an advertisement placed by the prominent Swedish goldsmith and court jeweller, C.G. Hallberg, which was looking for some fresh design talent. This piqued her strong artistic ambition and Stave submitted some design drawings to the firm, which then hired her. Around this time, she changed her surname from Gadd to Stave – which was her mother's new surname now that she had remarried.

The year after Stave moved to the Swedish capital, the landmark 1930 Stockholm Exhibition was staged, which provided an influential showcase of the new Functionalist movement in Sweden. She showed two designs at this event, a pewter and ebony chessboard and an enamelled silver box, both of which were purchased by the Nationalmuseum, thus sealing her professional credentials among her contemporaries. The following year, at the age of 23, she was promoted to the role of C.G. Hallberg's artistic director. Any previous training she had received prior to arriving in Stockholm still remains a mystery, but in all likelihood it was from her family. Certainly, in the mid-eighteenth century there were a number of goldsmiths based in Kristianstad with the surname Gadd, so it is highly probable she had learnt her trade within the context of a family-run workshop.

In 1933 Stave participated in an exhibition held in the atrium of the Nordiska Kompaniet (NK) department store in Stockholm, with her Modernist work being shown alongside that of two of the most celebrated Swedish designers of the day, Folke Arström and Rolf Engströmer. The next year, she exhibited numerous silver and silver-plated designs at the 'House and Home' exhibition held in Liljevalchs and, when Crown Prince Gustav Adolf acquired one of these pieces, an inkwell, Stave's reputation

soared. Her sleek, unadorned, minimalistic designs were also shown at the 1933 Century of Progress World's Fair held in Chicago, the 1934 Leipzig Trade Fair and at the 1937 'Exposition Internationale des Arts et Techniques dans le Vie Moderne' ('International Arts and Techniques in Modern Life') exhibition held in Paris. At this later event, one reviewer praised Stave's work for its 'elegant simplicity'.[2] Certainly, her designs, with their simple geometric forms and absence of superfluous decoration, exemplified the forward-looking and radical New Objectivity art and design movement of the interwar period.

But success can also breed conflict and, around 1937, Arström accused her of appropriating one of his designs for her creation of the royal tennis cup. Around this time Stave was accepted at the École des Beaux-Arts in Paris and so spent a year studying there before returning to Stockholm in 1939 to design what would become her last collection. The following year, she married a French doctor, René Agid, and, aged 31, gave up her flourishing career to become a housewife. Over the succeeding years, her remarkable body of work – equal in terms of forward-looking modernity to any of the iconic metalware designs of the Bauhaus – faded into almost complete obscurity. It was only thanks to Alessi, who re-editioned one of her designs in 1989, that there was a revival of interest in her work. This has since led to a complete re-elevation of her short but remarkable career, and a growing recognition that Stave was, without question, one of the greatest metalware designers of the interwar era.

VARVARA STEPANOVA

MODERNISM · GRAPHICS · CLOTHING

Russian
b. Kovno, Russia (now Kaunas, Lithuania), 1894
d. Moscow, Russia, 1958

A talented fine artist and photographer, Varvara Stepanova was also a pioneering revolutionary of Soviet design and by far the most prominent and prolific female artist to be associated with Russian Constructivism. Her soul mate, comrade and lifelong partner was the multi-talented artist and founder of Constructivism, Alexander Rodchenko, and together, they both worked effortlessly across a range of disciplines. In common with other Constructivists, she was ideologically committed to bringing art into everyday life through the creation of forward-looking utilitarian designs that met the social needs of the time, using, wherever possible, industrial means of production. She also used her exceptional design talents to promote the Soviet political cause through the creation of attention-grabbing propaganda materials. During her career she designed numerous pro-Soviet posters featuring innovative photomontage techniques, eye-catching books with bold typography and dynamic layouts, colourful and strikingly patterned textiles, as well as progressive workwear and sports clothing. She also worked as a theatrical designer, creating sets and costumes for many avant-garde productions.

Born to a peasant family, Varvara studied at the Kazan School of Fine Arts, from 1910 to 1913, which was where she first met Rodchenko. After completing her studies there, she moved to Moscow and worked as a bookkeeper and secretary in a factory for two years in order to make ends meet, while also studying at a private painting and drawing school founded by the artist Konstantin Yuon. Later, Rodchenko also moved to Moscow, where he and Varvara began living together in an apartment leased to them by the artist Wassily Kandinsky in 1916 (they did not marry until 1942). The Bolshevik Revolution of the following year marked a turning point for the couple and galvanized them into revolutionary action, with them calling on 'the proletarian of the brush' to unite in order to transform art into a tool for social progress. Initially, Varvara produced avant-garde poetry and paintings, but, like other artists associated with Constructivism, she increasingly concentrated on her design work or, as it was then known, production art, which was considered more socially worthy than the fine arts.

During this decade of intense social activity, Varvara was prolific: she designed covers for the journals *LEF* and *Novyi Lef*; devised experimental costumes for various plays, including Alexander Sukhovo-Kobylin's *The Death of Tarelkin*; produced over 150 textile designs with geometric patterning for Tsindel (the First State Textile Factory), many of which went into production; she also found the time to design many posters. In addition, she taught at the Krupskaya Academy of Communist Education and, from 1924, was a professor of textile design at VKhUTEMAS (Higher State Artistic and Technological Workshops), the progressive state-founded art and design school that was the USSR's answer to the Bauhaus. It is, however, her design of occupation-specific clothing for which she is now best remembered, especially her unisex sportswear designs that were cleverly devised to offer unrestricted movement and were patterned with bold graphics in order to help identify one team from another. A leading figure of the Russian avant-garde, Varvara's boldly innovative designs swept away the vestiges of the past with vigorous political zeal, and still – nearly a hundred years on – retain a remarkable vitality and refreshing originality.

NANNY STILL

Finnish
b. Helsinki, Finland, 1926
d. Brussels, Belgium, 2009

Nanny Still was one of the great Finnish form-givers of the twentieth century, who designed both art–glass and production glassware that exhibited a rare originality, especially in terms of form, function and technique.

As a child, Still loved to draw and determined at a very early age that she would follow a career in the arts. She took a teacher-training course in drawing and then an industrial-design course at the Taideteollinen Korkeakoulu (Central School of Industrial Design) in Helsinki. Although she specialized in metalwork as a student, she undertook a study trip to the glassworks in Riihimäki, north of Helsinki. This proved to be a very formative experience, prompting her to enter a glassware competition organized by Riihiamäki glassworks, and her submission, a herring plate, won a prize.

After graduating Still was hired as a designer by Riihimäen Lasi Oy in 1949. Over the next twenty-five years or so, she created a truly impressive body of work there, ranging from hand-blown art pieces to industrially produced glassware. When it came to the creation of practical glassware, Still ensured that her designs were well-thought through in terms of their utility – for, as she noted, 'I cannot make impractical objects. You must be able to wash them, and a beer glass must sit comfortably in the hand.'[1]

While working at the Riihimäki glassworks, she felt the urge to create new colours for glassware production and undertook a large amount of research in this area, collaborating closely with the glassworks' chemical laboratory. The remarkable spectrum of stunning smoky hues used for her Koristepullo bottles, produced from 1959 to 1968, testifies to her remarkable talents as a glass technician and colourist. One of the coloured glass hues she invented – a brilliant turquoise – was inspired by a shard of sea-glass found while on a trip to Capri. It was subsequently used for her extensive Harlekiini range (1958), which included jugs, decanters, stemware and covered bowls. This elegant glassware collection was also remarkable for its refined sculptural forms that had a strong graphic quality, a distinctive feature of Finnish design in general.

Throughout her career, Still imbued her functional glassware with a wonderful sculptural brio – from her early Pompadour vases (1945) with their strong undulating silhouettes, to her later and chunkier Grapponia (1968) and Fenomena (1968–72) ranges, whose highly textured surfaces reflected the increasing informality of the period. Throughout her career, Still managed to channel the very latest design trends into her glassware and, in many ways, helped define them, too. She continued designing for the Riihimäki glassworks until 1976, when it shut down its production of blow-moulded glass in order to concentrate on the mass production of utilitarian bottles and jars.

Although glass was Still's material of choice, she did explore the design possibilities of other materials with remarkable adeptness, demonstrating her versatility as a designer. Her teak-and-cane-handled salad servers (1954), for instance, received an award at the Milan Triennale, while her Good Morning breakfast set (c. 1964) was given a Signe d'Or prize and revealed her ability to work elegantly across different materials.

In 1958 Still married an American, George McKinney, and moved with him to Belgium the following year, where she remained for the rest of her life. Continuing to design for Riihimäen Lasi Oy, she also created glassware for Val Saint-Lambert and ceramics for Cérabel, both in Belgium, and ceramics for German producers Heinrich and Rosenthal. She also designed lighting for Dutch firm Raak, and plastic homewares for Sarvis and jewellery for Kultakeskus, both in Finland. In addition, Still was responsible for the sculptural Mango (1973) and plastic-handled Colorina (c. 1975) cutlery ranges manufactured by Finnish homeware firm, Hackman. In 1972 she was awarded a prestigious Pro Finlandia medal for her work 'that came straight from the heart' and, in 2006, the Ghent Design Museum staged a major retrospective exhibition of her work. This testified not only to Still's extraordinary design prolificacy, but also to her enduring love and technical mastery of glass – which, in her hands, was a material of extraordinary design possibilities.

Clockwise from right:
Model 1724 Grapponia
bottles, 1968, and Model
1720 Stella Polaris bottle,
1967, for Riihimäen Lasi;
Timantti (Diamond) vase
for Riihimäen Lasi, 1966
(also known as the Model
6493 Rubiini [Ruby] vase;
Koristepullo decanters/
bottles for Riihimäen
Lasi, 1959; Model 1192
Harlekiini (Harlequin)
covered bowls for
Riihimäen Lasi, 1958.

GUNTA STÖLZL

This page: 5 Choirs jacquard-woven wall panel, 1928.

Opposite: Slit Tapestry (red-green), executed in the weaving workshop of the Dessau Bauhaus, 1927–8.

MODERNISM · TEXTILES

German
b. Munich, Germany, 1897
d. Küsnacht, Switzerland, 1983

German textile designer and weaver, Gunta Stölzl, began her artistic education in 1914 at the local art school in Munich, where she studied a range of artistic disciplines under the noted Jugendstil designer, Richard Riemerschmid. In 1917 her training was interrupted by war, so she worked as a Red Cross nurse on the Italian and French fronts, producing an illustrated account of the conflict. Having resumed her studies, she undoubtedly benefitted from the art school's postwar curriculum reform, which resulted in her reading the Bauhaus manifesto. Instantly captivated by the new world described within – 'free of the divisive class pretensions that endeavoured to

raise a prideful barrier between craftsmen and artists'[1] – she applied to the Weimar Bauhaus as soon as she was able.

Her performance in the preliminary form and colour-theory workshops of painter Johannes Itten earned her a full scholarship, and she became one of the first students to join the new Bauhaus weaving workshop. She soon found, however, that course leader, Georg Muche, preferred to run the department as a laboratory for aesthetic experimentation, scarcely distinct from his own painting practice, rather than concentrating on the technical aspects of textile production. The craft itself, seen by many as 'women's work', was barely taught, but Stölzl's practical skill rendered her invaluable and she came to be seen as a de facto tutor. Her great talent was fusing fluency on the loom with the cutting-edge aesthetic ideas that buzzed through the corridors of the early Bauhaus. She attended lectures by artists Paul Klee and Wassily Kandinsky, and wove these influences into beautiful one-off tapestries. Stölzl drew inspiration from the arts and crafts traditions of various European cultures and her work was a subtle interplay between these earthy, rustic elements and the shocking modernity of the European Avant-Garde, exemplified by her African chair (1921), co-designed with Marcel Breuer – an Expressionist piece of ceremonial furniture.

Stölzl first exhibited her work publicly in Muche's Haus am Horn, a model dwelling produced for the landmark Bauhaus exhibition of 1923. The weaving department designed rugs, upholstery and wall hangings for this prototypical building and Stölzl's contribution played a part in her becoming technical director of her department, even as political pressure forced the school to relocate in 1926 to Dessau. With the Bauhaus no longer able to rely on state funding, sales of textiles produced under Stölzl's direction became a financial cornerstone of the school. Keen

to push this further, Muche introduced jacquard looms and urged students to increase production, but a student uprising ousted Muche and further cemented Stölzl's role as master of the weaving studio. By 1928, with assistance from Anni Albers, Otti Berger and Benita Otte, she had expanded the course to include advanced dye techniques, mathematics and the use of modern synthetic materials, such as *eisengarn* (iron yarn) and cellophane. There was a move away from abstract pictorial subjectivity towards a repeatable industrial aesthetic, which culminated in a commercial relationship with the manufacturer, Berlin Polytex.

Under pressure from the Nazis, Stölzl was dismissed in 1931 for being left-wing. The student body was so distraught that an entire issue of *Bauhaus* magazine was dedicated to her. That same year, her German citizenship was revoked because she had married the Jewish Israeli architect, Arieh Sharon, leaving her legally a citizen of Palestine. She decamped to Switzerland and became a key member of the Swiss Werkbund. Until her retirement, in 1967, Stölzl continued to develop her textile practice within a string of organizations, including the Society of Swiss Women Painters, Sculptors and Craftswomen. She also returned to the tapestry weaving of her youth.

Stölzl's polychromatic tapestry wall-hangings created at the Bauhaus broke new creative ground with their Expressionistic exuberance and are emblematic of the trailblazing experimentalism that this remarkable institution represented. Today, her designs are in the permanent collections of museums around the world, including MoMA, New York, the Busch-Reisinger Museum in Cambridge Massachusetts and London's Victoria and Albert Museum.

MARIANNE STRAUB

MID-CENTURY · TEXTILES

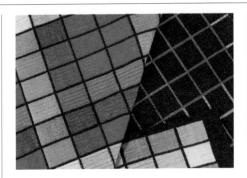

Swiss/British
b. Amriswil, Switzerland, 1909
d. Berlingen, Switzerland, 1994

One of Britain's leading commercial textile designers in the 1940s and 1950s, Marianne Straub was an influential advocate of democratic design who wanted to create 'things people could afford'.[1] Born in Switzerland, Straub spent four years of her childhood recuperating from tuberculosis in a hospital ward. During these periods of enforced immobility, she developed a strong memory for texture, colour and pattern. At 12 years old, she was given a narrow strip loom and began experimenting with different weaving techniques. She went on to study weaving at the Kunstgewerbeschule (School of Applied Arts), Zurich, from 1928 to 1931, under Heinz Otto Hürlimann, who had trained at the Bauhaus. After completing her studies, she returned to her home town to work as a technician in an industrialized cotton mill. She also set up a 16-shaft dobby loom at home and began hand-weaving domestic linens, such as bedspreads, curtains and cushion-covers. This balancing of craft and industry would, over the years, become a defining feature of her career and was prompted by her observation that 'to remain a hand-weaver did not seem satisfactory in this age of mass production'.[2]

Wanting to learn more about the technical and theoretical aspects of power weaving, Straub moved to Britain in 1932 to train at Bradford Technical College – as the two Swiss technical colleges offering courses in this field did not accept female students. She was only the third woman to study at Bradford, where she learnt 'textile maths, power spinning, weaving technology, cloth construction and raw materials'.[3] Because the college was in a wool town, emphasis was placed on woollen-cloth production and, as a result, Straub developed an enthusiasm for the

innumerable wool fibres available. She also became skilled in creating beautiful double-cloth weaves on power looms.

These interests led her to join Ethel Mairet's Gospels workshop in Ditchling, East Sussex, after completing her studies. It was renowned for its production of hand-woven textiles and there Straub learned hand-spinning techniques as well as how to concoct natural dyes. She also forged a lasting friendship with Mairet, which led to three trips abroad together and many return visits to Ditchling. Her association with Mairet also, undoubtedly, helped bolster Straub's credentials as an expert in her chosen craft. This led to her appointment as a design consultant to the Rural Industries Board, which looked after the interests of 72 wool mills in Wales. During her tenure (1934–37), she helped to revitalize the Welsh weaving industry through her in-depth technical knowledge and through her Modernist patterns, some of which were used as upholstery materials by the celebrated furniture designers Ernest Race and Gordon Russell.

In 1937, the Bolton-based textile company Helios appointed Straub its head designer. She later became the firm's managing director in 1946. After a takeover by Warner & Sons Ltd, in 1950, she moved her studio to Braintree, Essex, to be close to the Warner factory. She worked as a designer for Warner over the next two decades, becoming the company's representative in the Festival

Pattern Group, set up by the Council of Industrial Design for the 1951 Festival of Britain. Straub's famous rayon and wool Surrey textile (1951), with its eye-catching biomorphic patterning, was specifically designed for the group and inspired by an electron-density contour map of afwillite crystals created by the pioneering Irish crystallographer, Helen Megaw. This choice of motif reflected the burgeoning interest in molecular chemistry and crystallography in the postwar era. Likewise, Straub's Helmsley textile (1951) – also produced by Warner – was based on the atomic structure of nylon.

The renowned industrial design consultant, Misha Black, commissioned Straub to design textiles for ocean liners, including the *SS Oriana* (1960) as well as a moquette textile (*c.* 1965) for London Transport. Straub also designed fabrics for Heal's, taught at various design teaching institutions and published a book entitled *Hand Weaving and Cloth Design* (1977). Eventually, in recognition of her enormous contribution to the development of craft-inspired but industrially produced textiles, she was made a Royal Designer for Industry in 1972 and received a Sir Misha Black award in 1993.

Opposite: Reflections silk textile, 1981.

This page: Surrey furnishing textile for Warner & Sons (reissued by Humphries Weaving), 1951.

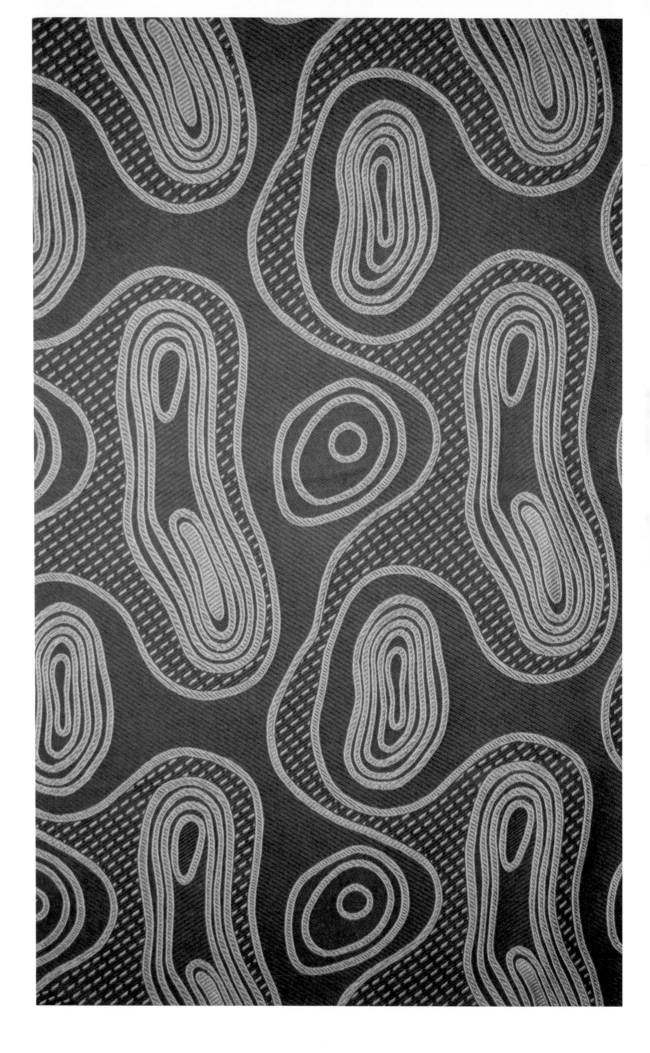

ANNE SWAINSON

American
b. Nevada, MI, USA, *c.* 1890
d. Chicago, IL, USA, 1955

Her name is largely unknown today, but Anne Swainson helped to fundamentally shape mainstream American design during the 1930s. A talented designer from a family of Swedish immigrants, she was also an influential design educator and corporate design manager. As the first woman in an executive position at the American retailing giant, Montgomery Ward & Co., she revolutionized the mail-order catalogue industry by replacing old-fashioned woodcuts with photographs of models wearing clothing and interacting with products. Her most influential success lay in employing strategic design thinking as a tool for commercial advantage.

Swainson took a bachelor's degree in education at the University of Missouri in 1909 and then a master's degree from Columbia University's Teachers College. In 1915 she was awarded an MA in household arts from the University of Chicago and, from 1915 to 1919, taught the applied arts at Illinois State University in Chicago. During this period, she also created exhibitions for Hull House, a socially progressive mission that promoted women's rights and trained them for male-dominated vocations.

In 1919 Swainson took up a teaching post at the University of California in Berkeley. There, she taught different aspects of design – textiles, ceramics, metalwork and jewellery – as well as a course specifically dedicated to the 'industrial arts'. She made several study trips to Europe that developed her expertise in designing for industry. In the French city of Lyons, she learnt about the economics of the textile industry and saw, firsthand, the negative effects industrialization could have on manufacturing standards.

Having moved to New York in 1923, she worked as a textile stylist for the Lord & Taylor department store. Her big career break came in 1930 when she was hired by the Chase Brass & Copper Company in Waterbury, Connecticut, as design director of its specialty sales department. Despite the economic woes of the interwar period, sales of Chase's stylish Moderne household items, designed by the likes of Russel Wright and Walter von Nessen, bucked the trend. It is thought that Swainson herself designed some of the unattributed wares in this line, specifically developed for more affordable home entertaining.

In 1932 Swainson was appointed head of Montgomery Ward's Bureau of Design. The mail-order company was suffering from declining sales because the Great Depression was beginning to bite and she was tasked with turning the company around. To this end, she instigated a redesign of the 40,000 items in the firm's product line,

to reflect the need for designs that were better suited to large-scale manufacture and that had a more modern appearance. In 1934 she described the Bureau's approach thus: 'First there is a thorough study of the needs, then rough preliminary sketches are developed; the merchandise division executives, and often the manufacturer, analyze these sketches with the design director, [and once approved] working drawings are made and turned over to the manufacturer.'[1]

Unusually, Swainson allowed her designers to patent their designs under their own names, rather than taking the credit herself. In 1940, the industrial-design consultant Harold Van Doren commended one of the firm's toasters for being 'inexpensive merchandise' that was 'simple [and] good'[2] – and that pretty much summed up the type of products that were created under Swainson's exacting design direction. During World War II, the manufacture of consumer products was restricted and so the Bureau's importance lessened and yet, in spite of the company's various management changes, Swainson remained its design director for 22 years. This was an astonishing accomplishment for a woman who had not even trained formally as a designer but who, nonetheless, understood the business of design far better than most of her male contemporaries.

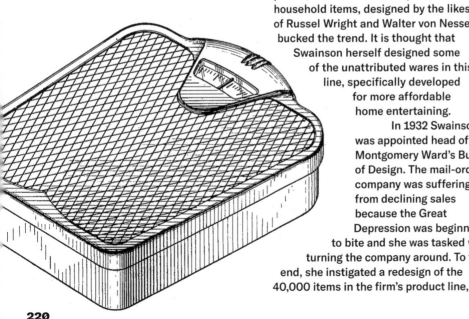

Opposite: Patent for bathroom scale, filed 1938.

This page, clockwise from top: Cover and interior of Montgomery Ward catalogue, Spring/Summer 1942; Roto-dial cabinet radio featured in Montgomery Ward catalogue, 1940; Airline radio featured in Montgomery Ward catalogue, 1940.

FAYE TOOGOOD

CONTEMPORARY · FASHION · FURNITURE

British
b. Rutland, UK, 1977

A self-confessed tinkerer, Faye Toogood is one of the most interesting present-day designer–artists, whose fascination with form-giving and materiality is expressed not only through the creation of eye-catching furniture, interiors, installations and sculptures, but also through the unisex workwear-inspired clothing that she designs with her younger sister, Erica. Working outside the industrial mainstream, Toogood sees her work as an 'antidote' to commercial mass production and seeks to produce designs that have an emotional resonance that are born out of 'pure self-expression and instinct'.[1]

She grew up in Rutland amid the verdant English countryside and, as a child, loved to make arrangements on the mantelpiece of her bedroom out of the 'sticks, stones and broken bones'[2] that she foraged compulsively in the nearby woods. In many ways, her current work is an evolution of this youthful fascination with collecting and constructing. For example, she groups her designed objects into collections of so-called Assemblages, which are themed according to the different materials and processes that have captivated her attention at that time. For each collection, she develops the individual designs themselves and, also, often conceives and constructs the spaces in which they can be exhibited, so that she is creating 'a single body of work with an intuitive and unified narrative'.[3]

Toogood's approach to design has a strong curatorial flavour, which is not so surprising given that, instead of coming from a traditional art and design vocational background, she studied art history at Bristol University, graduating in 1998. The following year, she began working for *World of Interiors* magazine, eventually becoming its decoration editor. In 2007 she left the magazine and the following year

established Studio Toogood in London. Initially, she worked as a stylist, designing exhibition stands for furniture designer Tom Dixon and in-store installations for clothing brand Comme des Garçons. But she soon branched out into designing objects, with a range of architectural hardware for Izé that cleverly took the realistic form of sticks, stones and bones. In 2010 she launched her inaugural furniture and lighting collection at the London Design Festival, which included sycamore versions of her Spade chair and Elements lamp. Initially, as Toogood happily admits with hindsight, she adopted quite a masculine, pared-down aesthetic, which she believes she subconsciously espoused in order to be taken seriously in an industry that was still largely male-dominated. The birth of her daughter, however, prompted her to adopt a more feminine and emotional approach to design – as she got 'fatter' with pregnancy, so the strict geometric angularity of her earlier furniture pieces was replaced with an altogether more curvaceous and voluptuous aesthetic.

The resulting Assemblage 4: Roly Poly collection was launched in Milan, in 2014, and comprised two chairs, a daybed and a table, developed using clay maquettes that were then translated into soft-toned white, cream and earth-coloured fibreglass. The chairs, with their low backs and chunky cylindrical legs, recall the forms of age-old African tribal stools, giving them a highly engaging new–old hybrid quality.

In 2015 Toogood designed 'The Cloakroom', a two-part installation at the Victoria and Albert Museum for the London Design Festival, which featured 150 coats each with sewn-in instructions of where to find a series of sculptural garments she had created.[4] This convergence of art and design is typical of Toogood's multi-faceted approach for, although she enjoys the creative freedom of art, she also revels in the functional constraints imposed by design. Today, her designs can be found in permanent museum collections around the world, while her fashion work goes from strength to strength.

This page, left: Roly-Poly chair, 2014; above; Spade chair, 2010.

Opposite: The Beekeeper unisex coat, 2014 (co-created with Erica Toogood).

VIVIANNA TORUN BÜLOW-HÜBE

1950S–1970S · JEWELLERY

Swedish
b. Malmö, Sweden, 1927
d. Copenhagen, Denmark, 2004

A legendary free spirit, Torun Bülow-Hube was one of the most influential jewellery designers of the twentieth century. Forging a new artistic sensibility within her chosen field, she was the first female silversmith to enjoy widespread international recognition. Throughout her career she created numerous pieces that are now considered icons of Modern Scandinavian design – from her distinctive Vivianna Bangle watch (1962) to her twisting and encircling Mobius brooch (1968).

'Torun', as she was always professionally known, grew up in a family with a strong artistic background, especially on her mother's side, with her maternal grandfather and grandmother being a painter and a singer respectively. Her mother, who was a sculptor, had grown up in an artist's colony on the island of Romanö, and it was here that Torun spent her childhood summers. As a teenager, Torun began designing and making jewellery and then later studied at the Konstfack (University College of Arts, Crafts and Design) in Stockholm under Baron Erik Fleming, the court silversmith to the King of Sweden. After graduating in 1945, she had a daughter the following year with a Danish journalist and they subsequently got married, but the union was short-lived. Around this time, she also set up her own workshop and had her first solo exhibition. In 1948 she travelled to Paris and Cannes, where she famously met Pablo Picasso on a beach while searching for pebbles to include in her 'anti-status jewellery' designs, which were meant to be worn casually.

In 1951 Torun married her second husband, the French architect Jean-Pierre Serbonnet, with whom she had a son. They divorced in 1956, and that same year

she moved to Biot in southern France with her third husband, the African-American painter Walter Coleman, presumably to escape the open racism that they encountered in Sweden. She established another studio there and in 1958 had a solo exhibition at the Picasso Museum in Antibes. She subsequently designed jewellery for many famous celebrities, including the singer Billie Holiday and the actresses Ingrid Bergman and Brigitte Bardot.

Torun and Coleman had two children together, but divorced in 1965. It was around this time, that she became involved with the Subud Brotherhood, a Sufism-related mystic fellowship with Indonesian origins. In 1967 she adopted the Subud name, 'Vivianna', and moved to Wolfsburg in Germany, where she lived in the spiritual group's communal residence for a while. That same year, Torun won the Lunning Prize for her game-changing jewellery designs, which broke new ground both functionally and aesthetically by having a distinctive easy-to-wear casual elegance that was the very antithesis of high jewellery. Her designs were also distinguished by a timeless quality for as she once noted, 'A piece of jewellery should be a symbol of love. It should enhance and move with the body so that it blends with you. It must not overwhelm, but enhance you. This is why it must be timeless. It shouldn't matter if you are 17 or 87 years old.'[1]

In 1967 Torun began working as a designer for Georg Jensen, eventually becoming the firm's most high-profile contemporary designer. This fruitful collaboration resulted in numerous understated yet beautifully sculptural jewellery pieces that had an innate wearability. It is testament to Torun's form-giving talents that many of these designs remain in production some fifty years after they were introduced, and enjoy as much popularity today as they ever did.

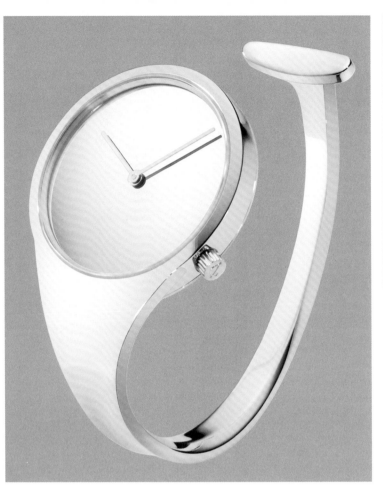

Opposite: Silver necklace with amber-coloured glass and stone pendants, c. 1955–56.

This page, clockwise from above left: Vivianna Bangle watch for Georg Jensen, 1962; Torun wearing a necklace and earrings of her own design, 1956; Mobius brooch for Georg Jensen, 1968.

NYNKE TYNAGEL

CONTEMPORARY · FURNITURE · LIGHTING · PRODUCT

Dutch/Belgian
b. Bergeijk, The Netherlands, 1977

Nynke Tynagel is a co-founding partner of Studio Job, which is internationally renowned for its provocative design-art pieces that push the boundaries of taste.

Although Tynagel grew up in a small village in the Southern Netherlands, she 'was brought up with design ... in a modernist environment'.[1] In fact, both her parents had studied design at the nearby Design Academy Eindhoven, and so from an early age she was aware of the progressive Dutch design scene.

After high school, she followed in her parents' footsteps studying at the Academy under the graphic designer Anthon Beeke. In 1996, while in a bar nearby to the school, she met Belgian-born Job Smeet who was also studying at the Academy. They started a relationship, which lasted twenty years romantically and professionally continues to this day. As Hannah Martin in *Architectural Digest* later insightfully noted, Tynagel 'turned out to be the perfect yin to Smeet's wily, enfant-terrible yang.'[2] In 1998 Smeet graduated and set up Studio Job and two years later, Tynagel, after graduating herself, became a full partner in this Antwerp-based practice. In many ways Studio Job's subsequent work represented the coming together of thought-provoking New Dutch Design with Belgian surrealistic eccentricity. Culturally savvy and aesthetically outré, both Studio Job's 2D and 3D work has a very distinctive look that is entirely attributable to Tynagel's strong graphic input.

In 2006 she and Smeet co-designed the Perished Collection, which comprises various furniture pieces executed in macassar ebony and hand-inlaid, with skeletal animal motifs rendered in bird's eye maple. This remarkable collection, which has a consciously Neo-Gothic overtone, was perfectly pitched towards the emerging design–art market of the mid-2000s. It also firmly established the couple's reputation as a significant post-Postmodern force within the globalized design world. Interested in exploring culture – both high and low – through the medium of design, rather than solving functional needs as a primary aim, many of Studio Job's 'New Gothic' pieces are made as one-offs and limited editions in their own atelier by a small team of skilled craftspeople and production specialists and then sold through a handful of selected galleries. That said, the duo have also designed more accessibly priced pieces for the likes of Moooi and Seletti.

One of the most impressive things about Tynagel is her ability to work across a broad range of design disciplines, from wallpaper, textiles, stained glass, furniture, lighting and ceramics to interiors, installations, branding and graphics. And while she is best known for her unique and limited edition pieces, she has also designed a Dutch postage stamp of which forty million examples have been printed. She similarly runs the gamut of materials and techniques, from the high-tech to the age-old, to produce designs with Smeet that are both sculptural and conceptual. Referencing playfully both high art and popular culture, Tynagel's work blurs subversively the traditional boundaries between fine art, graphics and product design, and is ultimately a potent form of transgressive expression. As she notes, 'Every expression is a statement' – and there are not many design statements as bold as those produced by Studio Job.

PATRICIA URQUIOLA

Spanish/Italian
b. Oviedo, Spain, 1961

Patricia Urquiola initially studied architecture at the Universidad Politécnica de Madrid (Technical University of Madrid), but decided to continue her studies in Italy at the renowned Politenico di Milano, graduating in 1989. Here, she was taught by one of the most creative Italian designers of all time, Achille Castiglioni. He became her mentor and oversaw her final dissertation, and later she became an assistant lecturer to him and to Eugenio Bettinelli, in Milan and Paris. In 1990 she met the Italian entrepreneur and furniture-company founder Maddalena de Padova, who hired her to head up her eponymous firm's

new product-development office, where Urquiola worked alongside another maestro of Italian design, Vico Magistretti. She later moved on to become head of the Lissoni Associati design group in 1996, and in this capacity developed designs for, among others, Alessi, Boffi, Cappellini, Cassina and Kartell.

At the suggestion of a friend, she made contact with Patrizia Moroso, art director of the Moroso family furniture company, as she had a prototype that she had been intending to show to another furniture company. They instantly established a rapport that would, over the coming years, result in a host of interesting and innovative seating solutions. When she opened her own architecture and design office in 2001, Urquiola already had an impressive track record, having worked previously with some of Italy's most progressive furniture manufacturing companies. It was, however, her early designs for Moroso, namely Antibodi (2006) and Tropicalia (2008) that really elevated her profile as a major creative force within the world of contemporary design. Sharing the same stainless-steel frames, these two collections epitomized the new craft sensibility that was emerging in product design, while also conveying an unashamedly feminine aesthetic. Urquiola would later note 'Moroso gave

me credibility',[1] and, certainly, it is a tribute to Patrizia Moroso's cultural awareness that she was prepared to take the commercial risk of putting such overtly female-centric designs into production.

Urquiola created the transparent polycarbonate Frilly chair (2008) for Kartell, which again expressed a lightness and charm, with its rippling wave-like surfaces and soft curves. She followed this with her Comback chair (2013) for Kartell, which cleverly reimagined the historic Windsor chair in an injection-moulded technopolymer. As one of the very few women to enjoy design renown at an international level, Urquiola has designed numerous different types of products for an impressive roster of manufacturers – from ceramics for Rosenthal and metalware for Georg Jensen, to textiles for Maharam and lighting for Flos – yet it is furniture that is still her standout specialism. She has also worked extensively as an interior architect designing hotels, showrooms, boutiques, restaurants and a host of exhibition installations.

In 2015 Urquiola was appointed art director of Cassina. Her first collection for the company included two of her own pieces, the Gender chair and the Beam sofa, alongside designs by Konstantin Grcic, Ora Ïto and Philippe Starck, which reflects a sensitive evolution and exploration of the company's cultural heritage. Harnessing a distinctly Spanish creative brio with an elegant Italian architectonic formalism, Urquiola's soft-edged designs possess a deeply satisfying functional and aesthetic logic.

Opposite: Tropicalia
daybed for Moroso, 2008.

This page, right: Antibodi
chair for Moroso, 2006;
below: Liquefy table for
Glas Italia, 2017.

MIMI VANDERMOLEN

1970S–1990S • AUTOMOTIVE

Dutch/American
b. Geleen, The Netherlands, 1946

Hailed as the genius behind Ford's 'rounded edge revolution', Mimi Vandermolen is an automotive designer who pioneered an ergonomic approach to car design. One of very few female design managers in the industry, she introduced a more female-focused outlook to Ford's design team, to enhance the driving experience of women through better design.

Born in Holland, Vandermolen was fascinated by cars even as a small child. In 1951 she moved to Toronto with her parents, seeking a new life. As she recalls, 'There is a photograph of the three of us in a little flat in Toronto with no furniture, the clothes on our back, a map of Toronto, and [our last] dollar bill!'[1] Her parents, however, both found work and she later credited her mother with making her realise it was 'okay for a woman to work'.[2] She studied at Ontario College of Art and Design in Toronto and, during her multidisciplinary first year, she so excelled in product design that her professors advised her to specialize in industrial design – one of the first women to do so. She worked on a range of products, from snow-blowers and screwdrivers to gas heaters and furniture, and, in her final year, was taught rendering techniques by Claude Gisman, a former Ford employee.

It was Gisman who introduced her to someone at Ford's design centre and she subsequently met the famed Ford car designer, John Najjar. He had just established the company's industrial-design group and Vandermolen started as a trainee. She also attended evening classes in automotive design at the Center for Creative Studies in Detroit, paid for by Ford, but, for a while, was the only female designer working at Ford's design centre. The 'studios' were male bastions, yet she never felt intimidated by their macho culture and, in due course, moved from

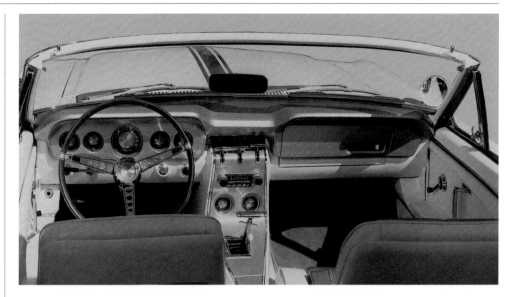

'products' to proper automotive design. She initially designed car interiors, including instrument panels and radios, before advancing to exteriors.

Having been promoted to senior designer level, she joined the Ford/Mercury studio and worked on the redesign of the 1975 Ford Granada. After a brief spell at Chrysler, she returned to Ford in 1978. She was quickly promoted to design specialist and began working with 'Team Taurus' on Ford's groundbreaking, soft-styled family sedan. Vandermolen approached the design of its interior ergonomically, introducing user-friendly innovations, including tactile, raised-bump controls and easy-to-use rotary dials for climate control. She replaced the traditional straight dashboard with a contoured one with centralized controls, which the driver could reach more safely. She and her team also painstakingly researched and developed an ergonomic seat shape to provide better lumbar support. At its launch, Ford described the Taurus as a 'rounded edge revolution', much of which can be credited to Vandermolen. More importantly, the American public loved this user-friendly

model and it soon became the country's bestselling car.

In 1987 Vandermolen was appointed design executive for small-car exteriors at Ford's North American design centre – a female-first in the automotive industry. In the Ford Probe (1993) she was able to introduce female-focused improvements, including a lighter weight trunk door and a lower front end for better visibility. She famously insisted that her male colleagues wear fake fingernails, resulting in, among other things, easily operated knobs and door handles. She also threatened to make them wear skirts unless they designed a model that was more practical for women to get in and out of. But perhaps even more important than the host of automotive design improvements instigated by Vandermolen was her position as a role model – her remarkable career demonstrating that 'glass ceilings' can be smashed, even in the most male-dominated areas of design.

Opposite: Interior for Ford
Mustang II concept car,
1963.

This page, from top to
bottom: Ford Probe, 1993;
Ford Probe V scale model,
1987; Ford Taurus LX
sedan/ saloon, 1986.

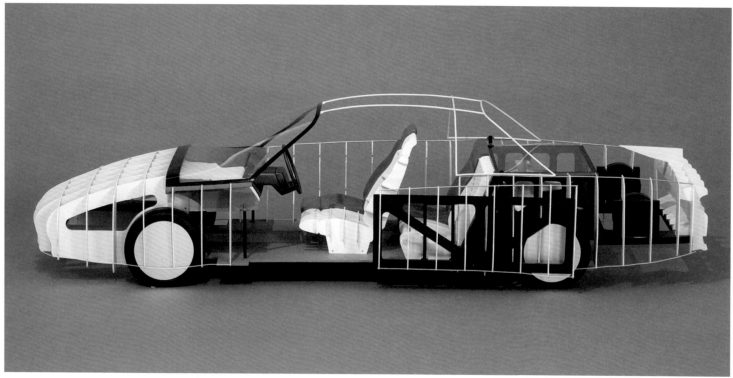

LELLA VIGNELLI

1960S–1990S · GRAPHICS · FURNITURE · PRODUCT

Italian/American
b. Udine, Italy, 1934
d. New York, USA, 2016

Lella Vignelli designed some of the most famous American corporate-identity programmes of the 1960s, 1970s and 1980s. She was also responsible for designing stylish and clever packaging for, among others, Barneys, Bloomingdale's, Saks Fifth Avenue and IBM. With her lifelong collaborator and husband, Massimo Vignelli, she introduced an elegant Italian Rationalist language of design to America's corporate visual-communications landscape. She also designed transportation graphics in the same stylistic vein, as well as pieces of furniture for Knoll and homewares for Heller.

For four decades, the Vignellis reigned supreme as New York's pre-eminent design power couple, giving the city its distinctive eye-catching graphic identity, including an iconic map in 1972 for the subway system. For them, graphic design was quite simply the 'organization of information' and they steered clear of more illustrative and narrative forms of visual communication in favour of bold

typographic clarity. Vignelli's work always possessed an almost architectonic sensibility that was quintessentially northern Italian in style, which is perhaps not surprising given she was born into a well-known family of Italian architects. Her father, Provino Valle, having established his own Udine-based practice in the 1920s, designed buildings in the Neoclassicizing Novecento style and her brothers, Gino and Nani, established their own highly respected partnership, Studio Architetti Valle, also in Udine. Following in her brothers' footsteps, Vignelli studied architecture at the Università di Architettura in Venice. In 1957 she met fellow student Massimo Vignelli at an architectural conference, and they married later that same year.

In 1958 the couple moved to the United States, as Vignelli had secured a fellowship to train at the Massachusetts Institute of Technology School of Architecture. Meanwhile, Massimo held a teaching post at the nearby Illinois Institute of Technology. After completing her studies, she worked in the interior design department of the prestigious Chicago-based architecture practice, Skidmore, Owings &

Merrill, giving her invaluable insight into designing for the American corporate world.

The couple struck out on their own in 1960 and established the Vignelli Office for Design and Architecture in Milan. Five years later, Massimo co-founded, with five other partners, the Unimark International design agency, with Vignelli heading up its interior design division. The following year, the couple moved back to New York to set up a sister branch of this pioneering design consultancy, specializing mainly in corporate identity work. Over the following decades, they worked together closely on countless projects, their personal and professional lives always completely intertwined. Together, they developed a distinctive, visually powerful design vocabulary that played with the ideas of clarity and ambiguity, and also always possessed an intellectual elegance. Whether it was a poster, a piece of furniture or a household product, their work always exhibited a careful balancing of form and function. For instance, their melamine tableware for Heller not only had a stylish architectonic feel but was also highly practical in that it stacked efficiently and was lightweight yet durable. As Massimo explained, 'Throughout our creative lives we have sifted through everything to select what we thought best. We sifted through materials to find those for which we have the closest affinity. We sifted through colors, textures, typefaces, images, and gradually we built a vocabulary of materials and experiences that enable us to express our solutions to given problems – our interpretations of reality.'[1]

It was Vignelli's creative intuition and formidable design-critiquing skills that provided their collaborations with the necessary 'structural strength',[2] as Massimo put it. Together, this talented duo of equals produced a remarkable body of work that quite simply transformed the identity of corporate America by giving it a contemporary Modernity that was syntactically appropriate and timelessly cool.

Opposite, from far left: Hellerware mugs for Heller Inc., 1964 (co-designed with Massimo Vignelli); Matchbox designed for the Palio restaurant in New York, 1985.

This page, from top to bottom: Poster for Knoll International, 1967 (co-designed with Massimo Vignelli); Knoll Textiles Collection 1 sample kit, c. 1967.

NANDA VIGO

1960S–1970S · LIGHTING · FURNITURE · INTERIORS

Italian
b. Milan, Italy, 1936

Nanda Vigo is a design virtuoso who skilfully plays with light and space, and is an influential pioneer of design–art. During the 1960s and 1970s her bold architectonic lighting designs introduced a new level of artistic sophistication. Her contemporaneous furniture and interior schemes, likewise, possessed a rare aesthetic refinement that sought to blur the boundaries between art and design. Vigo's work embodies the Milanese design sensibility – restrained yet stylish rationalism, with a twist of theatricality. From childhood, she possessed a keen love of the arts. It was, however, her early encounters with the buildings of Giuseppe Terragni that most inspired her, thanks to, as she puts it, their 'subtle employment of natural light'.[1]

Vigo studied architecture at the Swiss École Polytechnique (Federal Institute of Technology) in Lausanne, Switzerland, before working as an intern in San Francisco. In 1959 she returned

to Milan, opened her own studio and began visiting the studio of painter Lucio Fontana. She became friendly with the artist–founders of the Azimut Gallery in Milan – including Piero Manzoni, Enrico Castellani and Vincenzo Agnetti – and also met members of the radical Zero art group in Germany, Holland and France, who pioneered a form of kinetic art based on light and motion. These early associations enabled Vigo to exhibit her work in over 400 solo and group shows throughout Europe during her long and illustrious career.

In 1959 she began work on the design of the Zero House, or Casa Pellegrini, a completely white living space with walls adorned with artworks by Fontana and Castellani. This remarkable, forward-looking project was completed in 1962 and Vigo subsequently participated in 13 Zero exhibitions, curating the 'Zero Avant-garde' exhibition for Fontana in 1965. With Fontana, she created the Utopie installation for the 1964 Milan Triennale, which featured in *Domus* magazine. Her credibility established, Vigo went on to collaborate with the architect Giò Ponti on the Casa sotto una Foglia (1965–68), near Vicenza. The house was entirely white – inside and out – with Vigo responsible for its interior design. Covering the floors and walls with white ceramic tiles, she created built-in 'carpeted reliefs' upholstered in fake fur as an alternative to traditional seating. Neon-lit plastic tubes ran continuously along the ceiling perimeters of each room and Vigo enhanced the airy quality by incorporating glazed built-in cupboards, room-dividing glass screens and floor-to-ceiling mirrors.

In addition to interiors and light-art installations, Vigo organized the first performance-art–architecture 'happening'

to take place in Milan's Triennale building, in 1973. She also developed a series of lights for Arredoluce made of chrome-plated metal with a sculptural minimalist aesthetic, notably the Linea (1969), the Manhattan (1972) and the arching Golden Gate (1970) floor lamps – the latter receiving the New York Award for Industrial Design in 1974. She created tables, chairs, rugs and other household items with a space-age aesthetic, her Due Più chair (1971) for Conconi had a large-gauge tubular metal frame onto which two shaggy furred rollers were attached, providing a comfortable seat and backrest through minimal means.

It is, however, the Casa Museo (1971–73) – in which the artist and collector Remo Brindisi housed his collection of 1,800 contemporary artworks – that is Vigo's masterwork. Described by *Domus* as a 'dwelling museum', this exhibition-cum-living-space reflected Vigo's desire for *ambienti* (environments) that seamlessly blended design with architecture, and playfully explored the inter-relationship between space and light. Throughout her unconventional, decades-spanning career, Vigo has championed the convergence of art, design, architecture and environments, for she believes a creative, problem-solving approach 'unbounded by any disciplinary limits' provides the most fertile ground for 'spiritual and almost initiatory research'.[2] Her work is enduringly fascinating because it is motivated by philosophical thinking rather than any prescriptive doctrine.

Opposite: Geometral table light for Arredoluce, 1970.

This page, from top: Casa sotto una Foglia in Malo, near Vicenza, 1965–68; Golden Gate floor light for Arredoluce, 1970; Due Più chairs for Conconi, 1971.

VIVIENNE WESTWOOD

1980S–CONTEMPORARY · FASHION

British
b. Tintwistle, UK, 1941

Vivienne Westwood, England's most famed fashion radical, came from an unassuming background. She was born in a small Derbyshire town, where her father was a cobbler and her mother a cotton-mill worker. As a teenager she moved south with her family to Harrow, where she commenced and then quit a course in silversmithing. Without any hope of pursuing a career in the arts, she took up factory work to support herself while she did teacher training. In the early 1960s she married Derek Westwood with whom she had her first child, Benjamin.

An encounter with an idealistic art student named Malcolm McLaren in 1962 wrested the young Westwood from a life marked by working-class ordinariness. Leaving Derek, she moved to south London with McLaren, taking up residence in a council flat. In 1967 she had her second child, Joseph. She continued to teach in London, while becoming embedded in London's radical art and design scene and producing increasingly radical clothing, driven by concepts she developed with McLaren. In 1971 the pair opened a shop in the World's End area of Kings Road, Chelsea. The store was renamed several times during the following decade – being variously known as Let it Rock, Too Fast to Live Too Young to Die, Sex, Seditionaries and, finally, Worlds End.

The clothing on sale expressed the dissonant, aggressive nihilism that could be felt in the air as the Flower Power era reached its end. The pair's first big break came in around 1974 when McLaren became the impresario-like manager of punk progenitors, the Sex Pistols. The harsh, atonal brutality of their music created a singular impression when combined with Westwood's deconstructed, raggedly collaged clothing. While the Pistols' sound revolved around as few as three distorted chords, their outfits drew from a treasure-trove of visual references – BDSM leather pinned to Teddy Boy jackets to Celtic tartan. Given the ubiquity of her influence, it is natural that we now see these combinations as familiar tropes but, in its time, the look was positively alien.

Inherently self-destructive, punk's role at the cutting edge of fashion was short-lived. But Westwood was never wedded to a fixed style and, by the late 1970s, was experimenting with a more refined, historical approach. By irreverently mixing heritage fashion signifiers with avant-garde garment-craft, her designs gave the beguiling impression of existing outside history – perfectly appropriate for the Postmodern cultural zeitgeist of the 1980s. The Pirate collection of 1981 was a joyous 'dressing-up box' exploration of romantic silhouettes dating back to the seventeenth century. This dandyish range of outfits, intercut by graphic African-esque prints, inspired a wave of 'New Romantic' looks in popular culture.

Follow-on collections, including Nostalgia of Mud (often referred to as the Buffalo Girls collection, after being worn in the promo video for a catchy hip-hop single released by McLaren and the rap group The World's Famous Supreme Team in 1982), saw Westwood's sartorial imagination cast even further back into an earth-tone primitive past, referencing native North and South American costumes. Likewise, the interior of her short-lived Nostalgia of Mud store in St Christopher's Place, London, which operated from 1982 to 1983, channelled an earthy primal quality, which was the antithesis of the mainstream dayglo fashion vibe. In 1982 she released her Witches collection, a mysterious hybridization of occult costume and the graffiti patterns of American artist Keith Haring, which reflected McLaren's fascination with hip-hop culture and Westwood's love of the archaic. It was the pair's last collection together.

Without McLaren, Westwood's silhouettes softened. Collections such as Mini-Crini (1985), Harris Tweed (1987) and Time Machine (1988) were all lovingly eccentric homages to aspects of historical European costume and tailoring. Through these, she formed a critical symbiosis with the cultural establishment – equal parts rebellious outsider and national treasure.

The 1990s and 2000s saw huge commercial expansion of the Westwood brand, though never at the expense of critical success. Her range expanded to encompass accessories, knitwear and fragrances. She was awarded an OBE in 1992 and was further honoured with a damehood in 2006, formally cementing her role in British public life. Throughout this time, Westwood undertook roles as a spokeswoman for political and environmental causes, leveraging her celebrity status for social good. In order to fully focus on this, she stepped back from designing her main Gold Label line in 2017, handing the reins to her husband, Andreas Kronthaler, who has, under her watchful eye, successfully channelled her outré rebelliousness.

Opposite, top: Punched leather 'mock croc' platform shoes with blue ribbon laces, Autumn/Winter 1993–94 collection; bottom: Malcolm MacLaren and members of The World's Famous Supreme Team wearing items from the Buffalo Girls collection, 1983.

This page, left: Model outside the Worlds End shop, 1970s; below: Pirate ensemble, Autumn/Winter 1981–82 (co-created with McLaren).

YIQING YIN

Chinese
b. Beijing, China, 1985

Yiqing Yin is notable for being the first Chinese fashion designer to be accepted into the prestigious Parisian haute-couture establishment. She was born in Beijing to antique-dealer parents, the family moving often when she was young – most notably to Paris. Exposure to that city and her parents' trade in period artefacts furnished Yin with a wealth of visual references for use in later life.

She attended the renowned École Nationale Supérieure des Arts Décoratifs (National School of Decorative Arts) in Paris, initially training as a sculptor, but soon found she worked best with cloth and other textiles. Initially reluctant to make the huge leap into fashion design, Yin was convinced by a show from the experimental Japanese tailor, Yohji Yamamoto, that it was a risk worth taking. She set about creating elaborate experiments from the draping, pleating and sculptural form-giving of cloth.

Upon graduation, Yin undertook an internship at Cacharel, a ready-to-wear brand well known for its playfully feminine look. The world of standardized prêt-à-porter fashions, however, did not suit her particular vision, so, at the first opportunity, she developed an independent design practice. In the atelier culture of Paris, her imagination could blossom and she applied infinite care and creative nuance to every garment she produced. Redolent of the exquisite pleats found in Madame Grès's designs of decades earlier, Yin created fluid, dreamlike dresses that enveloped their wearers in a fluid fantasy of material. This has since become a signature of her work.

Her garments acknowledge the great tradition of Parisian decorative arts, formally referencing Art Nouveau and the organic forms of the early, floriated phase of Art Deco. In the same gown, one might find a network of threads, hung to resemble blood vessels, alongside furrowed silk reminiscent of mushroom-cap gills. These references are often oblique, dissolving into one another with the complex symmetry of a Rorschach ink-blot test. Her silhouettes are uniquely sensitive to the wearer's form, yet highly sculptural at the same time.

Her remarkable level of artistic maturity was validated by the fashion establishment in 2009, when Yin won the prestigious Grand Prix de la Création at the youthful age of 24. The following year, she showed her Exile collection at the Hyères International Festival, earning her the ANDAM prize. And, just a year later, she was given a time slot on the Paris haute-couture calendar by the Chambre Syndicale de la Haute Couture, the commission that determines which fashion houses deserve haute-couture status. In France, the very term 'haute couture' has legal status, so winning this mark of approval was highly prestigious. In 2013 Yin took a detour back into prêt-à-porter, as head of the ready-to-wear collections

of Leonard, but she left this position within two years to refocus on her own collections.

Despite her industriousness within the fashion world, Yin has also retained strong ties to the world of fine art and, specifically, sculpture. Her *In-Between* blood vessel work (2013) was shown at the Venice Biennale, and she has incorporated the gossamer, illuminated sculptures of contemporary artist, Bastien Carré, into her garments. She has also directed costume productions for both the Opera di Firenze (2014) and the New York City Ballet at Cartier Fifth Avenue (2016).

In 2018 Yin became creative director of the relaunched House of Poiret. The original 'King of Fashion', Paul Poiret was a giant of early-twentieth-century fashion, whose grand project to modernize French couture still looms large in the psyche of the sartorial establishment. That Yin has been entrusted to steward his remarkable legacy speaks volumes about the high regard in which she is held by those at the very apex of the fashion industry.

Opposite: Dress
from Spring of Nuwa
collection, Autumn/
Winter, 2012.

This page and overleaf
left: Dresses from Exil
collection, Spring/
Summer, 2011.

Overleaf right: Dress
from Spring of Nuwa
collection, Autumn/
Winter, 2012.

EVA ZEISEL

MODERNISM/MID-CENTURY • CERAMICS

Hungarian/American
b. Budapest, Hungary, 1906
d. Clarkstown, NY, USA, 2011

A doyenne of American design, Eva Zeisel always modestly described herself as a 'maker of useful things'. Her beautiful homeware designs certainly had an innate practicality, but what set them apart was their distinctive gracefulness. Her use of gestural fluid lines and abstracted organic forms gave her soft-edged designs a sculptural, almost sensual, quality.

From a wealthy and intellectual Hungarian-Jewish family, Zeisel spent her childhood in Budapest and Vienna – both epicentres of the New Art Movement. Drawn to the fine arts, at the age of 17 she studied painting at the Hungarian Magyar Művészeti Akadémia (Royal Academy of Fine Arts) in Budapest. She later undertook an apprenticeship with the master potter Jakob Karapancsik with a view to forging a more practical career, which would enable her to support her painting financially. The in-depth training she obtained was invaluable and, after gaining her journeyman certificate, she became a designer for the Kipester-Granit ceramics factory in Budapest, developing prototypes for industrial production. Having moved to Germany, she worked for the Hans Kunst Keramik company in Hamburg (1927–28) and for Majolika-Manufaktur in

Schramberg (1928–30), where she designed Constructivist-style wares with simple geometric forms and bold polychromatic decoration. In Berlin, from 1930, she worked as a freelance designer, out of her own studio, for Christian Carstenskommandit Gesellschaft – then the second largest ceramics manufactory in Germany. Like other Modernists working in Germany, Zeisel was interested in creating affordable, space-saving homewares. As she remarked in an article in the journal *Die Schaulade* in 1932, 'When designing in the modern style, one must ask what the practical use of the object will be!'[1]

That same year, she moved to Soviet Russia, where she became a designer for the state-run Lomonosov and Dulevo porcelain factories. She was appointed artistic director of the Russian Republic's porcelain industry in 1935, but the following year was imprisoned for 16 months after being falsely accused of conspiring in an assassination plot against Stalin. After her release, she returned to Budapest and married the sociologist Hans Zeisel and together they moved to the United States in 1938 to escape the Nazi occupation.

Once settled, Eva resumed her career as a ceramicist, designing practical

Modernist tableware for manufacturers including Stratoware and Bay Ridge Specialty Company. Initially, she took her inspiration from traditional Chinese ceramics, but became increasingly influenced by the new organic language of design that was being pioneered by the likes of Russel Wright, Isamu Noguchi and Charles and Ray Eames. She was also inspired by the free-form artworks of contemporary artists, such as Jean Arp and Joan Miró.

In 1942, New York's Museum of Modern Art and Castle China commissioned Zeisel to design an undecorated white dinner service, which was put into mass-production. Its success resulted in her being given the first ever one-woman exhibition at MoMA in 1946. The set, known as the Museum Service, also attracted the attention of Red Wing Potteries, for whom she later created her biomorphic Town and Country line (1947), which included her embracing salt and peppershakers, which thanks to their resemblance to Al Capp's cartoon character are often referred as 'schmoos'. She also designed her popular Tomorrow's Classic (1949–50) and Century (1955) dinnerware ranges for the Hall China Company. During the 1960s and 1970s, however, she took a career break in order to focus on various American history projects but returned to design in the 1980s and worked until she was 100 years old, creating new designs often based on her earlier wares for a new generation of manufacturers.

This page, left: Town and Country salt and pepper shakers for Red Wing Potteries, 1947; above: Geometric-patterned plate for Majolika-Manufaktur in Schramberg, Germany, c. 1928–30.

Opposite: Tomorrow's Classic creut set for Hallcraft/Hall China Company, 1949–50.

NIKA ZUPANC

CONTEMPORARY · FURNITURE · LIGHTING · PRODUCT

Slovenian
b. Ljubljana, Yugoslavia
(now Slovenia), 1974

The Slovenian designer Nika Zupanc is not afraid of playing with the idea of femininity in her work, ironically referencing colours and forms that are symbolically associated with the so-called 'fairer sex'. She positively relishes subverting feminine design clichés – Barbie pink, rose prints, glittery gold glamour, bows and frills – into ironic neo-Postmodern design statements. And she is not the slightest bit interested in adopting a masculine stance when it comes to design, instead delighting in bringing an overt female sensibility to the design of her furniture and lighting. She also refutes the Modernist mantra 'form follows function', preferring instead philosopher Ludwig Wittgenstein's dictum, 'meaning is use'. She incorporates into her work symbols that are emotionally connective: her ultra-feminine Ribbon chair (2016), for instance, with its bow-shaped back, alludes to gifting or a special occasion.

Raised in former Yugoslavia, Zupanc studied industrial design at the Academy of Fine Arts and Design, Ljubljana, under Saša Mächtig. She graduated with distinction in 2000 and, the following year, her thesis was awarded the prestigious Prešeren Award for Students – the highest accolade that can be given to any young Slovenian artist. After graduating, Zupanc began working as an independent designer and, in 2005, won the British Council's International Young Design Entrepreneur of the Year award for Slovenia. This helped to establish her professional design credentials.

In 2008 she broke onto the global design stage with her Lolita table lamp, which was launched by Moooi at the Milan Furniture Fair. Two years later, Moooi put her neo-retro 5 O'Clock table and chair into production. These were initially inspired by a late-afternoon visit the previous year to Tito's Teahouse at the Belvedere Pavilion on

Lake Bled. As Zupanc recalls, 'This place is able to take you back to the fragile times of forgotten values ... it was there when I first thought I just had to design a chair ... One that would radiate the beauty and the pain of [the] irreversibility of time.'[1] To do this, she chose the type of motif you would expect to find on a traditional English porcelain tea service, a pattern that was the antithesis of Modernist good form with decidedly nostalgic anti-Modernist connotations. But, as she explains, 'When something is forbidden, it becomes even more intriguing. For me, at least.'[2] The simple wooden frames of the 5 O'Clock pieces contrast markedly with the floral motif and are meant to allude to Japan and its culture of tea ceremonies.

Other notable seating designs include her Tailored Chair (2009) for Moroso, which references the form of a tailor's dummy, and her Golden Chair (2013) for Moooi that takes an archetypal low-brow 1950s-retro seating form and turns

it into a shimmering golden artefact. In addition to her work for various manufacturers, Zupanc also designs and self-produces an eponymous collection under the telling by-line 'La Femme et la Maison'.

It is her self-confessed girly rebelliousness that sets Zupanc's designs apart and challenges what she calls 'the boys' club' of design.[3] She takes hackneyed feminine symbols – for example, a bunch of cherries, a daisy form, a heart shape – and playfully incorporates them into functional design solutions, stylishly repositioning these visual clichés. Other designs of hers unashamedly hark back to more glamorous times, when more feminine-centric interiors were *de rigueur*. Through her work, she demonstrates that purist, simplified tastes are not a given and that, within the broad and varied landscape of contemporary design, there is just as much room for the electic and sensual as the functional.

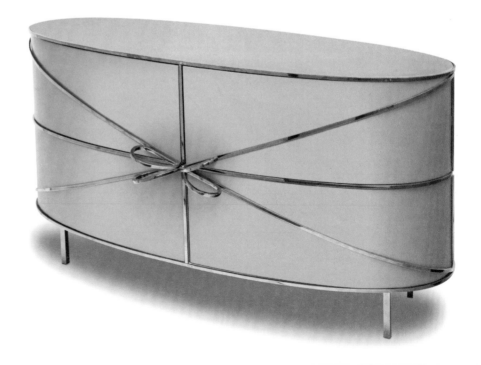

Opposite, top: Black Cherry light for Qeeboo, 2013; bottom: 88 Secrets sideboard for Scarlet Splendour, 2017.

This page, clockwise from above: 5 O'Clock table and chairs for Moooi, 2010; Lolita table lamp for Moooi, 2008; Ribbon chair for Qeeboo, 2016.

REFERENCES

PREFACE

1 'The Design Economy 2018' report, Design Council, London.
2 www.3percentmovement.com/mission.
3 www.designcouncil.org.uk/sites/default/files/asset/document/Design_Economy_2018.pdf.
4 'The Design Economy 2018' report, Design Council, London, 2018, p. 17.
5 www.design.upenn.edu/women-architecture.
6 Letter from Martine Bedin to the author, 6 December 2017.

INTRODUCTION

1 The historian, Jay Merrick asserted in 2012 that the first known woman architect was Lady Elizabeth Wilbraham, who was believed to have been a mentor to the young Christopher Wren, helping him design a number of churches. She is also thought to have designed around a dozen buildings for her family, including Weston Park in Staffordshire and Wotton House in Buckinghamshire. If this is indeed the case then she must be seen as an outlier, who was way ahead of her time, and as such had little relevance to larger the cause of women in design.
2 Seen through today's political lens, *A Vindication of the Rights of Woman* could be considered a rather problematic text, yet it still gives a rare insight into how women were widely viewed in the late eighteenth century and the subordinate role they played in society. Despite the importance of this text, however, Mary Wollstonecraft is now probably better known as the mother of Mary Shelley, who famously wrote *Frankenstein* in 1818.
3 Later becoming the National Art Training School, and then the Royal College of Art.
4 James P. Cramer and Jennifer Evans (eds), *Almanac of Architecture & Design 2006* (Greenway Group Inc., Norcross, GA, 2006), p. 372.
5 www.branchcollective.org/?ps_articles-imogen-hart-on-the-first-arts-and-crafts-exhibition.
6 Catherine W. Zipf, *Professional Pursuits: Women and the American Arts and Crafts Movement* (University of Tennessee Press, Knoxville, TN, 2008).
7 Anton Kaes (ed.), *The Weimar Republic Sourcebook* (University of California Press, Oakland, CA, 1995), p. 438.
8 Bruno Taut, *Die Neue Wohnung, Die Frau als Schopferin*, 1924.
9 Ibid.
10 www.nytimes.com/2011/12/31/arts/design/eva-zeisel-ceramic-artist-and-designer-dies-at-105.
11 www.youtube.com/watch?v=IBLMoMhlAfM.
12 www.nber.org/papers/w7527.pdf.
13 https://broadly.vice.com/en_us/article/bj8mz4/how-spare-rib-magazine-revolutionized-womens-publishing.
14 See http://designschoolarchive.calarts.edu/post/154430726483/item-title-icographic-the-womens-design (*Icographic*, no. 6, The International Council of Graphic Design, London, 1973).
15 Natasha Walter, *The New Feminism* (Little, Brown & Company, London, 1998), pp. 174-75.
16 Constance Smith, *Damsels in Design – Women Pioneers in the Automotive Industry, 1939-1959*, (Schiffer Publishing, Atglen, PA, 2017), p. 7.
17 www.telegraph.co.uk/women/womens-business/10011974/Zaha-Hadid-interview-Women-are-always-told-they-wont-make-it.

AINO AALTO

1 Louna Lahti, *Aalto* (Taschen, Cologne, 2007), p. 19.

ANNI ALBERS

1 Ulrike Müller, *Bauhaus Women: Art, Handicraft, Design* (Flammarion, London, 2009).

LINA BO BARDI

1 Zeuler Lima, 'Preservation as Conservation: The Work of Lina Bo Bardi', from *Future Anterior: Journal of Historic Preservation, History, Theory and Criticism*, vol. 2, no. 2 (Winter 2005), p. 24.

CINI BOERI

1 www.klatmagazine.com/en/architecture-en/cini-boeri/32943.
2 Ibid.
3 www.domusweb.it/en/interviews/2012/05/09/cini-boeri-designing-is-a-joy-but-also-a-commitment.

IRMA BOOM

1 www.eyemagazine.com/feature/article/reputations-irma-boom.

MARGARET CALVERT

1 www.theguardian.com/artanddesign/shortcuts/2015/sep/18/way-to-go-the-woman-whoinvented-britains-road-signs.

LOUISE CAMPBELL

1 www.louisecampbell.com/work/prince-chair.
2 Ibid.
3 www.bonluxat.com/a/Louise_Campbell_Veryround_Armchair.html.

CASTELLI FERRIERI

1 Julie V. Iovine, Castelli Ferrieri obituary: www.nytimes.com/2006/06/28/arts/design/anna-castelli-ferrieri-87-force-in-postwar-modern-italian.

KIM COLIN

1 The first women to receive the RSA's Royal Design for Industry (RDI) award was the weaver and textile designer Ethel Mairet in 1937. Her chosen fields of endeavour were traditionally seen as being more appropriate for women to pursue than other areas of design.
2 www.iconeye.com/design/features/item/10087-profile-industrial-facility.
3 www.industrialfacility.co.uk.
4 www.disegnodaily.com/article/kim-colin-royal-design-for-industry-award.

COLLIER CAMPBELL

1 www.theguardian.com/artanddesign/2011/may/15/susan-collier-obituary.

MURIEL COOPER

1 https://medium.com/mit-media-lab/muriel-coopers-lasting-imprint-b7a8b5d9d19a.
2 Cited in http://adcglobal.org/hall-of-fame/muriel-cooper.
3 https://medium.com/mit-media-lab/muriel-coopers-lasting-imprint-b7a8b5d9d19a.

4 www.nytimes.com/2007/09/28/style/28iht-design11.1.7670693.

MATALI CRASSET

1 http://frenchculture.org/art-and-design/2832-interview-designer-matali-crasset.
2 Ibid.

CARLOTTA DE BEVILACQUA

1 www.nowness.com/series/in-residence/carlotta-de-bevilacqua-milan.

SONIA DELAUNAY

1 Cited in www.tate.org.uk/whats-on/tate-modern/exhibition/ey-exhibition-sonia-delaunay/delaunay-introduction.

ELSIE DE WOLFE

1 Elsie de Wolfe, *After All* (William Heinemann, Portsmouth, NH, 1935).
2 Before de Wolfe, there had been a number of high-profile interior decorating firms in America.
3 De Wolfe once reputedly declared, 'I'm going to make everything around me beautiful, that will be my life.'
4 Elsie de Wolfe, 'The House in Good Taste', 1913, Chap. 1. www.gutenberg.org/files/14715/14715-h/14715-h.
5 *The Standard and Vanity Fair* (9 June 1905), n.p.
6 The Colony Club was designed by the architect Stanford White.
7 Elsie de Wolfe, 'The House in Good Taste', 1913: title of Chapter 2.

ELIZABETH DILLER

1 http://time.com/collection/most-influential-people-2018/5217632/elizabeth-diller.
2 This position is still held by Diller, who also became the department's head of graduate studies in 1993.
3 www.ft.com/content/e4f80782-97ae-11e7-b83c-9588e51488a0.
4 In 2003, the practice was renamed Diller Scofidio + Renfro, when Charles Renfro (who joined the office in 1997) became a partner.

NANNA DITZEL

1 Charlotte and Peter Fiell, *Modern Scandinavian Design* (Laurence King, London, 2017), p. 156.

DOROTHY DRAPER

1 www.architecturaldigest.com/story/draper-article-052006.
2 Elsie de Wolfe was the only high-profile female interior designer prior to this.
3 Wendy Moonan, 'Be Bold, Confident and Larger Than Life (But Never Clash)', *The New York Times* (19 May 2006).
4 *Decorating Is Fun! How to be Your Own Decorator* (Literary Guild of America, Inc., New York, 1939), pp. 29 and 63.
5 Cited in Carleton Varney, *The Draper Touch: The High Life and High Style of Dorothy Draper* (Simon & Schuster, New York, 1988).

CLARA DRISCOLL

1 Prior to this, George A. Kemeny and Donald Miller published a book entitled *Tiffany Desk Treasures* in 2002, which had ascribed the design of the Dragonfly lamp to Driscoll, and named her as a significant designer working for Tiffany Studios.
2 Clara briefly left Tiffany Studios in 1896, when he became engaged to Edwin Waldo, however, during a pre-wedding trip to the Mid-West, he disappeared and as a result she returned to former employment. Six years later, however, Waldo re-emerged, claiming that he had been suffering from temporary amnesia, but Clara was decidedly unmoved by this tale and the relationship was not resumed.

FRONT

1 www.dezeen.com/2016/08/17/video-interview-front-lifesize-horse-lamp-animal-collection-moooi-experiment-movie.
2 www.frontdesign.se/about.

'GEORGIE' GEORGINA GASKIN

1 Cited in a footnote, in William Morris, 'The Collected Letters of William Morris', vol. IV [1893-96] (Princeton University Press, Princeton, NJ, 2014), p. 150.

GENERAL MOTORS' 'DAMSELS OF DESIGN'

1 Cited in www.core77.com/posts/49498/The-Story-Behind-GMs-Celebrated-Damsels-of-Design.
2 Frigidaire was a subsidiary of General Motors.

SOPHIE GIMBEL

1 *Time* magazine (15 September 1947), p. 88.
2 The New School, Parsons, press release, 2013, see: www.newschool.edu/pressroom/pressreleases/2012/sophiegimbel.htm.
3 www.nytimes.com/1981/11/29/obituaries/sophie-gimbel-leading-american-designer-for-40-years-dies-at-83.

THE GLASGOW GIRLS

1 This ethereal otherworldly tendency, which was inspired by the contemporary fascination with Spiritualism, gained 'The Four' the moniker 'Spook School'.
2 Juliet Ash and Elizabeth Wilson, *Chic Thrills: A Fashion Reader* (Canongate, Edinburgh, 1990), pp. 215-17.
3 A suffrage activist, Ann Macbeth was eventually imprisoned and forcibly fed for her militant action in circa 1912, although it is not known what form it took as it is believed she gave a false name when she was arrested.

LONNEKE GORDIJN

1 www.studiodrift.com/about/studio.

APRIL GRIEMAN

1 www.aiga.org/medalist-arminhofmann.
2 http://archive.madeinspace.la/subversion.
3 April Grieman, *Hybrid Imagery: The Fusion of Graphic Design and Technology* (Watson-Guptill, New York, 1990), p. 45.

ZAHA HADID

1 Other co-founders of OMA included Madelon Vriesendorm, Elia Zenghelis and Zoe Zenghelis.
2 www.zaha-hadid.com/architecture/the-peak-leisure-club.
3 www.zaha-hadid.com/architecture/vitra-fire-station-2.
4 www.theguardian.com/artanddesign/2013/sep/08/zaha-hadid-serpentine-sackler-profile.

INEKE HANS

1 Iittala Press Release for Plektra, April 2015.
2 www.inekehans.com/studio/work/ordinary-furniture-sets.
3 Iittala Press Release for Plektra, April 2015.

GRETE JALK

1 *Scandinavian Review*, vol. 78 (Amercian-Scandinavian Foundation, New York, 1990), p. 142.

2 Decorative Art in Modern Interiors, vol. 54, (Viking Press, New York, 1964), p. 7.

GERTRUDE JEKYLL
1 Cited in M.J. Tooley (ed), *Gertrude Jekyll: Artist, Gardener, Craftswoman* (Michemas Books, 1985), p. 33.
2 Gertrude Jekyll, *Wood and Garden – Notes and Thoughts, Practical and Critical, of a Working Amateur* (Longmans, Green & Co., London/New York, 1899), p. 7 (Introduction).

BETTY JOEL
1 Derek Patmore, 'British Interior Architects of To-Day. 6. Betty Joel', *The Studio*, no. 104 (1932), p. 276.
2 *Nottingham Evening Post* (17 May 1937).
3 *The Studio*, vol. 14 (London, 1937), p. 165.

HELLA JONGERIUS
1 www.jongeriuslab.com/work/long-neck-and-groove-bottles.

ILONKA KARASZ
1 Cited in www.core77.com/posts/47403/Ilonka-Kárász-20th-Century-Design-Polymath.
2 Ibid.

SUSAN KARE
1 www.wired.com/2013/04/susan-kare.
2 Biography sent to author by Susan Kare Design, 2018.
3 www.wired.com/2013/04/susan-kare.

FLORENCE KNOLL BASSETT
1 Eric Larabee and Massimo Vignelli, *Knoll Design* (Abrams Books, New York, 1981), p. 80.
2 Ibid., p. 77.

FLORENCE KOEHLER
1 https://americanart.si.edu/artist/florence-koehler-2677.
2 http://snaccooperative.org/ark:/99166/w6tz7bjw.
3 https://archive.org/stream/jstor-25505399/25505399_djvu.txt.
4 http://myweb.tiscali.co.uk/speel/otherart/fisher2.htm.

BELLE KOGAN
1 Pat Kirkham, *Women Designers in the USA, 1900-2000: Diversity and Difference* (Yale University Press, New Haven, CT, 2002), p. 271.
2 Ibid., p. 272.

VALENTINA KULAGINA
1 http://russia-ic.com/people/general/k/829.

LORA LAMM
1 Lamm was following in the footsteps of other Swiss designers, most notably Xanti Schawinsky, Max Huber and Walter Ballmer, all of who had found employment in Antonio Boggeri's influential Milanese studio during the 1930s and 1940s.

ESTELLE LAVERNE
1 www.nytimes.com/2004/04/18/magazine/the-invisibles.

AMANDA LEVETE
1 www.theguardian.com/theguardian/2011/apr/09/amanda-levete-architecture-practice.
2 www.architectsjournal.co.uk/news/amanda-levete-the-social-networker/8670158.article.
3 www.theguardian.com/theguardian/2011/apr/09/amanda-levete-architecture-practice.
4 www.architectsjournal.co.uk/news/amanda-levete-awarded-jane-drew-prize/10027671.

article?blocktitle=NEW-HOMEPAGE-BIG-PIC&contentID=19632.

SHELIA LEVRANT DE BRETTEVILLE
1 http://sheliastudio.us.
2 Email to author, June 2018.

ELAINE LUSTIG COHEN
1 Aaris Sherin, *Elaine Lustig Cohen: Modernism Reimagined* (RIT Press, Rochester, NY, 2014), pp. 12–13.

MÄRTA MÅÅS-FJETTERSTRÖM
1 Cited in www.fjhakimian.com/blog/house-m-rta-built.
2 Cited in www.mmf.se/story/artists/maerta-maas-fjetterstroem.

CECILIE MANZ
1 www.ceciliemanz.com/content/about-cecilie-manz.

ENID MARX
1 http://arts.brighton.ac.uk/collections/design-archives/resources/rdis-at-britain-can-make-it,-1946/enid-marx.

GRETHE MEYER
1 Cited in Charlotte and Peter Fiell, *Scandinavian Design* (Taschen, Cologne, 2002), p. 452.
2 www.grethemeyerdesign.dk/en/grethes-tale.

MAY MORRIS
1 Janis Londraville, *On Poetry, Painting and Politics: The Letters of May Morris and John Quinn* (Susquehana University, Selinsgrove/Associated University Press, London, 1997), p. 69.
2 Cited in ibid., p. 28.

NERI OXMAN
1 https://dspace.mit.edu/handle/1721.1/59192.
2 www.materialecology.com/neri-oxman.

MARIA PERGAY
1 Cited in a press release sent by Demisch Danant to the author, 2017.
2 Ibid.

CHARLOTTE PERRIAND
1 Cited in Stefano Brusaporci (ed.), *Handbook of Research on Emerging Digital Tools for Architectural Survey* (IGI Global, Hershey, PA, 2015), p. 517.
2 Ibid., p. 516.
3 Charlotte Perriand, *Charlotte Perriand: A Life of Creation* (Monacelli Press, New York, 2003), p. 20.
4 Cited in *Architectural Digest*, vol. 63 (2006), p. 17.

MIUCCIA PRADA
1 www.britishfashioncouncil.co.uk/pressreleases/Miuccia-Prada-to-be-Honoured-with-the-Outstanding-Achievement-Award--at-The-Fashion-Awards-2018.

MARY QUANT
1 Nigel Whiteley, *Pop Design: Modernism to Mod* (Design Council, London, 1987), p. 96.

INGEGERD RÅMAN
1 Marcus Engmann, Bo Madestrand and Ingegerd Råman, *It's Nothing but It's Still Something*, (IKEA of Sweden, Almhult, 2016), p. 64.
2 Ibid., pp. 68–9.
3 Ibid., p. 5.

RUTH REEVES
1 Robert Mumford and Robert Wojtowicz, *Mumford on Modern Art in the 1930s* (University of California Press, Berkeley, CA, 2007), p. 154.

LILY REICH
1 John S. Elmo, *Designing Women, Dialogue with Pioneering Women Designers* (Friesen Press, Victoria, BC, 2015), chapter 11, no p.n.
2 Ibid.

LUCIE RIE
1 One of Lucie's father's friends was Sigmund Freud, who he played chess with on a regular basis. His Viennese surgery was decorated in an innovative Modernist style.
2 From Lucie's 'Credo' statement given to Fritz Lampl and transcribed by him in circa 1950, cited in C. Frankel, *Modern Pots: Hans Coper, Lucie Rie, and their contemporaries: The Lisa Sainsbury Collection* (University of East Anglia Sainsbury Centre for Visual Arts, Norwich, 2000), p. 67.

ASTRID SAMPE
1 *Surface Design Journal*, vols 16–17 (Surface Design Association, Oakland, CA, 1991), p. 16.
2 Ibid.
3 Ibid.

PAULA SCHER
1 http://adcglobal.org/hall-of-fame/paula-scher.
2 Ibid.

MARGARETE SCHÜTTE-LIHOTZHY
1 Anne Commire and Deborah Klezmer, *Women in World History* (Yorkin Publications, Waterford, CT, 2002), p. 14.
2 Cited in www.nytimes.com/2006/07/14/arts/design/a-forwardlooking-kitchen-by-a-woman-of-the-20s.
3 See www.west86th.bgc.bard.edu/translatedtext/passages-from-why-i-became-an-architect-by-margarete-schutte-lihotzky.
4 Cited in www.theatlantic.com/health/archive/2010/05/the-first-functional-modern-kitchen/57305.

DENISE SCOTT BROWN
1 Cited on www.designersandbooks.com/blog/1968-learning-las-vegas-studio-revisited.
2 Biography sent by Denise Scott Brown to author, 2018.

ALISON SMITHSON
1 *Daily Mail* (March 1956), p. 61.

SYLVIA STAVE
1 Micael Ernstell and Magnus Olausson, 'Sylvia Stave in the Nationalmuseum', Art Bulletin of the Nationalmuseum Stockholm, vol. 20, p. 43.
2 Ibid., p. 45.

NANNY STILL
1 Cited in Charlotte and Peter Fiell, *Design of the 20th Century* (Taschen, Cologne, 2012).

GUNTA STÖLZL
1 Walter Gropius, 'Manifesto and Programme of the Weimar State Bauhaus' (April 1919).

MARIANNE STRAUB
1 May Schoeser, *Marianne Straub*, (Design Council, London, 1984), p. 16.
2 Ibid.
3 Margot Coatts (ed.), *Pioneers of Modern Craft*, (Manchester University Press, Manchester, 1997), p. 83.

ANNE SWAINSON
1 Victoria Matranga and William E. Meehan Jr, 'Anne Swainson, The Making of a Design Pioneer', *Innovation* (Spring 2016), p. 24.
2 Ibid.

FAYE TOOGOOD
1 Biography sent by Faye Toogood to author, 2018.
2 https://matildabathurst.wordpress.com/2018/01/25/interview-with-the-designer-faye-toogood.
3 Biography to author.
4 In 2013, Faye and her sister Erica launched the Toogood fashion label, which takes its inspiration from traditional workwear.

VIVIANNA TORUN BÜLOW-HÜBE
1 www.bonhams.com/auctions/22761/lot/217.

NYNKE TYNAGEL
1 www.telegraph.co.uk/luxury/design/studio-job-interview.
2 www.architecturaldigest.com/story/meet-job-smeets-and-nynke-tynagel-of-studio-job.

PATRICIA URQUIOLA
1 www.dezeen.com/2015/08/28/movie-moroso-gave-me-credibility-as-designer-patricia-urquiola.

MIMI VANDERMOLEN
1 www.autolife.umd.umich.edu/Design/Vandermolen_interview.
2 Ibid.

LELLA VIGNELLI
1 Vignelli, Massimo, *The Vignelli Canon* (Lars Müller Publishers, Zurich, 2015), p. 14.
2 Ibid.

NANDA VIGO
1 Biography sent by Nanda Vigo's office to author, 2017.
2 Ibid.

EVA ZEISEL
1 Cited in Pat Kirkham (ed.), *Eva Zeisel: Life, Design, and Beauty* (Chronicle Books, San Francisco, CA, 2013), p. 54.

NIKA ZUPANC
1 www.dezeen.com/2010/04/26/5-oclock-chair-by-nika-zupanc-for-moooi.
2 Ibid.
3 http://babyology.com.au/news/nika-zupancs-astonishing-cradle-car-and-storage-box.

INDEX

PICTURE CREDITS

PICTURE CREDITS

FURTHER READING

Books

Attfield, Jude, and Pat Kirkham, *A View from the Interior, Feminism, Women and Design*, The Women's Press Ltd, London, 1989

Burkhauser, Jude, *Glasgow Girls: Women in Art and Design, 1880–1920*, Canongate Books, Edinburgh, 2001

Callen, Anthea, *Women Artists of the Arts and Crafts Movement, 1870–1914*, Pantheon Books, New York, 1979

Coatts, Margot (ed.), *Pioneers of Modern Craft: Twelve Essays Profiling Key Figures in the History of Twentieth Century Craft*, Manchester University Press, Manchester, 1997

Fernández Garcia, Ana María (ed), *MoMoWo: 100 Works in 100 Years, European Women in Architecture and Design, 1918–2018*, Zalozba ZRC, Ljubljana, 2016

Fiell, Charlotte, and Peter Fiell, *Design of the 20th Century*, Taschen, Cologne, 1999

—, Design Museum: *A to Z of Design and Designers*, Goodman Fiell, London, 2016

—, *Scandinavian Design*, Taschen, Cologne, 2002

—, *The Story of Design, from the Paleolithic to the Present*, Goodman Fiell, London, 2013/The Monacelli Press, New York, 2016

Kirkham, Pat, *Charles and Ray Eames: Designers of the Twentieth Century*, MIT Press, Cambridge, MA, 1995

Kirkham, Pat, *Women Designers in the USA, 1900–2000: Diversity and Difference*, Yale University Press, New Haven, CN, 2002

McQuiston, Liz, *Women in Design: A Contemporary View*, Trefoil, London, 1988

Müller, Ulrike, *Bauhaus Women: Art, Handicraft, Design*, Flammarion, Paris (English edn), 2009

Smith, Constance, *Damsels in Design: Women Pioneers in the Automotive Industry, 1939–1959*, Schiffer Publishing, Atglen, PA, 2018

Elmo, John S., *Designing Women, Dialogue with Pioneering Women Designers*, Friesen Press, Victoria, BC, 2015

Sherin, Aaris, *Elaine Lustig Cohen: Modernism Reimagined*, RIT Press, Rochester, NY, 2014

Walter, Natasha, *The New Feminism*, Little, Brown and Company, London, 1998

Zeisel, Eva, and Pat Kirkham (eds), *Eva Zeisel: Life, Design, and Beauty*, Chronicle Books, San Francisco, CA, 2013

Zipf, Catherine W., *Professional Pursuits: Women and the American Arts and Crafts Movement*, University of Tennessee Press, Knoxville, TN, 2008

Journals

Innovation, ISDA, Spring 2016 (Designing Women issue)

ACKNOWLEDGMENTS

This book has been a colossal undertaking and as such has involved a lot of teamwork, and we would, therefore, like to thank everyone involved in its successful outcome.

Our thanks go to the staff at Laurence King Publishing who we worked so closely with: Jo Lightfoot and Sophie Drysdale for commissioning this book in the first place; Blanche Craig for her good-natured editorial management of the project; Jessica McCarthy for her skillful copy-editing; Anjali Bulley for her thoughtful proofreading; Julia Ruxton and Cheryl Thomas for their help with additional picture sourcing and image permissions clearances; Angus Hyland for his invaluable creative direction; Davina Cheung for overseeing its exacting production; and Vicki Robinson for her careful indexing. We are also grateful to Sam Wolfson of BLOK design for her eye-catching graphic design work and Alex Coco for his assistance in the final stages of the design.

Likewise, we would like to express our immense gratitude to all the manufacturers, museums, galleries, auction houses, picture libraries and designers' estates that allowed us to use their imagery. Our heartfelt thanks also go to all the many designers and design studios who so kindly provided us with invaluable information and sent us beautiful images to illustrate their entries. We sincerely hope that we have done justice to your remarkable design stories.

And lastly but by no means least, we would like to offer our most profound thanks to Peter Fiell and Samuel Morley for their helpful copy-editing and proof reading, insightful feedback and sustaining love – you will never know how much your support is appreciated.

This book is dedicated to all the unsung women of design – both past and present.

ABOUT THE AUTHORS

Charlotte Fiell is a leading authority on the history, theory and criticism of design and has written sixty books on the subject. She initially trained at the British Institute in Florence, before studying at Camberwell College of Arts (UAL), London, from which she received a BA (Hons) in the History of Drawing and Printmaking with Material Science. She later trained at Sotheby's Institute of Art in London. In the late 1980s with her husband, Peter, she opened a pioneering design gallery in London's King's Road and through this acquired a rare hands-on knowledge of modern design. In 1991, the Fiells' first book *Modern Furniture Classics since 1945* was published to widespread acclaim. Since then, the Fiells have concentrated on communicating design more widely through authorship, curation, and teaching. Charlotte also works as a consultant on design legacy management and is currently undertaking, in conjunction with the National Trust, a PhD in History at the University of Reading. Her most recent titles include: *Modern Scandinavian Design*, *100 Ideas that Changed Design* and *Contemporary Chinese Furniture Design* – all published by Laurence King

Clementine Fiell is a London-based writer, editor and researcher. She received a first-class BA Honours in Fashion Communication with Promotion at Central Saint Martins (UAL). While there, she was awarded the prestigious Felicity Green Award for Fashion Journalism. She has since held various editorial and art direction roles at a number of titles and organizations including: *Vice*, *POP Magazine*, *Arena Homme Plus*, Mario Testino and Vivienne Westwood. *Women in Design* is her first book.